Assessment Practices

Edited by Christine A. Coombe
and Nancy J. Hubley

Case Studies in TESOL Practice Series

Jill Burton, Series Editor

Teachers of English to Speakers of Other Languages, Inc.

Typeset in Berkeley and Belwe
by Capitol Communication Systems, Inc., Crofton, Maryland USA
Printed by Kirby Lithographic Company, Inc., Arlington, Virginia USA
Indexed by Coughlin Indexing Services, Annapolis, Maryland USA

Teachers of English to Speakers of Other Languages, Inc.
700 South Washington Street, Suite 200
Alexandria, Virginia 22314 USA
Tel 703-836-0774 • Fax 703-836-6447 • E-mail info@tesol.org • http://www.tesol.org/

Director of Department of Publishing: Paul Gibbs
Managing Editor: Marilyn Kupetz
Copy Editor: Marcella Weiner
Cover Design: Capitol Communications Systems, Inc.

ISBN 1931185077
Library of Congress Control No. 2002115361

Table of Contents

Series Editor's Preface   v

INTRODUCTION: Themes in Language Assessment   1
  Christine A. Coombe and Nancy J. Hubley

PART 1: COMPREHENSIVE ASSESSMENT

CHAPTER 1: Creating a Complete Language-Testing Program   9
  James Dean Brown

PART 2: CURRICULUM WASHBACK

CHAPTER 2: Developing an English Proficiency Test for
Japanese Secondary Students   27
  Caryl Lyons, Sandra Bolton, and Stephen Gaies

CHAPTER 3: Deconstructing the Making of Japanese
University Entrance Exams   41
  Tim Murphey and Kazuyoshi Sato

CHAPTER 4: Cooperative ESP Assessment at a Japanese University   49
  Mitchell Goodman

PART 3: IN-PROGRAM ASSESSMENT

CHAPTER 5: Linking Assessments With Instruction in a
Multilingual Elementary School   63
  Nancy Frey and Douglas Fisher

CHAPTER 6: From Paper and Pencil to the Web:
A Testing and Technology Partnership   75
  Greta J. Gorsuch and Katherine A. Austin

CHAPTER 7: Beyond the Individual Speaker in New Zealand   91
  Helen Basturkmen

CHAPTER 8: A Quest for the Perfect Portfolio   103
   Barbara Dogger, Jeff Moy, and Manny Nogami

PART 4: END-OF-PROGRAM ASSESSMENT

CHAPTER 9: Multiple-Measures Assessment: Using Visas to Assess
Students' Achievement of Learning Outcomes   121
   Peter Davidson and David Dalton

CHAPTER 10: Assessing English for Employment in Hong Kong   135
   Tom Lumley and David Qian

PART 5: PROGRAM EVALUATION

CHAPTER 11: A Curriculum Review of an ESL Composition Program 151
   Edwina S. Carreon

CHAPTER 12: Evaluation of Training in an ELT Project in Egypt 165
   Barbara Thornton, Robert Burch, and Dina El-Araby

CHAPTER 13: Consensus, Control, and Continuity in a
University ESOL Program   177
   James Campbell, Julie Howard, Judith A. Kent, Ana King,
   Kristin Lems, and Gale Stam

References   189

Index   199

Series Editor's Preface

The Case Studies in TESOL Practice series offers innovative and effective examples of practice from the point of view of the practitioner. The series brings together from around the world communities of practitioners who have reflected and written on particular aspects of their teaching. Each volume in the series covers one specialized teaching focus.

◈ CASE STUDIES

Why a TESOL series focusing on case studies of teaching practice?

Much has been written about case studies and where they fit in a mainstream research tradition (e.g., Nunan, 1992; Stake, 1995; Yin, 1994). Perhaps more important, case studies publicly recognize the value of teachers' reflection on their practice and also constitute a new form of teacher research or teacher valuing. Case studies support teachers in valuing the uniqueness of their classes, learning from them, and showing how their experience and knowledge can be made accessible to other practitioners in simple but disciplined ways. They are particularly suited to practitioners who want to understand and solve teaching problems in their own contexts.

These case studies are written by practitioners who are able to portray real experience by providing detailed descriptions of teaching practice. These qualities invest the cases with teacher credibility and make them convincing and professionally interesting. The cases also represent multiple views and offer immediate solutions, thus providing perspective on the issues and examples of useful approaches. Informative by nature, they can provide an initial database for further, sustained research. Accessible to wider audiences than many traditional research reports, however, case studies have democratic appeal.

◈ HOW THIS SERIES CAN BE USED

The case studies lend themselves to pre- and in-service teacher education. Because the context of each case is described in detail, it is easy for readers to compare the cases with and evaluate them against their own circumstances. To respond to the wide range of settings in which TESOL functions, cases have been selected from diverse EFL and ESL settings around the world.

The 12 or so case studies in each volume are easy to follow. Teacher writers describe their teaching context and analyze its distinctive features: the particular demands of their context, the issues they have encountered, how they have effectively addressed the issues, and what they have learned. Each case study also offers readers practical suggestions developed from teaching experience to adapt and apply to their own teaching.

Already published or in preparation are volumes on

- academic writing programs
- action research
- bilingual education
- community partnerships
- content-based language instruction
- distance learning
- English for specific purposes
- gender and TESOL
- grammar teaching in teacher education
- intensive English programs
- interaction and language learning
- international teaching assistants
- journal writing
- literature in language teaching and learning
- mainstreaming
- teacher education
- teaching English as a foreign language in primary schools
- teaching English from a global perspective
- teaching English to the world
- technology in the classroom

◈ THIS VOLUME

This exciting volume showcases assessment in its myriad forms: classroom assessment, formal testing, program evaluation, curriculum renewal, and self-assessment of teaching and learning. The studies, set in Egypt, Hong Kong, Japan, New Zealand, and the United States, document and analyze assessment design and development, implementation, and review. This volume will interest teachers, testers, and language educators alike.

Jill Burton
University of South Australia, Adelaide

INTRODUCTION

Themes in Language Assessment

Christine A. Coombe and Nancy J. Hubley

Assessment in English language teaching has come a long way from the days when it was merely synonymous with discrete-point, objective testing. Granted, that form of assessment is still appropriate for certain purposes, but now assessment includes a broad range of tools and techniques that range from testing an individual student's ability to evaluating an entire language teaching program. The case studies in this volume represent innovative assessment techniques and reflect current practice. The studies showcase interesting new approaches to assessment so that English teachers around the globe can benefit from the experience of others. The volume as a whole offers a broad introduction to assessment literacy for those who are new to the field, whereas each case study offers practical ideas for implementing the type of assessment that it describes.

◈ ORGANIZATION OF CASE STUDIES

The chapters in this volume are generally organized by the stage of assessment within a program, ranging from admissions and placement testing through in-program assessment and exit tests to whole-program evaluation.

In Part 1, Brown (chapter 1) describes a comprehensive testing program that encompasses all the assessment measures that pertain to a student at his university.

Part 2 contains three chapters that deal with assessment in Japan, where the preparation for high-stakes English exams has significant washback on the processes of teaching and learning. Lyons, Bolton, and Gaies (chapter 2) describe an innovative testing program for secondary students, whereas Murphey and Sato (chapter 3) focus on assessment issues in the Japanese university system. Goodman's case study (chapter 4) of collaborative test taking in a university-level English for specific purposes (ESP) course concludes the Japanese section.

Part 3 deals with different forms of in-program assessment. Frey and Fisher (chapter 5) describe assessment philosophy and techniques used in a multicultural primary school. In that setting of ethnic diversity with 39 languages, assessment is an integral part of what goes on regularly in the classroom. Gorsuch and Austin (chapter 6) explain the computer adaptation of a paper-and-pencil proficiency test used at their university to determine the needs of international students. They describe the process and provide practical suggestions for computer test administration. Basturkmen (chapter 7) reports on developing appropriate strategies to assess discussion skills in an academic speaking course at a New Zealand university. She notes that most assessment of speaking focuses on presentation skills instead of interlocutor skills in groups. Finally, Dogger, Moy, and Nogami (chapter 8) detail the process of developing writing portfolios that are used to determine whether English for speakers of other languages (ESOL) college students are ready for the first-year composition course or need further remediation. After a period of experimentation and self-examination, teachers developed a system that enhanced student success in writing.

In Part 4, two chapters deal with assessment at the end of academic programs. Davidson and Dalton (chapter 9) describe the "visa system" of assessment that is used to determine if students at a Middle Eastern university have met the outcomes of the English as a Foreign Language (EFL) Readiness Program and are prepared to move on to their major academic programs. Lumley and Qian (chapter 10) discuss an exit test that was developed to ensure the language proficiency standard of university graduates in Hong Kong.

Part 5 contains three case studies of program evaluation. Carreon (chapter 11) documents in considerable detail the process of reflection involved in self-study by an American academic department. By contrast, Thornton, Burch, and El-Araby (chapter 12) are concerned with monitoring and evaluating an EFL train-the-trainer program in a developing country. Kent and her colleagues (chapter 13) conclude the volume with their case study of ways in which a university ESOL program maintains high standards through a complex system of coordination.

◈ WHERE NEXT?

Language assessment is such a burgeoning field that many teachers find it difficult to keep pace with current developments. As you read the case studies in this volume and are motivated to pursue a topic further, you might consider visiting one of several excellent Internet sites that provide up-to-date resources and links to assessment topics. Glenn Fulcher at the University of Dundee maintains a Web site devoted specifically to assessment in English language teaching (Fulcher, 2003). Another comprehensive Internet resource is the Educational Resources Information Center's (ERIC's) site (http://www.ericae.net/) on assessment, evaluation, and research. Although it is not specific to TESOL, the ERIC site provides educators with ideas and resources from many fields.

◈ THEMES

Three main themes are threaded through most of the case studies:

- multiple-measures assessment
- assessment in context
- cyclical nature of assessment

Together, the threaded studies describe teachers' experiences in introducing novel forms of assessment in schools, universities, and training programs around the world.

Multiple-Measures Assessment

Brown (chapter 1) describes the creation of an integrated testing program that utilizes a variety of measures. Long an advocate of multiple-measures assessment, Brown is explicit about the function and purpose of different types of assessment and argues cogently for basing decisions about students on multiple sources of information. Despite his insistence on high standards for test development and analysis, Brown keeps the end user, the student, always in focus. To maintain standards and thereby treat students fairly, Brown urges teachers to annually review all aspects of a testing program, from item analysis of tests themselves to their articulation with the curriculum.

Assessing the full range of academic speaking skills is not easy, as Basturkmen and her colleagues (chapter 7) found at the University of Auckland. In developing a viable approach to assessing spontaneous participation in discussions as well as preplanned presentations, it became evident to Basturkmen that it was necessary to develop a new approach. The resultant scheme was task based and included a self-assessment component for the students. Teachers found that using multiple measures gave a more comprehensive picture of students' oral skills.

In Japan, where the focus of most assessment is on high-stakes examinations, Goodman (chapter 4) builds a case for using a variety of evaluation techniques at the classroom level where teachers have more scope for experimentation. In his ESP classes at a university, Goodman has extended the idea of cooperative learning to cooperative written tests, a technique that fosters teamwork and peer interaction. Additional advantages of this approach are that the affective barrier is lowered and that students are more likely to take risks than they would in higher stakes tests. By assessing in a variety of ways, Goodman feels that he addresses the diverse learning styles of his students and motivates them to learn more successfully.

Dogger, Moy, and Nogami (chapter 8) explain the development of a system of portfolio assessment used at Richland College in Texas for ESOL students embarking on their degree programs. Key features of the Richland portfolios are the use of multiple-trait scoring as well as double-blind scoring to ensure interrater reliability. Despite the importance of standardized marking, this institution has chosen to balance student assessment by giving equal weight to teachers' grades so that important decisions do not rest solely on one form of assessment.

Davidson and Dalton's case study (chapter 9) shows in considerable detail the multiple measures used in their university preparatory program to ascertain that EFL students are prepared to embark on a full-fledged academic program. The measures include the Test of English as a Foreign Language (TOEFL), listening and summary writing in a lecture context, reading and reporting on academic material, demonstrating information literacy skills, and participating in academic discussions. In addition to measuring English language skills, the different instruments also assess academic study skills and critical-thinking skills as well as learner independence.

Assessment in Context

Tailoring assessment to the context in which it is used is this volume's second theme. Context has many meanings. In the classroom, it means developing assessment that is appropriate for the language level and cultural background of students within a particular program. At a higher stage, it involves the institutional culture in which the program is situated. For example, a vocational college might value competency-based or performance-based assessment more highly than formal examinations. At a still higher level, assessment is subject to cultural norms and values. In some regions of the world, assessment at critical points in life is accepted as a deciding factor in who will be allowed to move on to further education and who will be diverted into the workforce. At the highest level, high-stakes, standardized assessment has become a cultural entity of its own with features that transcend national and ethnic boundaries. Scores on major standardized tests such as the International English Language Testing System (IELTS) or TOEFL are reified into much more than exam results. Educational institutions and employers make life-altering decisions based on candidates' scores. Clearly, the choice of assessment type and the exact nature of the material used will depend on all these contextual factors.

The case studies in this volume describe a variety of responses to the context of assessment. For example, much of chapter 2 by Lyons, Bolton, and Gaies is devoted to the careful process they went through in identifying the cultural factors that affected the development of a test for Japanese secondary students. They started by raising questions about every aspect of the exam and then examined the underlying assumptions that test developers from different cultures might bring to these issues. Later, they took advantage of opportunities for cross-cultural exchanges and actively brought Japanese teachers into the process of test development. In training North American raters, they made every effort to raise their awareness of cultural differences such as the differences between EFL and native-speaker writing styles.

In an era when computer use is taken for granted, computer-based testing is still not widespread. From their experience with converting a printed proficiency test to a computerized delivery format, Gorsuch and Austin (chapter 6) explain the contextual factors associated with this use of technology. To reap the benefits of computer scoring and data analysis while maintaining reliability, the authors took special measures to ensure that candidates' performances were not affected by the delivery mechanism. Their case study emphasizes the importance of developing a detailed implementation plan, preparing students for the computer exam, and having a responsive team of technicians available for support.

In developing an exit test to document the English proficiency of graduates from a Hong Kong university, Lumley and Qian (chapter 10) considered numerous contextual issues. First, they ascertained what information the consumers of the exam needed: practical information about the productive capabilities of potential employees in speaking and writing English. Second, they took into account the candidate population. Although the graduating students initially seemed to form a homogeneous population, on closer inspection, the differences were even more important than the similarities. Third, in developing specifications for the assessed tasks, Lumley and Qian tried to replicate authentic situations that the candidates would encounter in the workplace. Finally, the test developers were aware of the broad range of stakeholders in the exam, who included not only candidates and potential employers but also the university, government oversight agencies, and funding sources for English training.

When Thornton, Burch, and El-Araby (chapter 12) conducted an evaluation of an English language training program in Egypt, they used an evaluation model that was designed to assess Western businesses. However, in their adaptation, local educators were involved in every stage of the program from planning to program review. Consequently, the evaluation program itself became incorporated as part of the training and eventually cascaded down to all the stakeholders. Thus, assessment was contextualized both in terms of EFL and in its cultural setting.

Cyclical Nature of Assessment

The book's third theme is seeing assessment as an ongoing, cyclic process in which the techniques and instruments used are constantly monitored and reevaluated before being used again. Just as an individual student's progress in learning English is tracked and documented at many different points, so are the means of assessing students and programs.

Frey and Fisher (chapter 5) describe an elementary school in California where teachers see assessment and instruction as recursive. At that school, assessment has its roots in daily classroom instruction and is used to further inform instruction in an endless circle. Teachers conduct multifaceted assessment on an ongoing basis as part of their teaching to get information about their students' literacy. This helps the teachers plan appropriate lessons. Thus, assessment is embedded in the classroom experience instead of being separate from it.

Murphey and Sato's case (chapter 3) on the Japanese examination system and its effect on teaching and learning strongly advocates greater assessment literacy. For them, this entails a more professional approach to exam construction as well as careful analysis of examinations. The authors assert that a haphazard approach to exam development in a system where high-stakes exams are ubiquitous is not fair to students.

Sometimes the cycles of assessment are long. Carreon (chapter 11) describes a self-study undertaken by a university ESL composition program that had been last assessed more than 40 years ago. The faculty undertook the evaluation of their own program to gather information about its strengths and weaknesses so that they would have an informed basis for decision making. Within the self-study, the assessment instruments used actually emerged from the program itself and were developed organically as the study progressed. At the conclusion of the self-study, it was natural that the information gleaned was fed back into improving the program.

Kent and her colleagues (chapter 13) describe a coordinated network of assessment at National-Louis University in Chicago that monitors the quality of student performance, instruction, and curriculum. Quality assurance is built into the functioning of the ESOL program at the university and is carried out on an ongoing basis. The structure of evaluation includes tracking the progress of students who have graduated from the program to determine whether the program has met their needs.

Lyons, Bolton, and Gaies (chapter 2) examine the evolutionary process of test development with reflection and reevaluation at every stage. Another cyclic aspect of their case study is the way in which the test developer moves beyond testing to teaching, using the results of the exam to help candidates understand good strategies for reading, listening, and writing.

◈ CONTRIBUTORS

Christine Coombe and Nancy Hubley are English faculty members at Dubai Men's College and Sharjah Women's College respectively. They serve as systemwide assessment leaders for the United Arab Emirates' Higher Colleges of Technology (HCT). In 1997, they founded the Current Trends in English Language Testing conference, now an annual international event. They specialize in assessment training and have been English language specialists for the U.S. Department of State.

Christine is past president of TESOL Arabia and winner of the 2002 Educational Testing Service (ETS) Outstanding Young Scholar Award and the Mary Spann Fellowship. Her current research is on test preparation strategies.

In 2001 Nancy received the HCT Chancellor's Award as Teacher of the Year. Her interests include computer-based testing and materials writing.

PART 1

Comprehensive Assessment

CHAPTER 1

Creating a Complete Language-Testing Program

James Dean Brown

◈ INTRODUCTION

The perfect language test for many administrators and teachers would be an aptitude-proficiency-placement-diagnostic-progress-achievement test that does not take too long to administer and is easy to score. For such people, the dream test would be one that does everything and does it painlessly. As I have explained elsewhere (e.g., Brown, 1989, 1990, 1995, 1996b), such a test is simply not possible because the purposes of the different types of tests vary in many systematic ways. In general, language tests can be designed for either norm-referenced or criterion-referenced tests.

Norm-referenced tests are designed to compare the performance of each student with the performances of all the other students in a norm group and do so across a continuum of general language abilities. Thus, norm-referenced tests are not designed to determine how much students have learned in a specific setting, but rather to compare students with other students (usually from many different institutions), even if they all know a great deal or very little. Norm-referenced tests are typically used for three different purposes, which differ in the degree of specificity of what they are measuring:

1. Language aptitude purposes: determining each student's relative standing in terms of his or her overall ability to learn languages (usually for purposes of deciding who would be the best investment for language study); measuring very broadly but not in any particular language

2. Language proficiency purposes: determining each student's relative standing in terms of his or her overall ability in a particular language (usually for purposes of moving students from one institution to another as in university admissions decisions); still measuring broadly but at least within a specific language

3. Language placement purposes: determining each student's relative standing in terms of the appropriate level of study in a particular language program (usually for purposes of creating classrooms of students with relatively homogeneous ability levels); measuring only at the specific levels of ability involved in the placement decisions

Because norm-referenced tests are referenced to a norm group, the three purposes usually cannot be accomplished with the same test. A language aptitude test would typically be designed for a general norm group without reference to a particular language (e.g., the Defense Language Aptitude Test is normed to all new military personnel, who presumably differ considerably in their aptitudes to learn languages). A language proficiency test would also typically be designed for a general norm group, but in this case, only people who have learned a particular language (e.g., the Test of English as a Foreign Language [TOEFL] is normed to a wide range of abilities from virtually no English language proficiency to nativelike proficiency). A language placement test is more specific in that the norm group would be students in the range of abilities found at a particular institution (e.g., the English Language Institute Placement Test at the University of Hawaii at Manoa is normed to the rather restricted range of students who fall between 500 and 600 on the TOEFL). In short, aptitude, proficiency, and placement tests are designed to compare students with each other for purposes of grouping them into those who (a) will or will not be a good investment for language study (aptitude); (b) will or will not be admitted to a particular institution (proficiency); or (c) will study at the elementary, intermediate, or advanced levels or be exempted altogether (placement).

Instead of being designed to compare students with each other for purposes of grouping them, criterion-referenced tests are designed to measure the percentage of material each student has learned or acquired, most often based on the specific objectives of a particular language course. Criterion-referenced tests can be used for three different purposes, which differ in terms of when in the learning process they are administered:

1. Diagnostic purposes: determining each student's strengths and weaknesses vis-à-vis the objectives at the beginning of the course (usually for purposes of giving feedback to students and teachers on where they should focus their energies)

2. Progress purposes: determining how much progress each student has made in learning each of the objectives in the middle of the course (usually for purposes of giving feedback to students on how they are progressing and how they should refocus their energies)

3. Achievement purposes: determining how much each student has learned across all the objectives at the end of the course (usually for grading, promotion, or graduation purposes)

Once such a criterion-referenced test is designed, the three functions can be accomplished with the same test administered at different times (i.e., in the beginning, middle, and end of a course). However, for security reasons, different forms of the test are typically used for these three functions, or better yet, different forms of the test are created and then administered in a counterbalanced manner (i.e., at the diagnostic testing point, some students take Form A, others take Form B, and still others take Form C; at the progress testing point, each of the three groups takes a different form of the test; then at the achievement testing point, each of the three groups takes the third form of the test that they have not previously seen). In short, diagnostic, progress, and achievement tests are all designed to measure how much of a particular set of objectives the students have mastered, but they differ in their purposes and timing.

This case study is of a comprehensive language-testing program in the English Language Institute (ELI), University of Hawaii at Manoa (UHM), that was implemented during my tenure as director. This comprehensive testing program combined and integrated norm-referenced tests (proficiency and placement) and criterion-referenced tests (diagnostic and achievement) into a single language-testing program.[1]

❖ CONTEXT

As shown in Figure 1, the ELI regularly offered seven courses in three skill areas: (a) academic listening (ELI 70 and ELI 80), (b) reading (ELI 72 and ELI 82), and (c) writing (ELI 73, and ELI 83 for graduate students; English as a second language [ESL] 100 for undergraduate students). All of these courses (except ESL 100) were credit equivalent (i.e., students received credit for enrollment and financial aid purposes only). ESL 100 was the credit-bearing equivalent of the regular English composition course.

The curriculum for each course was developed following the model shown in Figure 2, which included six interrelated curriculum components: (a) needs analysis; (b) goals and objectives specification; (c) test development and improvement; (d) materials adoption, adaptation, or development; (e) teacher support; and (f) regularly conducted formative evaluation (for more information on these topics, see Brown, 1995).

After several years, we had completed each of the components shown in Figure 2 for each of the courses, so we set about revisiting the components on a

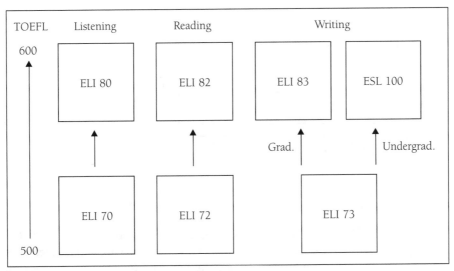

FIGURE 1. English Language Institute Courses

(From *Testing in Language Programs*, p. 282, by J. D. Brown, 1996, Upper Saddle River, NJ: Prentice Hall Regents. Copyright © 2001 by J. D. Brown. Adapted with permission.)

---

[1] Note that aptitude testing was not a political option in a program that must accept all students who are admitted to the university, and progress testing was left entirely up to the individual teachers.

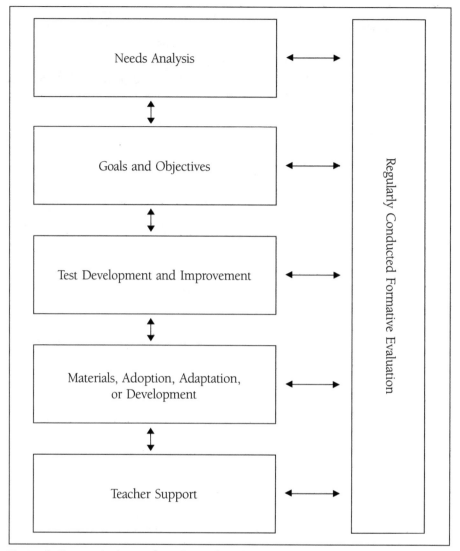

FIGURE 2. Systematic Approach to Curriculum Design

(From *Testing in Language Programs*, p. 27, by J. D. Brown, 1996, Upper Saddle River, NJ: Prentice Hall Regents. Copyright © 2001 by J. D. Brown. Adapted with permission.)

cyclical basis in what we called our ongoing formative evaluation. Every autumn, the curriculum committee (made up of the director, assistant director, and lead teachers for listening, reading, writing, and testing), working with the teachers in each skill area, would revisit the needs analysis, objectives, and criterion-referenced tests (i.e., classroom assessment procedures) to determine the degree to which they still matched the needs of our teachers, students, and administrators. If revision was needed, the needs analysis, objectives, and criterion-referenced tests were revised together as a unit for implementation during the following semester. Each spring, the same was done for the materials adoption, adaptation, or development component as well as for the teacher support component of the curriculum. In addition, every spring, the ELI director analyzed all of the norm-referenced ELI Placement Test (ELIPT) results from the previous year (usually for about 800 students) and presented an extended report to the curriculum committee with an abbreviated report to the ELI faculty. Both reports covered item analysis, descriptive statistics, reliability analysis, and arguments for the validity of our placement testing procedures, as well as suggestions for revising the test for the following autumn. During the summer, the director also revised and updated the teacher orientation materials for the yearly teacher orientation meeting.

This case study will focus on the test development and improvement portion of the curriculum development processes and show how the proficiency, placement, diagnostic, and achievement testing became an interlocking system of information useful for both teachers and administrators.

❖ DESCRIPTION

An Institutional Point of View

As director of the ELI, it was my duty to make sure all students were working at the appropriate level in each skill area (i.e., listening, reading, or writing) and that they were progressing satisfactorily through the courses. To those ends, a testing program (shown in Figure 3) evolved to include four distinct stages. They include the initial screening stage, the placement stage, the 2nd-week assessment stage, and the end-of-course achievement procedures.

Initial Screening Stage

Before being admitted to UHM, the admissions staff screened all international students by examining their previous academic records, letters of recommendation, TOEFL scores, and financial statements. To be accepted into any degree program at UHM, students were required to have a score of at least 500 on the TOEFL.

International students admitted to UHM were informed of that fact in a letter that also directed them to report to the ELI as soon as they arrived at UHM. They also received a separate letter from the ELI explaining how this requirement worked: We could either give them clearance (if they had 600 or higher on the TOEFL) or assess their need for further ELI courses (if they fell in the range between 500 and 599 on the TOEFL). Thus, students could be entirely exempted from ELI courses or be required to take between one and six 3-unit courses during their first 2 years at UHM. The students were allowed to take these ELI courses in tandem with their other content-area courses at the university. According to UHM policy, ELI courses took precedence over other course work. However, as a matter of ELI policy, we did not usually require students to take more than two ELI courses in any given semester.

At any point in this initial screening stage, students could request an interview with the ELI director for further consideration. This allowed a modicum of flexibility and an opportunity to identify students who could be exempted from ELI training without any further testing. For example, students who were born in foreign countries but did all of their K-12 education in Hawaii or students from India who did all of their education in English-medium schools could be exempted in an

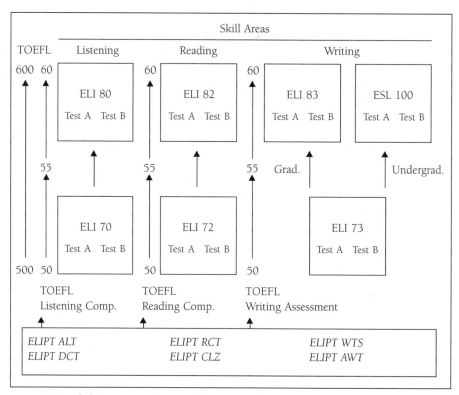

FIGURE 3. English Language Institute Placement Test

(From *Testing in Language Programs*, p. 133, by J. D. Brown, 1996, Upper Saddle River, NJ: Prentice Hall Regents. Copyright © 2001 by J. D. Brown. Adapted with permission.)

interview after examining their high school transcripts. In Hawaii, many different and interesting language background situations arose, and the decisions in these cases could only be made on a one-to-one basis in an interview with the student. In cases where I was in doubt or felt that I did not have enough information, I would have the students take the ELIPT to obtain more information.

Placement Stage

In most cases, students who scored between 500 and 599 on the TOEFL were required to take the ELIPT as soon as they arrived because the ELIPT

- gave us more precise and comprehensive information than the TOEFL scores did

- provided more recent information than the TOEFL scores did (TOEFL scores could be as much as 2 years old)

- pinpointed how the students fit into our particular ESL program in terms of their level of ability in each of the skill areas

The placement stage was particularly important to the ELI program because the ELIPT focused specifically on the skills and levels of ability that were found in the ELI courses.

The ELIPT was a 3-hour battery of six tests, including the:

1. Academic Listening Test (ALT)
2. Dictation (DCT)
3. Reading Comprehension Test (RCT)
4. Cloze Procedure (CLZ)
5. Writing Sample (WTS)
6. Academic Writing Test (AWT)

The ALT and DCT scores served as the basis for placing students into the listening courses (as indicated by the arrows just to the left of ELI 70 and ELI 80 in Figure 3) with the TOEFL listening comprehension subtest scores used as backup information. The RCT and CLZ served as the basis for our reading placement decisions (as indicated by the arrows to the left of ELI 72 and ELI 82 in Figure 3) with the TOEFL reading comprehension subtest scores used as a backup. Finally, the AWT and WTS served as the basis for placing students into writing courses (as indicated by the arrows to the left of ELI 73, ELI 83, and ESL 100 in Figure 3) with the TOEFL writing and analysis subtest scores used as a backup. Note that placement into each skill area was done independently of the other skills. A student, therefore, could end up in ELI 80 for advanced listening, ELI 72 for intermediate reading, and be exempt in writing, though it was much more common for students to place into the same level in all three skills. Note also that each skill-area placement was based on two ELIPT test scores with a TOEFL subtest score as a backup. Thus we had information from three points of view on each student's abilities within each skill area.

Even with all that information, the listening, reading, and writing skill placement decisions were not simple mechanical judgments based on the students' test scores. Each student's placement decisions were made in an individual interview with an ELI teacher or administrator. The interviewers had the student's file and test scores in front of them. They were told to base each skill-area placement decision on the appropriate ELIPT and TOEFL scores as well as to consider any other applicable information (e.g., the length of English language study, speaking ability during the interview, grades in high school). In those cases where an instructor could not make a decision or the student disputed the decision, the instructor sent the student to talk to the ELI director or assistant director for further evaluation and a final decision.

Second-Week Assessment Stage

After the final course withdrawal date in the 2nd week of classes, the teachers were asked to administer two forms of a criterion-referenced test designed to test the objectives of their particular course. These criterion-referenced tests were developed in two forms (cleverly labeled Forms A and B) so they could be administered in a counterbalanced manner. This pattern of counterbalancing is shown inside each of the course boxes in Figure 3. We administered these criterion-referenced tests to

*   determine which students, if any, had been misplaced by the ELIPT
*   identify students who already knew the material covered in the course objectives so well that the course would do them no good (such students were either promoted to the next level or exempted from further study in that skill area)

- provide the teachers with diagnostic information that would help them to identify the strengths and weaknesses of each student

- emphasize to the students what the objectives of the course would be and how they would be assessed

- permit the curriculum committee to examine the degree to which the students actually needed to learn each of the course objectives

At this point, our placement and 2nd-week assessment procedures had provided the teachers with groups of students who (a) were fairly similar in overall English language proficiency and (b) needed to learn at least some of the objectives of the course.

Achievement Procedures

At the end of the course, to complete the counterbalancing, the teachers administered the opposite form of the criterion-referenced test to each student. We found that putting their names on the forms in advance (instead of trying to decide on the spot who had taken which form and giving them the other one) helped a great deal to avoid confusion.

The teachers' final grades in the courses for each student were based on this test score, as well as on the student's attendance, classroom performance, and other tests and quizzes given by the teacher. In all of the courses except ESL 100 (where students received letter grades), the students were graded "pass," "fail," or "pass and exempt from the next level of study" in that particular skill area. In cases where students failed the final achievement test or otherwise were failing the course, it was my job as ELI director to arrange interviews with the students to advise them that they were failing and to inform them that they would need to repeat the course during the next semester. This took some of the pressure off the teachers.

In all cases, teachers filled out a performance report form for each student. On that form, the teacher filled in the student's grade, a recommendation for what level of ELI course the student should take next, ratings of the student's performance on six different scales (attendance, participation, content mastery, etc.), and a prose description of the student's achievements in the course. These performance reports were copied and sent to the students' academic departments so that their content-area advisors would know how they had performed. In this way, we treated all students equally, whereas those who had achieved more than their fellow students were identified so that adjustments could be made in their subsequent placement.

This system of four assessment stages depended on the information provided by our various types of tests. The initial screening stage depended primarily on the overall norm-referenced proficiency scores provided by the TOEFL. The placement stage relied principally on the norm-referenced placement results of the ELIPT. The 2nd-week assessment stage was based mainly on the criterion-referenced diagnostic test given in the 2nd week of each course, and the achievement stage was based partially on the students' scores of the end-of-term criterion-referenced test.

A Student's Point of View

To review the testing program from a different perspective, I would like to take the point of view of the ultimate consumer of our language teaching services, the student. Consider for a moment the case of Xiao Lao (a hypothetical student), who wanted to study for a business degree at UHM.

Xiao Lao began the process by filling out an application form, statement of purpose, and financial statement. She also had to get three letters of reference; have transcripts of her previous studies in China officially translated, copied, and sent to UHM; and take the TOEFL test. Once she completed her application and all the other parts had been received (including her TOEFL score of 571), the admissions office decided to admit Xiao Lao.

Once Xiao Lao was admitted, the admissions office immediately (in the bureaucratic sense of that word) sent her TOEFL proficiency test results to the ELI office. If she had scored over 600, she would have automatically been exempted from ELI training. However, her score was 571, so we had to consider whether she needed further ESL instruction. In her letter of acceptance, Xiao Lao had been informed that she would have to report to the ELI office before she could register. She also had received a letter from the ELI telling her very much the same thing but with more details. Unfortunately, she only read the acceptance letter as far as the words "Congratulations, you have been admitted. . . ." Similarly, she glanced at the letter from the ELI but then proceeded to forget all about it.

When Xiao Lao tried to register after standing in a long line, she found that she could not do so because something called the ELI had put a hold on her registration with the message to report to the ELI. Needless to say, she was hot, tired, and irritated when she finally located and reported to the ELI. At that point, she found herself talking to an overworked and busy secretary who asked her to talk to the ELI director. When she did so, she discovered that she would have to take the ELIPT 3 days later and would not be able to register until after that examination—by which time she was sure all of the courses she wanted to take would be closed. Against her wishes, she went back to the ELI secretary and signed up for the ELIPT. At that time, the secretary gave her a pamphlet describing the various parts of the ELIPT. Xiao Lao read this information carefully so that she would know what to expect when she took the ELIPT.

Xiao Lao went to the designated language laboratory to take the placement examination at 7:30 a.m. and took all six tests. ELI teachers were proctoring the ELIPT and this was Xiao Lao's first contact with these instructors. She finished the test battery about 11:00 a.m. and went to lunch. She had to return to the ELI office area at 1:30 p.m. for a placement interview conducted by one of the instructors. In that interview, the instructor told Xiao Lao that she was exempt from any further reading courses (as indicated by her ELIPT scores) but that she would have to take the advanced listening course (ELI 80) and the advanced writing course for graduate students (ELI 83). She reluctantly agreed to sign up for the courses. She was reluctant because she was in a hurry to finish her degree due to financial constraints and these ELI course requirements would slow her down. However, because she had no choice, she agreed to sign up for the two ELI courses at the same time as she registered for some of her other degree courses.

During the 2nd week of each of her ELI classes, she found herself taking another test in each class. Xiao Lao noticed that she was taking Form B in the listening class and wondered what that meant. In the directions for the tests, the teachers told her that any students who did very well would be exempted from the course, so Xiao Lao did her best on the test but did not do well enough on either test to be exempted.

However, she did notice that one student in her listening class and two in her writing class were exempted. Based on this 2nd-week diagnostic test, both teachers told Xiao Lao about her specific strengths and weaknesses in the skill area involved. For instance, in her writing course, she was told that her grammar was excellent but that she should concentrate on improving her organization and mechanics. Xiao Lao took the advanced listening and writing courses for 15 weeks. In the listening course, she learned about listening skills, did a great deal of listening to English, and gave a speech. In her writing course, she learned word-processing skills and practiced writing, proofreading, and revising her written English.

In the 16th week, at the end of her courses, Xiao Lao had to take another test to measure her achievement in each course. Xiao Lao noticed that the test was similar to the test she had taken at the beginning of the course but was not exactly the same. She noticed that the one in her listening course was labeled Form A. She did very well on these achievement tests, which was good because she knew that she had to pass these achievement tests to pass the courses. In addition, these achievement test scores would account for 20% of her grade in each course. Xiao Lao's overall performance in the course was recorded by the teacher and reported to her Business School advisor. Thus, Xiao Lao had completed all of her ELI requirements.

◈ DISTINGUISHING FEATURES

One central message in this case study is that, from the ELI's point of view, testing was an important and integral part of the curriculum. In addition, all program participants (students, teachers, and administrators,) benefited from the testing.

Because the placement test was essentially norm-referenced and used for administrative decision making, I took primary responsibility (in my role as ELI director) for developing and revising it.[2] As mentioned above, I reported annually on the ELIPT to the ELI staff as a means of quality assurance. In this report, I examined the item characteristics; descriptive statistics; and reliability, validity, and practicality of the various tests and suggested ways the test could be revised and improved. At the same time, I sought feedback from the teachers on any aspects of the tests they thought were problematic.

The development of the criterion-referenced diagnostic and achievement tests was even more cooperative. The lead teacher for testing worked with the teachers in each of the skill areas to write these tests. As a result, each and every test item came directly from the teachers. Thus, they had a large stake in the testing process.

Another central message in this case study was that the student's point of view was considered important. The ELI administrators and teachers never forgot that students were affected by the tests and the decisions based on those tests. Even though there was a great deal of testing, to Xiao Lao the testing appeared to be a natural part of the way things were done in the ELI. I think this was true only because the testing was set up as an important and integral part of the overall curriculum.

---

[2] Teachers were in no sense excluded from the norm-referenced testing. Indeed, they often needed to explain the ELI admissions and placement procedures to students and were a crucial part of the proctoring, scoring, and interviewing/placing processes during the actual ELIPT admissions.

The following characteristics of this testing program distinguished it from the testing that goes on in most language programs:

- Both norm-referenced (TOEFL and ELIPT) and criterion-referenced tests (diagnostic and achievement) were included in the testing program.

- The different types of tests were integrated into one continuous assessment and decision-making process that included admissions, placement, diagnostic, and achievement decisions.

- Teachers were involved in the placement testing (as proctors, scorers, interviewers, and critics).

- Each year, one teacher was given release time as lead teacher for testing to coordinate the development, administration, analysis, and revision of the criterion-referenced tests for diagnosis and achievement.

- Administrators were supportive of test development for classroom purposes as evidenced by the marshalling of resources (e.g., release time for a lead teacher for testing).

- Teachers were integrally involved in developing the items for the diagnostic and achievement tests in each course (as item writers, proctors, scorers, interviewers, and critics) and understood that to be part of their jobs.

- All placement tests were regularly and appropriately analyzed (for norm-referenced item characteristics, reliability, and validity) and revised (e.g., see Brown, 1989).

- All diagnostic and achievement tests were regularly and appropriately analyzed (for criterion-referenced item characteristics, dependability, and validity) and revised (e.g., see Brown, 1993).

- Students were not forgotten in the testing process. The students' points of view on the testing were considered important.

- Testing was important, but every effort was made to keep it from becoming intrusive.

◈ PRACTICAL IDEAS

To avoid creating a blissful picture of curriculum perfection, in this final section, I will discuss some of the problems we had in developing our comprehensive language-testing program and how we overcame them.

Get the Work Done

Testing is often an afterthought in language teaching. Such an attitude is too prevalent in language programs and, from my point of view, irresponsible. Tests are too important in terms of the significant decisions we make with them to be treated so cavalierly. Unfortunately, an integrated testing program (complete with a six-test placement battery and seven different classroom-oriented criterion-referenced tests in two forms each) is not easy to develop, implement, and maintain. Indeed, such a project across many courses requires an extraordinary amount of work. Nonetheless, a group of administrators, lead teachers, and teachers did create just such a testing program.

Can we count on teachers to do all that work on their own? Indeed, can we count on teachers to independently do any sort of coherent curriculum development across courses? No, we probably cannot, unless their work is coordinated and supported at the institutional level. Fortunately, the cost of such support need not be very high. The sole costs of our coherent testing program were constant attention from one ELI director, the appointment of a lead teacher for testing, and the cooperation of all teachers.

Appoint a Lead Teacher for Testing

The lead teacher for testing was given 50 percent release time (amounting to a one course reduction) to help the administrators and teachers develop, administer, score, analyze, and revise all the ELI tests. At the beginning of each semester, during the norm-referenced placement testing, the lead teacher for testing took responsibility for administering the tests, while the assistant director took charge of logistical matters and the director did the scoring and analysis of the results as each test was completed.

During the remainder of the semester, when our attention turned to the diagnostic and achievement tests, the lead teacher was in charge of the testing logistics, which included:

- getting teachers to write the items
- putting them together into a test
- proofreading the items
- getting the ELI director to proofread the items
- revising and compiling the pilot items into two forms
- photocopying the tests
- distributing the tests to teachers for in-class administration
- collecting the tests after they were administered
- scoring the tests
- getting the results back to the teachers (within 24 hours if possible)
- analyzing the items for revision purposes
- analyzing the tests for dependability and validity

As for the importance of fancy statistics, I would like to emphasize that the lead teacher for testing needed only the knowledge about language-testing programs provided in a book such as Brown (1996b). With basic understanding of item analysis techniques, any language teaching professional should be able to get a good start on developing such tests.

Get All Teachers on Board

At first, getting teachers to cooperate in this testing effort was difficult. Many teachers felt they worked too hard and did not want to do anything extra. A number of strategies were used to overcome this attitude, but the primary and most successful strategy involved clearly outlining the teachers' duties.

The curriculum committee began this process by first outlining their duties and responsibilities. These descriptions were discussed with the teachers and revised based on their comments. The committee was then in a good position to develop a description of the teachers' duties and responsibilities. Using the graduate division's description of the duties of graduate assistants (all ELI teachers fell in this category at that time), the curriculum committee proposed a draft set of duties, which included the graduate division's requirement that they work 20 hours a week. We divided the 20 hours as follows:

- 6 hours of classroom teaching
- 6 hours for preparation time
- 2 office hours
- 1 hour for meetings
- 5 hours for curriculum development

Thus, curriculum development (and therefore testing) was included as an integral part of the teachers' job description. In the discussions that followed, some teachers were unhappy about what they (correctly) perceived as a trick to get them to do more work. But that unrest soon settled down, when everybody realized that they were seldom asked to do any more than an hour or two of curriculum work each week. In addition, the teachers realized that they received a great deal from these curriculum development efforts.

Anticipate Surprise Problems

As in so many human endeavors, we often did not learn what we set out to learn in the process of developing our tests. For example, we chose to develop two forms of the ELI 72 reading test as our first criterion-referenced diagnostic and achievement tests. We carefully developed them to match the course objectives and administered them with some excitement in the 2nd week of classes. Unfortunately, the scores of the students for each and every objective indicated that the students already knew virtually all of the material we were planning to teach them—at the beginning of the course. We found ourselves facing the uncomfortable fact that our objectives, which had been used for many years, were targeted at a level far too low for the abilities of our students.

As a result, we had no choice but to discard our tests and revise our objectives considerably. In this particular case, we were able to use similar objectives by applying the existing objectives to considerably more difficult reading texts. Initially, we had been devastated to realize that our first criterion-referenced test development efforts were in vain, but, in retrospect, this early attempt at developing diagnostic and achievement tests (even though it failed) helped us to change our views of the students' language abilities and learning needs. This failure benefited not only the single reading course but all the other courses as well.

Thereafter, we never had such a wholesale failure of our curriculum, though in virtually every course, we did get detailed information from our criterion-referenced tests about objectives that (a) were not being tested well, (b) were not being taught at all, (c) were not being taught well, or (d) were not teachable at the level of proficiency involved. All of which, on an objective-by-objective basis was useful information for curriculum-revision purposes.

Rely on Multiple Measures of Assessment

Although we did everything possible to ensure that our testing program appropriately admitted, placed, diagnosed, and promoted most of the students served by the ELI, we recognized that such decisions are made by human beings and that, even when based on something as seemingly scientific as test scores, the human judgments involved are hardly perfect. One way a comprehensive testing program like that described here helps to safeguard against errors in judgment is by relying on multiple sources of information. Admissions decisions were never based solely on the proficiency test scores but rather on multiple sources of information including grades, letters of recommendation, statements of purpose, financial statements, and TOEFL scores. Similarly, placement decisions for each skill area were based on two ELIPT test scores with a TOEFL subtest score as backup and other information gathered during a personal interview with each student. The classroom diagnostic and achievement criterion-referenced decisions were each based on a single test score. However, at the achievement decision point, the diagnostic and achievement test results were examined together and teachers were encouraged to gather information of their own including homework, quizzes, midterm exams, attendance, and additional final examination testing.

◈ CONCLUSION

In sum, we viewed our admissions, placement, diagnostics, and achievement decisions as important: An incorrect decision could cost a student a great deal in extra time and tuition for studying in the ELI. Thus, we took those decisions seriously and based them on the best available information taken from a variety of sources including test scores.

Such a testing program certainly entails considerable effort on the part of the administrators, lead teachers, and teachers, but the benefits derived from effective and fair testing procedures accrue to the entire curriculum and to everyone involved in the language learning process.

◈ ACKNOWLEDGMENTS

I would like to personally thank for their dedication and hard work the three testing lead teachers who served while I was director of the ELI: Charles Lockhardt, who is a well-known author and professor in Hong Kong; Gary Cook, who recently completed a doctorate in educational testing at the University of Michigan; and Yuichi Watanabe, who just completed his dissertation defense at UHM and is working as a professor at the Kanda Institute of Foreign Studies in Japan.

◈ CONTRIBUTOR

James Dean ("JD") Brown is a professor in the Department of Second Language Studies at the University of Hawaii at Manoa. He has published 13 books and numerous articles in the areas of language testing, curriculum design, and research methods.

PART 2

Curriculum
Washback

CHAPTER 2

Developing an English Proficiency Test for Japanese Secondary Students

Caryl Lyons, Sandra Bolton, and Stephen Gaies

◈ INTRODUCTION

In 1997, the Benesse Corporation in Japan contracted with ACT, Inc., a not-for-profit testing company in the United States, to develop a test for Japanese high school students studying English in Japan. This case study describes the development of the Benesse Proficiency Test of English Communication (PTEC), a test measuring Japanese students' progress in reading, writing, and listening in English. This case study focuses on multicultural variables that critically affect the test development process. It emphasizes the writing section of the PTEC because this subtest best illustrates the intercultural issues that emerged during the test development process.

◈ CONTEXT

Why the PTEC Was Developed

Benesse's main intention was to help schools and teachers advance toward the newly stated goal of the Japanese Ministry of Education, Culture, Sports and Science (Monbusho) to move English language teaching in a more communicative direction (Ministry of Education, 1989, 1990).[1] Traditionally, English language education in Japan has emphasized reading and grammar. Reading usually has been taught through translating, memorizing vocabulary, and sometimes reading aloud repetitively. Japanese teachers of English usually have explicated reading texts in detail, primarily using Japanese rather than English. Writing has most often consisted of single sentences translated from an original Japanese version (LoCastro, 1996). None of these activities fits into a model of communicative language teaching.

Several factors motivated the Ministry to create the new curriculum. As more Japanese students studied abroad and went on homestays, it was increasingly recognized that the English taught in school was not practical for common communication (i.e., listening and speaking). It became evident that students needed to be able to understand spoken English and to speak English well themselves if they

---

[1] In 2001, the Ministry of Education, Culture, Sports and Science (Monbusho) merged with the Science and Technology Agency to become the Ministry of Education, Culture, Sports, Science and Technology (Monbukagakusho). See http://www.mext.go.jp/english/ for additional information on the Monbukagakusho.

were to succeed in business, government, science, and many other fields, as well as to succeed in studying abroad in English-speaking countries. Furthermore, Japanese students' test scores on the Test of English as a Foreign Language (TOEFL) and the Test of English for International Communication (TOEIC) were consistently lower than those of students in other Asian countries (Mulvey, 1999). In response, the Ministry began changing its guidelines for English proficiency. Today some Japanese universities have altered their entrance requirements to reflect the acknowledged need for communicative English and have begun to test speaking and listening skills. For example, the prestigious University of Tokyo has introduced a listening comprehension component in its entrance exam (LoCastro, 1996).

Consequently, Japanese secondary schools have come under pressure to provide more instruction in listening and speaking and in writing for communication. Teachers are being required to teach more communicatively, but many have never been taught communicative methods of teaching and some teachers are unsure of their own communicative English skills.

Communicative Testing and the PTEC

Among the definitions of communicative language teaching and testing are those mentioned by Kitao and Kitao (1996): (a) students should develop the ability to use language in real-life situations; (b) tests should reflect communicative situations in which testees are likely to find themselves or social situations in which they might be in a position to use English; and (c) the receptive skills of listening and reading should emphasize understanding the communicative intent of the speaker or writer. Additional emphasis on real-world communication comes from the Australian Board of Senior School Secondary Studies, which notes that communicative testing should use authentic texts and give students the opportunity to speak and write from their own experiences (Sato & Kleinsasser, 1999).

The PTEC was developed in response to the new communicative curriculum. It aims to test language that is used in authentic communication and to test this language in a more communicative manner. Because it is possible to enhance the communicative nature of a test through the use of materials and tasks that students might encounter in the real English-speaking world, the three subtests contain various authentic elements.

The listening portion of the test reflects authentic American speech patterns, syntactically and phonetically, and a large percentage of the items replicate real-life situations. The reading items are based on reading skills used in real life: skimming, scanning, and deciphering the meaning of words from context. Also, the majority of the reading texts are based on authentic materials originally written for native English speakers. In general, the PTEC focuses on the meaning intended by the language rather than on the structure of the language.

A direct writing assessment is the third subtest of the PTEC. A direct writing assessment involves communication between the writer and the rater (or scorer). The PTEC writing assessment is additionally communicative because it evaluates primarily the content rather than the grammatical accuracy of student writing.

◈ DESCRIPTION

The Test Development Process

Many decisions must be made when developing test specifications for a standardized English as a second language/English as a foreign language (ESL/EFL) assessment. Some of the questions that ACT and Benesse considered in each of the tested skill areas are listed below. How a number of these questions were answered for the PTEC emerges throughout the rest of this case study.

Listening

- What are the purposes of the listening test (e.g., understanding content, distinguishing sounds)?
- What microskills should be tested?
- Should the vocabulary be controlled or uncontrolled?
- Should the test use only one variety of English or a variety of Englishes?
- How many elisions or reductions should there be?
- What should be the speed of the recorded speech?
- Should students be able to listen more than once?
- How long should pauses for answering questions be?
- How many types of items should there be?
- How many items of each type should there be?

Reading

- What microskills should be tested?
- Should the vocabulary be controlled or uncontrolled?
- How much time should be allowed for various parts of the test?
- What topics are suitable for the population of students to be tested?
- How many item types should there be?
- How many items of each type should there be?

Writing

- What decisions are being made on the basis of the writing test?
- Should students have a choice of prompt?
- What type of writing should be assessed (e.g., descriptive, narrative, persuasive)?
- Should more than one type of writing be assessed?
- Should a scenario be given and/or an audience designated?
- Should stimulus materials accompany the prompt?
- Should the rating be holistic or analytic?

- What scoring features should be included in the rubric?
- What level of confidence is necessary for the results?
- Should students have access to the rubric?
- What kinds of feedback could the assessment give to students in addition to a score?
- Should raters be native English speakers? From which country?
- What special considerations should be taken into account when native speaker scorers assess writings of nonnative speakers?
- How much time should students have for writing?
- How many prompts should there be?

Other Considerations When Developing a Test

In addition to the specifications for each subtest, test developers must consider broader issues of how the assessment will likely be used and for whom the assessment is intended.

What Are the Assessment's Purposes?

Will the assessment be used

- for admission?
- to place students in classes?
- to motivate students?
- to monitor and track proficiency?
- to help students learn by providing study materials?
- to lead or change instruction (positive washback)?
- to evaluate teachers?
- to evaluate programs or schools?
- to compare students within a school?
- to compare students nationally or internationally?
- to compare schools or countries with other schools or countries?

The PTEC has several purposes. The test is intended to influence instruction, providing positive washback by encouraging teachers to use more communicative activities in their classrooms and to spend more class time on listening, speaking, and communicative writing activities. Other envisioned uses were (a) to motivate students by providing them with a variety of authentic materials similar to what they might read or hear when traveling or living in an English-speaking environment; (b) to monitor or track student proficiency by giving students and their teachers reports that show student progress on the PTEC from year to year; and (c) to help students learn by providing study materials. After each operational test, Benesse has provided students with study materials that show them the test items and the correct answers as well as give them information about how to locate the correct answers in the stimulus material.

Who Is the Assessment For?

- Is it for students, to help them learn their strengths and locate their weaknesses?

- Is it for teachers and administrators, to help them assess their own programs or teaching?

- Is it for parents, to help them evaluate their children's skills and potential?

- Is it for admissions officers, to help them select or eliminate students for admission?

The PTEC, a low-stakes test, gives information to all of the above except admissions officers. Currently, the test is not used for admissions purposes, although it can be used to study for tests that, in turn, will be used for admissions. The PTEC is intended to help students monitor their own progress in English; to help teachers see the strengths and weaknesses of all their students, particularly in the area of writing; and to help local school administrators see how their students are performing compared to previous administrations of the test.

The PTEC

The test was developed based on the points listed above. The actual test that evolved from these discussions is described in Table 1. All items on the Benesse test are field tested, and, on the basis of the field-test results, items are selected for constructing the operational test forms.

Listening Subtest

The listening subtest, which is made up of four sections (Parts A through D) is 25 minutes long. There are 40 multiple-choice listening items (10 items per part), enough items to gain an accurate measure of students' listening abilities. Moreover, careful adherence to an approved vocabulary list, assembled from words and idiomatic phrases found in English language textbooks used in secondary schools in Japan, helps to ensure that the test will not be too difficult. This is important because too many low scores do not permit adequate differentiation among lower level students. There is no repetition of spoken stimuli (i.e., conversations and mono-logues) or the response options that students hear on tape, but students may take notes in the margins of the test book.

The subtest tries to simulate authentic spoken American English. Therefore, in the stimuli and options that are recorded, words are naturally linked, and some contractions and phonetic changes (assimilations and reductions) are used. Graphics play a significant role in the subtest—half the test items include either photos or illustrations—in an effort to come closer to real-life listening situations, which usually provide visual cues for listeners.

In Part C items, for example, most of the illustrations depict a silhouette of a human figure representing the examinee who will carry out the task. In addition, young speakers are used in the recordings to represent the Japanese student (the test taker) who must perform the task. This helps draw the test taker into the dialogues by making them seem more relevant and immediate. To answer the questions, students must recognize discrete information, or details, as well as be able to understand the interaction among the details.

TABLE 1. THE PROFICIENCY TEST OF ENGLISH COMMUNICATION (PTEC)

Listening		
Part A	25 min	Students choose the best statement out of three recorded statements they hear to match with a photograph. The photographs permit the testing of descriptive language as well as inferencing skills.
Part B		Students hear a short question and three responses and then quickly choose the correct response to the question.
Part C		Students perform real-world tasks in which English would naturally be used between a Japanese student and a native English speaker. The recorded conversation is based on a scenario that students can read in Japanese. Students choose the correct option out of four options represented in an illustration. Questions are printed in the test book.
Part D		Students find specific information by listening to short conversations (four-to-six-turn dialogues) and monologues. The language is denser and more complex than in the other parts. Questions are printed in the test book.
Reading		
Part A	7 min	Students select the appropriate vocabulary word to fit into a one- or two-sentence context. Items are specifically designed to test vocabulary knowledge rather than grammatical knowledge.
Part B	14 min	There are two types of items in Part B. For the skimming items, students read an approximately 100-word paragraph to determine the main idea, the only question that is asked. For the scanning items, students are directed to read the two questions associated with a word-and-graphic stimulus (e.g., schedule, advertisement, brochure) and must scan the information to find the answers to the questions. Usually students must put together two pieces of information found in the stimulus to answer the questions.
Part C	24 min	Students read three 300- to 325-word passages and answer five questions about each passage. These are standard question types for a reading test (e.g., recognizing main ideas, understanding details and relationships, figuring out vocabulary from context). The passages are adapted from authentic fiction and nonfiction materials in English.
Writing		
One Prompt	20 min	Students write in English in response to one prompt, writing as much as the time allows. The writing includes a variety of forms, such as an essay, an e-mail message, or a draft of a speech. The prompts present a real-world scenario (e.g., a homestay, a classroom in the United States) in which students would naturally use English to communicate in writing. Photographs or illustrations accompany each prompt as stimulus material.

Reading Subtest

The reading subtest is in some ways a traditional test of reading, but the materials are nearly all adaptations of authentic materials. As stated earlier, the reading subtest is communicative in that it uses authentic materials and that it asks students to use real-life reading skills such as skimming and scanning in addition to the usual close-reading skills. The reading subtest uses basically the same vocabulary list as the listening subtest.

The scanning items in Part B are based on authentic materials such as schedules, advertisements, and brochures, which students examine to locate specific information. In one example, the authentic material is a schedule for riverboat rides. Students are directed to read two questions first and then scan the stimulus material for the answers, rather than to read the entire schedule. In most cases, students have to access at least two pieces of information to answer a question.

Writing Subtest

The writing subtest is a communicative experience for students because the prompts create authentic situations for using English, and the students' essays are returned to them with the handwritten comments of the raters of their essays in the United States.

At Benesse's direction, the writing subtest gives students 20 minutes to respond to one prompt. A brief scenario is included that may ask students to think of going abroad for a homestay, giving a brief introductory speech to a class, or responding to an e-mail from an American friend. The purpose of the brief scenario is to attempt to give students a real-world purpose and audience for writing. The types of writing include expository, descriptive, and persuasive writing. Photographs or illustrations accompany each prompt as stimulus material.

Developing the subtest entailed a number of specific issues that became key factors in our case study. These include prompt construction, rubric development, and rater training.

Prompt Construction

The construction of prompts for a large-scale writing assessment presents many questions to the test developer. This is especially true when designing an assessment to measure EFL writing competence. The test developer from another culture must be aware that students bring personal and cultural experiences to the task that may affect their ability to demonstrate proficiency under testing conditions. Therefore, the prompt topic must be as fair as possible, not privileging one specific set of cultural experiences over another. Further, the prompt should be clearly written, using an appropriate level of vocabulary or being printed in the student's first language (L1) as well as the student's second language (L2) to ensure that writing skill, not reading ability, is the skill being tested. Finally, the prompt topic must walk a fine line between being broad enough to allow a range of student responses yet not so broad that it elicits responses too divergent to compare on the same rating scale.

The main purpose of the writing subtest, designed primarily for instructional purposes, is to measure students' developing ability to write in English. The form of the PTEC prompts evolved over time. However, the general characteristics remained the same:

- The topic of the prompt should relate to the experience and knowledge of Japanese students and be of interest to them.

- The topic of the prompt should require only background knowledge that the majority of the intended student population is likely to possess.

- The prompt should require only a level of English vocabulary that Japanese students are likely to know or English words provided in the translation of the prompt.

- The prompt should allow a broad range of student response so it does not limit the content of student essays.

It was also agreed that the topics should not evoke an emotional response in the student population; hence, the test avoids topics such as death, suicide, domestic violence, bullying, divorce, religion, drugs and alcohol, and race or ethnicity. Each prompt is printed in Japanese as well as English to ensure that students are able to understand the writing task.

To ensure the highest quality and integrity of writing assessment, field testing the writing prompts is an essential step in any large-scale testing process. Field testing can reveal problems with accessibility, student interest level, and prompts that do not discriminate clearly among student ability levels. The operational prompts that appear on the writing subtest were field tested using Japanese secondary students, the same population as those taking the test. The operational prompts were then selected using statistical means to ensure comparability across administrations and using content analysis by ESL and writing test specialists as well as by raters who scored the field-test papers.

Holistic Rubric Construction

The writing subtest uses a six-point holistic rubric, or scoring scheme, because early field testing showed that the writing could support this number of distinctions. A holistic rubric was chosen for two main reasons. First, the holistic scoring approach tends to reward what students are doing well (Wolcott & Legg, 1998), especially important in a second-language assessment, and can perhaps more evenly weigh rhetorical ability with grammatical knowledge. In addition, rater comments would provide diagnostic information for classroom use. The measurable components in the PTEC rubric are idea development, organizational pattern, sentence structure, and word choice. Functional fluency is more highly valued than formal accuracy for this population of second-language learners, so mechanics are considered only as they may or may not interfere with communication of thoughts and ideas.

The rubric is designed as a two-decision rubric, which means that the rater makes two decisions about each piece of writing. First, the rater must decide whether the writing is basically lower level (closer to a 2), or basically upper level (closer to a 5) based on the well-developed criteria for these two points. Then, the rater must decide whether the writing precisely meets the criteria for a 5 or a 2, or whether instead it is better or worse than a 5 or a 2. Criteria for scores 6 and 4 are written so that they are relative to the criteria for a 5, and criteria for scores of 3 and 1 are written so that they are relative to the criteria for a 2.

Along with a numerical score, raters provide handwritten comments, selected from a menu of comments, on each paper. The comments are categorized into "praise" and "suggestions for improvement." Students receive comments from each category, and sentences or words in their essays that correspond to the improvement category are underlined. All papers are returned to student writers in their individual classrooms, where, it is hoped, teachers and students work together to use the comments to improve the students' writing.

Raters have given comments in some form from the beginning; however, as with the writing prompts, the comment form has evolved, driven by the wishes of the test users. In the beginning, raters simply selected comments from a prescribed list and filled in numbers on the score sheet that corresponded to the comment number. The move toward more personalized, text-specific comments came as a result of teachers and students wanting a closer link between reader and writer and wishing, perhaps, for more direct help in improving student writing.

Rater Training

Evaluators must be made aware of cross-cultural differences before beginning to score second language writing (Wolcott & Legg, 1998). In preparation for scoring the Japanese student papers, rater training for the PTEC begins with a discussion of special considerations when rating EFL writing. These considerations include how EFL writing may differ from native speaker writing in, for example, sentence structure, use of prepositions and articles, word choice, and tone. The difference is emphasized between global errors that interfere with meaning such as syntactic errors, and local errors, such as misuse of articles (see, for example, Sweedler-Brown, 1993), that do not interfere with communication. Raters are made aware of how many years of study and practice it takes second language learners to come close to mastering the finer points of the English language (e.g., the use of prepositions and articles).

After this introduction to scoring second language writing, the raters read and discuss previously scored benchmark papers whose scores have been determined during the range-finding process. Then raters reach consensus, through small and large group discussion, on papers they score individually. The last part of the training session is devoted to the practice of giving handwritten comments of praise and suggestions for improvement on each student paper. For this purpose, legibility, a positive tone, and a careful choice of appropriate vocabulary are stressed. As is common in most large-scale writing assessments, each paper is scored twice by independent raters, with scores resolved by a third rater if they are more than one point apart.

❖ DISTINGUISHING FEATURES

Assessment, like everything else connected to ESL/EFL, has cultural implications. What underlying assumptions are the test makers unaware of that might affect student performance? How do the assumptions of the two cultures involved in creating the test differ? Many competing priorities emerged in the process of developing the PTEC, such as differing cultural assumptions and the need to maintain good test development practices while remaining flexible in meeting test-taker needs.

Balancing these competing priorities led to some of the fine lines that Benesse and ACT walked during the development process.

Balancing Competing Priorities: Walking the Fine Lines

The Fine Line Between Cultures

Negotiating everything from content to costs has been interesting. Questions arose concerning what types of stimuli were appropriate for use with Japanese students, and what subjects should be avoided because they were either too familiar or too inaccessible to these students. It was decided that all test stimuli and items would be reviewed by a group of Japanese teachers to ensure that they were linguistically and culturally accessible to the students and that the difficulty level was appropriate. Whenever there were disagreements, however, the company commissioning the test had the final say.

Japanese teachers of English reviewed all the items on the test, specifically looking for cultural misunderstandings that might arise from certain reading passages or listening dialogues. Feedback from Japanese reviewers has helped the test developers avoid questions that pose daunting problems for even the best Japanese students.

Communicative Test Versus Noncommunicative Training

Another fine line exists between the desire of ACT and Benesse to produce a communicative test and the degree of communicative training of many Japanese teachers of English. Many Japanese teachers have been trained in the grammar-translation method of teaching English. Many have not had an opportunity to live and study in an English-speaking environment and are understandably reluctant to be forced into a type of teaching for which they have not been trained. Nunan (2002) has recently documented the gap, across a number of Asian countries, between an official sanctioning of communicative teaching and the reality: that communicative teaching rarely happens in classrooms.

Old Versus New Item Types

Walking the line between old and new item types happens in all sections of the test, with the goal being to provide a test that looks familiar to teachers and students but is also communicative. The reading subtest includes traditional item types such as passages for close reading and vocabulary items in brief contexts. However, a more innovative section tests skimming and scanning skills. Skimming skills are tested by asking students to determine only the main idea in a short article, whereas scanning skills are tested by asking students to locate information in authentic stimuli such as advertisements, brochures, recipes, and directions.

On the listening subtest, many items are traditional. Most are either dialogues or monologues followed by either spoken or printed questions and answer options. Part C items, though, are task based: Students read a scenario (in Japanese) that places a Japanese student in a situation in which he or she would naturally use English, such as a homestay. Students then hear a dialogue or monologue in English while looking at an illustration. They must respond as the Japanese student who is supposed to do something in the illustration (e.g., find a person, locate something to give to someone, follow directions to a specific place). These situations are intended to be especially communicative.

Many considerations were discussed as the test specifications were being developed. For example, what percentage of words could be unknown words (i.e., words that are not on the official word lists printed by the Ministry or do not appear in commonly used student textbooks)? Teachers have a vested interest in testing their students on words they have learned so that the students do well on the test, but a communicative test seeks to challenge students to use context clues in reading authentic materials. We finally allowed 5% of unknown words in the close reading passages and a higher percentage of unknown words in the authentic skimming and scanning materials.

Reliability

A fourth fine line relates to reliability. Across the test as a whole, the number of questions on each part had to be determined so that there were enough questions for each part to be valid and have an acceptable level of reliability but few enough so that the total test could be administered in two 45-minute class periods. Each of these decisions was discussed at length, and compromises were made to allow for an optimum number of questions and variety of question types.

Maintaining Consistency and Meeting Client Needs

Finally, there is the fine line between maintaining consistency and meeting client needs with flexibility. This test was set up to give students an ongoing report on their progress from year to year. To have stability of information, it is better that test specifications remain unchanged from year to year. Yet, in setting up a new test, it is necessary to maintain some flexibility so that the test can be responsive both to the results of the test and to the wishes of the clientele, namely, the schools and the teachers who decide to purchase the test.

The need for flexibility has allowed minor adjustments to wording and placement of items in the reading and listening subtests. However, in the writing subtest, flexibility has been a constant. From the beginning, the goal has been to have the writing tasks be accessible, interesting, and culturally appropriate to encourage students to write as much as possible within the 20-minute time frame. Over time, the prompt format has evolved both in the kind of writing students do and in the stimulus materials designed to aid students' writing. At first, students wrote both descriptive and persuasive essays, with two photographs accompanying the descriptive prompt. Later, charts and graphs were added to the persuasive prompt and then dropped. During the developmental process, the scoring rubric has provided the consistency necessary for comparisons across the various models.

The PTEC Versus Other Large-Scale Proficiency Tests

Several features distinguish the PTEC from other large-scale national and international assessments:

- The test was designed to be more communicative than traditional English proficiency tests in Japan.

- Following the test, detailed explanations of the correct answers and the reasons for them are provided to the teachers and students to enhance learning and to create positive washback.

- In the direct writing assessment, students receive personalized narrative feedback as well as numerical scores.

- The raters of the writing essays are trained to score ESL writing focusing on the content of the writing rather than on grammatical accuracy.

◈ PRACTICAL IDEAS

Recognize and Appreciate That Cultural Differences Will Exist

While developing the PTEC, ACT staff traveled to Japan to meet with Japanese teachers and to learn about Japanese culture firsthand; the Benesse staff regularly visited the United States and participated in cultural events as well as business meetings. One ACT staff member made a presentation at the Japan Association of Language Teachers (JALT) conference. Benesse furnished ACT with a subscription to an English-language Japanese newspaper, and many ACT staff members regularly read books and articles about Japanese education and culture.

Keep the Channels of Communication Open

Modern technology was indispensable in the daily communication that was necessary throughout the entire process of the PTEC's development and implementation. In addition to almost daily e-mail communication, faxes were exchanged regularly, and teleconferences and videoconferences were occasionally held. In addition, rapid mail delivery companies allowed the timely exchange of longer documents and confidential materials.

Reach Agreement on Sharing Information and Data for Research

The frequency distribution of rater comments formed the basis for one research study (Bolton, 2000). Other studies examined the correlations among the reading, listening, and writing components of the test (Gaies, Bolton, & Lyons, 2002; Gaies, Johnson, Lyons, & Bolton, 2001). The possibilities for research based on cross-cultural, collaborative test development are rich and potentially fruitful for the field of EFL assessment.

◈ CONCLUSION

Developing the PTEC is as much a case study in cultural dialogue as an instance of test development. Throughout the process of test development, it was necessary to maintain a balance between adhering to traditional principles of test development and acknowledging particular aspects of the cultural context for which the test was developed, ever mindful of the fine line between flexibility and consistency. The result is an assessment instrument that measures Japanese students' language proficiency in ways that promote more communicative teaching of English.

◈ CONTRIBUTORS

Caryl Lyons is a test development associate at ACT, Inc., in Iowa City, Iowa. She has taught in intensive English programs and rhetoric and writing labs at the university level as well as in secondary school and adult education programs.

Sandra Bolton is a senior test development associate at ACT, Inc. She has taught at the high school and college levels and has facilitated summer workshops for the Iowa Writing Project.

Stephen J. Gaies is a professor of TESOL and applied linguistics at the University of Northern Iowa. For more than 25 years, he has been involved in second language assessment in several capacities: as a researcher, as a presenter in in-service teacher education, and as an item writer and test-development consultant. He is a former editor of *TESOL Quarterly*.

CHAPTER 3

Deconstructing the Making of Japanese University Entrance Exams

Tim Murphey and Kazuyoshi Sato

❖ INTRODUCTION

This case study describes the university entrance exam system in Japan, our attempts to improve entrance exam construction, and the impact of entrance exams on participants in the system. We recount our personal experiences to familiarize readers with the situation and provide views from other researchers to corroborate what we describe. Examination construction methods described in this case study have been replicated throughout Japan for a long time and will probably continue for some time to come. Our goal in describing the conditions under which teachers work on these exams is not meant to embarrass or hurt any institution or individuals but to permit more open views of the situation so that changes can occur more quickly to improve the system. Indeed, we hope to contribute to a healthier entrance system by writing this case study. Our main point is that the fossilized reification of the exam system is being used to guide multiple practices that produce questionable evaluations of students' abilities and suitability for entrance to universities. We consider these practices unethical vis-à-vis the youth of Japan and harmful to the country's education system as a whole, and, thus, to Japanese society. We argue for greater assessment literacy as the way to improve the situation.

We would like to note that there are at least three positive things happening in the university entrance exam system. First, the Center Test from Japan's Ministry of Education, Culture, Sports, Science, and Technology[1] and some of the national university tests have been improving, according to several recent analyses (Guest, 2000; Mulvey, 1999).

Second, 31% of national universities now include listening sections on university entrance exams. However, only 9% of all private universities have listening exams. Because individual faculties or departments at each university often have their own exams, this is somewhat misleading. Altogether, 199 out of 1,629 entrance exams (12%) now have listening sections (Y. Yagi, personal communication, July, 26, 2001; see also "Eigo Listening Juushi," 1999). The Ministry has reportedly also decided to add a listening comprehension section to the Center Test as early as 2006 ("Colleges Add Hearing Skills," 2000).

---

[1] In 2001, the Ministry of Education, Culture, Sports, and Science merged with the Science and Technology Agency to become the Ministry of Education, Culture, Sports, Science, and Technology. See http://www.mext.go.jp/english/ for additional information.

The third positive development is that some universities are beginning to use an admissions office (AO) type of entrance evaluation for at least a small portion of their students; that is, evaluating students using more than one instrument. However, some lower-level schools admit nearly all AO candidates and "recommended" applicants automatically to secure early commitment in the competition for more students ("The Good and Bad of AO exams," 2001; "Universities Strive," 1999).

◈ CONTEXT

Japanese University Entrance Examinations

Takeo Niwa, the director of research at Kawai Juku, Japan's largest and most powerful cram school chain, says that the positive efforts described above are good but affect only a small number of universities (personal communication, July 24, 2001). The private university system, accounting for more than 70% of the total number of universities, is still not making many changes. Niwa (2000), whose book criticizes many universities' exams in detail, says one of the main problems is that university professors are not trained to write exams (see also Ito, 2001). Kawai Juku trains students year round to pass entrance exams, regularly constructs its own piloted mock tests, and has researched the exams extensively. Niwa sees exam making and preparation as a full-time professional job. In fact, Kawai Juku began offering its exam experience to universities and made 20 entrance exams for various low-, middle-, and high-level universities for the February 2001 session and doubled the number for 2002. Some exams are only for a department, whereas others are for the whole university with about 50% being English exams. Although this has reportedly been met with mixed feelings by the Ministry ("Ministry Against Setting Exam," 2000), Niwa says Kawai Juku has been encouraged by the Ministry in private. Still, he laments the fact that the universities refuse to share the data after the exams so that the test developers at Kawai Juku can see how well the exams perform to weed out bad questions. This disregard for analyzing tests is even more serious with the ones universities make themselves, developed by rotating committees of co-opted teachers.

However, those with power to change the procedures for the design of entrance examinations at many universities are possibly unfamiliar with assessment literacy (Fullan, 1999) or are not professional test developers (Niwa, 2000). They simply repeat what has been done before and follow Ministry guidelines when they must. Although some teachers are assessment literate and have ideas to improve the system, they are often forced to be silent by a hierarchical educational system.

Doyon (2001), in an informative review of higher education reform in Japan, says:

> Of all the problems inherent in the Japanese education system, probably the most unwieldy and most often criticized have been the "entrance examination system" and "educational credentialism." Despite numerous deliberations and efforts to reform the entrance examination system, little has changed in the negative effects that it levels at society and education. (p. 462)

The U.S. Department of Education (1998) case study on Japanese education concluded that "severe competition on the entrance exams for admission to elite schools continues to create educational overheating." Chapter 2 of the same case study reports:

> The pressures of the entrance examinations are seen as contributing to a variety of school-related problems, including an over-dependence on *juku* by students, bullying (*ijime*), school refusal syndrome (*tokokyohi*) and a host of other problems.

Throughout the year students take practice exams in high schools and cram schools (*juku* and *yobiko*). In fact, students are socialized into the exam system early on, with some students taking exams for kindergarten and elementary school, and most taking exams for junior and senior high schools. These are definitely high-stakes exams that not only determine the futures of young people to a great degree but also determine much of the content of junior and senior high school education (Gorsuch, 2000, 2001). Taking university entrance exams is considered by many to be one of the greatest events in determining one's life, both before and after taking them (Doyon, 2001).

Economics

In 2001, 590,000 students took the Center Test, 9,000 more than in the year 2000, because more private universities started to use the test ("Kokkouritsu Daigaku Nyuushi," 2001). A small portion of the students who take the Center Test and score especially high may be admitted directly to some universities. Most students, however, are given another test created by the individual teachers in specific departments at each university, both public and private. The students are not given their actual scores nor do they know which answers the universities count as correct. Brown (1996a) states that "the high schools and universities make a great deal of money from the exams, especially from the 80 to 90 percent of students who fail" (p.15). Although a good, small (e.g., 6,000 students) university may earn 6 to 7 million U.S. dollars each year in 5 days of entrance exams, larger, more popular universities earn two or three times as much.

Revenue is high at popular universities because each student usually takes as many as 6 or 7 tests (and some may take as many as 10 or 12) for different departments within one or several universities. The students usually pay $100 to $400 for each exam (Brown, 1996a). After the examination period, copies of the tests are collected and published in the newspapers. The large cram schools publish the tests in books, which are typically used to train candidates for future tests for the different universities. This publishing of the test is seen as extremely open and fair in Japan, because this is regarded as a potential form of critical review from the public and media. The testers, however, never publish validity or reliability data on the tests, contending this would be releasing information that is private to the test takers.

◈ DESCRIPTION

A University Teacher's Perspective: Tim Murphey

I was involved at a Japanese university for 11 years and on the English exam-making committee four times, the last time as assistant chair. My understanding of the system also comes from working with thousands of junior and senior high school teachers who train their students for the tests. I interacted with these teachers at Ministry-organized teacher-leader camps for 6 years and gave numerous invited presentations to Japanese teachers of English and assistant language teachers (native speakers with bachelor's degrees from a variety of countries) at the city and prefecture level. I was also involved with my own university's summer teacher training courses, observed graduating seniors practicing teaching each year, and taught graduate school courses. In addition, my perspective is informed by responses from more than 200 undergraduates each year from whom I requested feedback on entrance exams in their action logs (Murphey, 1993) and language learning histories (Murphey, 1998; Oxford & Green, 1996).

Throughout the 1990s, I suggested changes in entrance examinations at the private Japanese university at which I was working and tried to engage others in dialogue about assessment practices in my university and with colleagues at other schools. In February 1999, while on sabbatical in the United States, I received an e-mail from the private university asking me to chair the English entrance exam committee for the following year. I responded that I would not chair the committee until we began testing our tests. When I returned to Japan, I was told I could have the data on the previous year's English tests in exchange for agreeing to be assistant chair that year as well as chair in 2000. This looked like progress to me, as normally no one was on the committee for 2 consecutive years. I was hopeful that I could make changes from within. As Buell (1996) reports, usually a new group of test makers "redesign the tests from scratch each time; it's a classic case of having not thirty years experience, but one year's experience thirty times" (p. 24).

I agreed with the university's proposal, and I eventually received data for the previous 5 years of exams. I, like most of the faculty, had no idea that these data were even available for the five sets of English exams given each year. (Note that it is the English department at this university that is responsible for making the English exams for all faculties.) I discovered that cumulatively for the 5 years of English exams, only 36% of the discrete point vocabulary and grammar questions discriminated adequately according to published standards (Brown, 1996b). For reading, 66% of the questions discriminated adequately, and 75% of the listening did on the 20% of exams that had listening each year. However, it was the first category, grammar and vocabulary, that was weighted most heavily, whereas listening was weighted the least. I presented these data to our English department faculty, and they agreed to increase the weight given to listening on the one exam that contained this subtest. However, the administration still refused to allow me to add listening to the other English exams for the following year when I was supposed to be English exam chair. Moreover, the administration did not inform the chairs of the other departments of these data so that they could consider changing the weighting of the English exams that we were designing for them or consider adding a listening portion. According to regulations, the administration reported, any large-scale change had to be announced 2 years beforehand so that teachers could prepare their students appropriately. Later, I was told that this was not a regulation but a rule of thumb.

When I thought about creating and administering untested exams repeatedly for the rest of my career, I decided I did not want to make those agonized compromises. It was considered unfair if I did not take the chair role because I was the only full professor who had not served in that capacity. I, therefore, decided to resign from my position and submitted a letter to that effect in September 1999 (Murphey, 2001a, 2001b, 2001c). The administration asked me to stay an extra year (2000–2001) and decided during this time that foreign staff would not have to be chairs. Because native speakers would still be spending a third of their professional time on unprofessional entrance exam work, I decided I would not be happy working under those conditions. My resignation was finally accepted in the autumn of 2000, and I left the school in the summer of 2001 for another university in Taiwan. In an effort to give the issue more attention, I presented the TESOL Resolution on English Entrance Exams at Schools and Universities at the 2000 TESOL Convention in Vancouver, which was supported by many scholars and passed (TESOL, 2000).

A High School Teacher's Perspective: Kazuyoshi Sato

I started my career as a high school teacher of English. For 7 years, I prepared my students for university entrance exams. I then went to Australia for my master's and doctoral degrees. Upon my return to Japan, I began university teaching and, since 1999, have been an associate professor (at a different school than the one depicted above). I have remained involved in researching English education in high schools by establishing a regular study group with high school teachers and researching curriculum change through teacher development.

My graduate research concerned communicative language teaching in Japanese high schools. Surprisingly, my research revealed that the teachers in the high school I observed during my graduate studies taught the same way as we had 8 years before, paying even more attention to examination-oriented English (Sato, 2002). Although the Ministry introduced new guidelines for communication-oriented English in high schools in 1994, the teachers I observed were confused about how to teach. One experienced teacher reported:

> I agree that the purpose of English is developing students' communicative skills, so being able to get across one's intentions, read, and understand what people say are ideals. . . . It is necessary and is an ideal to be able to speak and listen. But, we cannot ignore university entrance examinations. That's another problem. If entrance exams were removed, it would be time that we started to think about alternatives. (Sato, 2000, p. 102)

Classroom observation data showed that teachers, regardless of age and teaching experience, conformed to a pattern of teaching with heavy emphasis on grammar explanation and translation. Even in oral communication classes, teachers taught listening and grammar without any interactions among students in English. Even occasional visiting native speaker teachers had difficulty getting students to interact and communicate in English. Teachers took it for granted that they should follow the hidden departmental goal of examination-oriented English.

In short, a homogeneous teaching pattern supported teachers' beliefs that classroom order was very important and that grammar points and translation were necessary for university entrance examinations. Both interview and observation data revealed that these teachers ignored the new guidelines by the Ministry and continued to teach the same way to prepare students for university entrance examinations.

◈ DISTINGUISHING FEATURES

Brown (1996a) listed eight characteristics of the exam system in Japan with a forceful plea for change. We find these still relevant in 2002:

1. The entrance exams are not piloted. Thus, the questions are of unknown quality, difficulty and discrimination.

2. The reliability of the entrance exams is generally unknown and is not reported publicly, so a certain unknown amount of inaccuracy is affecting decisions about the futures of Japanese students.

3. The validity of the exams (translation or otherwise) is not studied, or reported on publicly, so the test developers are not sure what they are testing (monolingual, bilingual or otherwise).

4. The exams are expensive (from 10,000 to 40,000 yen [about 100 to 400 U.S. dollars] each), and students take many exams.

5. The high schools and universities make a great deal of money from the exams, especially from the 80 to 90 percent of students who fail. Thus, administrators, teachers, and professors have a vested interest in maintaining the current "traditional" system.

6. The cram schools and publishers make a great deal of money from the students preparing for the exams, and from the many *ronin* who fail, so they too have a vested interest.

7. Many Japanese would like to see the present examination system changed.

8. The entrance procedures in Japan have changed in the past and can be changed in the future. (p. 15)

Although there is a general consensus among all the participants that the system is stressful and harmful, especially to the youth of Japan, each group of participants has its own reasons not to want change. For the juku and universities, the system is financially rewarding. Both also have invested huge resources in the system as it is now and have a whole administrative bureaucracy built around it. Note, however, that Brown and many others are not asking universities to forego the income but merely to make the tests more valid and professional.

The Ministry would become unpopular if it tried to insist on too much change. If change really did happen, things might be chaotic for several years as teachers would need retraining and curricula rewriting. Thus, Ministry officials can ask others to change on the one hand, and then be glad that things are not changing too fast because that probably would be a long, administrative headache.

In addition, there are the already overstressed high school teachers. By keeping spoken English out of the classroom, they do not have to learn a new way of teaching. As Ehrman and Dornyei (1998) so aptly say, "the finding that leaders tend more to behave in an authoritarian manner in stressful than in non-stressful situations and manage anxiety by seeking to close off options may explain why many teachers so often adopt an authoritarian style" (p. 162). Not only is spoken English seldom heard, interaction, the bread and butter of progressive language learning, in high school classrooms is extremely rare.

Finally, there are the high school students who suffer from learned helplessness (Seligman, 1990) entrained by a pedagogy for silence (Yoneyama, 1999). Alas, they often know no better and have no basis for comparison. They, and the future of Japan, are the true victims in this game of passivity. Students who have been schooled abroad for a while have another frame of reference. Because they do not usually fit back into traditional Japanese high schools anymore, these students go to special international schools.

Japan has finally started noticing the brain drain that this way of educating has created as many scholars find they are better treated abroad ("Fair Assessment," 2000). We hope that this is the difference that makes the difference so that the Ministry will not only accept changes in one standard for all but also encourage more diversity.

◈ PRACTICAL IDEAS

Treat Test Making as a Valid and Developing Professional Field

Assessment literate teachers seek ways to improve examinations to provide valid data to decision makers and create more ethical practices for test takers. We need to realize that "the act of language testing is not neutral. Rather, it is a product and agent of cultural, social, political, educational and ideological agendas that shape the lives of individual participants, teachers, and learners" (Shohamy, 1997a, p. 2).

Create and Use Item Banks

The creation and use of item banks would mean that items with good statistical validity could be reused in future exam administrations.

Give Adequate Time and Resources to Inform Change

Invite knowledgeable personnel to spend longer terms on testing committees with release time. This will help foster a culture of change.

Do More Holistic Evaluations of Candidates

Train professional, full-time staff to look at a range of criteria in addition to tests, including high school records, portfolios, letters of recommendation, and public service achievements.

Use Multiples Measures When Rating Institutions

Rate universities and departments on a multitude of qualitative criteria (e.g., student/ teacher ratio, size of library), rather than simply on the performance of students on their entrance exams.

Fight for What You Believe In

As a TESOL professional, lobby actively for better testing practices and encourage community stakeholders to do so as well.

◈ CONCLUSION

Assessment literacy, like all education, should be a lifelong concern for teachers. It is something that you continue to learn and develop. Tests in other countries and the ways of conducting them have their own sets of problems. Following another country's lead is not necessarily the best way. Assessment literacy means continually reflecting on better ways to assess in one's own context. It should be the goal of professional educators to align their values with their actions (Murphey, 1999) and to look at testing practices critically (Shohamy, 1997a).

Comparing one's own practices with those of other schools and countries simply gives us points of comparison to better understand what we are doing. Ignoring what others are doing keeps us isolated and dangerously ethnocentric. We need to study how our work can continually become more professionally justified and ethically correct for the advancement of our field and for the fair treatment of all participants.

We do not expect our doctors to know everything there is about medicine—there is too much out there. We do, however, expect doctors to continually study to keep up with the changes in best practices. Nothing less should be required of educators. Teaching is the learning profession (Darling-Hammond & Sykes, 1999).

◈ CONTRIBUTORS

Tim Murphey has taught in Switzerland, Japan, and Taiwan. He has published books with Longman, Oxford University Press, Peter Lang, and MacMillan LanguageHouse. He presents workshops internationally on interactive and alternative language learning methods, and researches Vygotskian sociocultural theory. He is the series editor for the *Professional Development in Language Education* series (TESOL, 2003). He currently teaches at Dokkyo University, in Japan.

Kazuyoshi Sato teaches at Nagoya University of Foreign Studies. He has published articles on communicative language teaching and teacher education. His current research interests include teacher development, teaching culture, and learning strategies.

CHAPTER 4

Cooperative ESP Assessment at a Japanese University

Mitchell Goodman

◈ INTRODUCTION

To test or not to test is a question that many teachers have had to ask themselves, and for better or worse, the answer has often been in the affirmative. How else are the teachers to assess the masses of students passing through their classrooms? In Japan, written testing of the masses is certainly nothing new. These days, 4- and 5-year-olds are given examinations to screen them for entrance into prestigious elementary schools, and parents are forced to tutor their children at a very early age, generating substantial anxiety in students and stress on families. An educational industry of preparatory or cram schools known as *juku* functions as a shadow educational system to prepare students to reach each successive rung of the educational ladder. Cramming continues through to the university level.

But after one has passed the university entrance examinations, the educational environment changes from a high-stakes to a low-stakes endeavor. There are no more entrance examinations to cram for because college is the top rung of the educational ladder. Recently, however, there has been a shift toward more accountability and evaluation at the tertiary level as a result of guidance from the Monbukagakusho (Japan's Ministry of Education, Culture, Sports, Science, and Technology).[1] Hence, many schools are now instituting the Test of English for International Communication (TOEIC) and offering or requiring TOEIC classes. Despite this trend, the university has been and still is regarded by students primarily as a place to establish a network of lifelong friends and contacts and take a break from the examination treadmill.

After graduation from a university, the emphasis on testing resumes because companies commonly administer tests to job applicants. As universities do not prepare their students for these company-administered examinations, special preparatory schools called *yobiko* are there to do the job. Some companies also require supplementary qualifications of long-term employees, including TOEIC scores. Companies use test scores for making personnel decisions, which impact an employee's job description and security.

---

[1] In 2001, the Ministry of Education, Culture, Sports, and Science (Monbusho) merged with the Science and Technology Agency to become the Ministry of Education, Culture, Sports, Science, and Technology (Monbukagakusho). See http://www.mext.go.jp/english/ for additional information on the Monbukagakusho.

In contrast to this emphasis on high-stakes testing in Japan, this case study advocates the ideals of creativity, interaction, and learner-centeredness in assessment design. It details a cooperative written test and feedback methods used at a Japanese university in an English for specific purposes (ESP) course focusing on computers. The methods include a cooperative written test and formal and informal ongoing feedback. This case study paints a background picture of the Japanese educational environment and then profiles the students and their attitudes toward university training. The evolution of the cooperative assessment process has played an important formative role in the course over the past few years through an interactive process of trial and revision. Using the Japanese university cultural context, student profile, and course description as a background, this case study identifies the distinguishing features of the assessment methods and makes suggestions for their implementation.

◈ CONTEXT

Japanese students enter the university English classroom after years of grammar-translation practice (usually from English to Japanese) and memorization of grammar rules and lexical items for their entrance examinations. Most students have never heard, uttered, or read in any meaningful context most of the words they have memorized before entering the classroom. Even after 6 years of English study in junior and senior high school, Japanese students are false beginners in the true sense, with few productive language skills but a great deal of potential (Reischauer, 1988/ 1977). They do have grounding in English, but, unfortunately, it is fragmented and based predominantly on receptive skills that place emphasis on visual recognition of discrete lexical items.

Much of this is due to the nature of university entrance examinations. Norm-referenced university entrance exams usually consist of discrete-point, multiple-choice items (Brown & Yamashita, 1995) so they can be easily graded by computer. Furthermore, there may be native-speaker-level reading passages with complex comprehension questions. Gorsuch (1999) argues that high school textbooks, which must be sanctioned by the Monbukagakusho, are geared toward preparing students for the discrete items found on these tests. They, therefore, do not promote the use of communicative teaching, which some Monbukagakusho guidelines seek to foster. Mulvey (1999) argues that Monbukagakusho-sanctioned textbooks barely prepare the students for the entrance exam reading passages, which can be so complex that even the one thousand hours of study students receive before attending a university is not nearly sufficient. Both parents and students pressure teachers and schools to teach to entrance examinations, because these tests entail such high stakes. The reason the stakes are so high is that prospective employers, although not always interested in grades, usually take into account what school an applicant has graduated from. Students, therefore, desperately want to get into the best schools. Most important, examinations and textbooks of the kind mentioned here generate a tremendous amount of capital for the textbook publishers and the institutions administering the tests. Although it is not apparent what influence universities and publishers have on Monbukagakusho policy with regards to the entrance examinations, they clearly have a vested interest in the perpetuation of the system.

Students take a dim view of paper-and-pencil tests and understandably see them as a crude system of ranking their personal worth with scores and grades. Faced with these kinds of tests, they tend to treat their own minds like temporary storage cabinets, cramming essential information in and cleaning out unessential information immediately after the exam (Leamnson, 1999). Although most teachers agree that some form of testing is useful, they question whether this purely discrete-point form of individual assessment is what students really need and whether there is some alternative or hybrid method of testing that would be more desirable. This case study describes an attempt at a different model of assessment.

◈ DESCRIPTION

The locus of this case study is alternative assessment in a mandatory, one-credit university ESP class in the engineering department that focuses on computers. Students may take as many as 15 other classes, and some may be worth more credits. Thus, this course may not be their prime educational concern. The majority of the students are between the ages of 18 and 20, and female students constitute approximately 20% of the enrollment. Each class lasts 90 minutes, and the classes meet approximately 13 times in both the spring and fall semesters, for a total of 26 lessons. The classes consist of approximately 40 first-year students who closely fit the previously described student profile. Exceptions are returnees from overseas who generally have a much higher level of comprehension and communicative ability, and repeaters who previously failed the class and have a lower level of ability. Repeat students also tend to have less effective study habits and often fail because of poor attendance.

The educational materials consist of two textbooks and a video. The textbooks are quite thorough with many useful illustrations of the concepts and components being studied. The video is a BBC television production, made for a native-speaking audience. It includes people such as Bill Gates, speaking at native speed. The language is therefore authentic, quite varied, and rather difficult for the students to understand. The overall course aim is to broaden the students' technical English vocabulary and develop language skills by analyzing, discussing, and assimilating concepts related to the computer through the use of the course materials. The first or spring semester is devoted to hardware. This includes the definition of a computer, types of computers, input and output devices, computer components, integrated circuits, transistors, binary code, memory, storage devices, networks, and telecommunications. The fall semester is devoted to software. This module includes the definition of a program, system versus application software, types of applications, software languages, flowcharts, e-mail, and the Internet. A quick perusal of this list clearly shows that there is an overabundance of material to be covered in an insufficient amount of time. The engineering department and instructors assemble the curriculum, which is given to the students at the beginning of the term. It calls for four written tests each semester or one every 3 weeks. However, teachers have a good deal of autonomy with regard to assessment and can create any additional or alternative assessment instruments they feel are suitable.

A densely packed university classroom, and a low-stakes, one-credit, difficult curriculum such as that described above poses challenges for both students and instructors, including

- inadequate comprehension due to the difficult course content
- difficulty in comprehending the materials, leading to discouragement, lack of interest, and low motivation
- insufficient instructor time for individual students
- insufficient time to complete all the course material
- insufficient space for students to move around in the classroom
- low prioritization of the course as students' motivation wanes
- negative student feedback

Faced with such a plethora of problems, I thought a radical change from traditional teaching approaches was necessary. Cooperative learning is an alternative approach that addresses many of these problems. This approach consists of breaking the students up into small groups and having them work together to solve problems and complete certain tasks. It promotes social and educational interaction through the use of positive interdependence (Johnson & Johnson, 1994, 1999; Kluge, 1994). By assessing a group as one unit and assigning group grades, a feeling develops that the group sinks or swims together (Cohen, 1994). Furthermore, when a group of students is positively interdependent, the students not only help each other but also hold each other responsible for their respective share of the group's tasks. There is an increase in both individual and group accountability and in peer tutoring. Students who are able to understand certain difficult concepts explain them to others who cannot, making it easier for all of them to comprehend a higher order of conceptual material. This concurrent social interaction very often results in close friendships. Tutoring and encouragement by fellow classmates lead to better comprehension and lift the students' confidence levels and spirits. Social interaction of this kind can motivate students to attend class, pay attention, ask questions, do homework, and, in optimal cases, work autonomously.

Cooperative learning is therefore a very efficient form of instruction from both the instructor's viewpoint as well as the student's standpoint. Instructors are able to have more intimate contact with each group of students than they would with individuals, so students actually receive more comprehensible input in the form of personal interaction from the instructor. Worksheets and projects done by groups are easier for the instructor to evaluate and respond to in depth, simply because of the smaller number of papers to review.

The goal of all of these cooperative activities is to recycle and process ideas more intensely to generate a diverse, well-rounded understanding of them. However, what is more important is to give the students an exciting educational experience to remember beyond the straightforward course content. As van Lier (1996) points out, such memories of happy classroom experiences no doubt "far outlast the memorized items addressed in test questions" (p. 120). Cooperative written tests create a challenging yet memorable atmosphere in which the students can describe what they have learned.

Cooperative Written Tests as Assessment

The idea of teaching progressively or creating a progressive vehicle for assessment does not mean abandoning everything traditional (Dewey, 1938/1997). Japanese students are accustomed to and fairly skilled at multiple-choice paper-and-pencil tests. It is part of their educational culture. A sudden, total departure from this regimen would be disorienting for some students. Furthermore, inasmuch as this is a knowledge-based content course with well-defined content, these tests lend themselves rather well to the goal of assessment. There is a body of key concepts and lexical items for the students to learn, and one of the purposes of the tests is to ascertain whether that learning is taking place.

My challenge was how to design a paper-and-pencil test that maintained a link to traditional pedagogical assessments and yet progressed beyond them in ways that made the testing more motivational and interactive. This problem reflects Dewey's insistence on the significance of experience in learning. Learning begins with students' preschool experiences that they bring to the classroom. Classroom learning then proceeds through cognitive processing of the experiences that occur there. In the best of cases, students are motivated to keep on learning autonomously long after a course has ended.

At the same time, learning takes place naturally outside the classroom without any formal instruction or assessment. Teachers need to find ways to bring this natural acquisition into the classroom. One of the goals of the cooperative test is to create an atmosphere in which learners can be naturally engaged and less conscious of the formal nature of the event. Most people faced with challenges will turn to family or friends for help or advice because they prefer accomplishing challenging tasks with others. So why should students not enjoy an educational challenge such as completing a paper-and-pencil test together? The suggestion that such a test could be interesting to students may sound like a contradiction. However, tests are multi-faceted, and gradual alterations to some of their facets may be able to alter students' perceptions of tests.

Test Content

The tests in question comprehensively cover the computer concepts and lexical items that were taught. All of the test items test class material. These tests are therefore domain referenced in that they are about computers, and objectives referenced in that they are constructed based on what all of the students have been exposed to in past lessons (Genesee & Upshur, 1996).

Apart from ensuring that the test sample is comprehensive, I also recycle items from previous tests. Students often balk at this aspect of the examination, because it means they can no longer empty their minds of previously learned concepts and language. The recycling of course concepts and language items forces the students to keep their notes and old examination papers. By the end of a term, this material should be organized as a portfolio of notes, worksheet exercises, and examinations to refer to—more important than this body of evidence, though, is the academic process students go through to collect and systematize the material.

Test Specifications

The tests take about 30 minutes, are three pages in length, and have two basic parts. The first part consists of objective questions such as multiple choice, true or false, word matching, cloze, and item sequencing. This accounts for two-thirds of the test and point value. The objective questions assay the students' ability to recognize key concepts learned in the course and are structured in such a way as to give the test takers some hints and vocabulary they can use in the writing section that follows. The written part of the test requires students to demonstrate their understanding of conceptual and factual information by answering questions in complete written sentences. Each section has clear written instructions and point-value explanations.

The importance of including written response questions on the test cannot be stressed enough with regard to university students (Leamnson, 1999). Japanese students are well versed in taking multiple-choice examinations, but they are weak at expressing themselves. This essential ability to communicate in writing is something that multiple-choice questions cannot measure. The production of written English, furthermore, is essential for academic students because it promotes thinking (Krashen, 1992). Through writing, one interacts with one's thoughts. Unfortunately, paper-and-pencil tests that are taken individually do not enable social interaction. Negotiation of meaning in these situations is indeed a lonely affair.

Test Method: Response Format

If one teaches cooperatively and believes that teaching and assessment should exist together, then it is logical to also test cooperatively. Negotiation on this kind of test then becomes three-way with increased potential for cross-analysis. The key to fomenting this cooperative interaction on the test lies in the following procedure:

- Students take the test in their base groups of three, facing front and sitting one behind the other.
- Each student must use a different colored pen (pencils and erasers are prohibited).
- There is no talking allowed during the test.
- At the start of the test, students A, B, and C receive pages 1, 2, and 3 respectively.
- Several minutes after the test starts, a timer goes off. When the timer sounds, A's paper is passed to B, B's paper is passed to C, and C's paper is passed to A (Figure 1).
- The instructor resets the timer at 3- to 4-minute intervals. Thus, one complete cycle of the test papers takes 9 to 12 minutes.
- The process of recycling the test papers continues for approximately 30 minutes until the test is finished and the papers are collected.
- Tests are graded, given back to the students to discuss, and whole-class review focuses on the most confusing items.

This format has several major advantages for the students. First, there is a tremendous amount of academic interaction and peer correction, which entails both bottom-up and top-down processing not only of the test questions but also of each

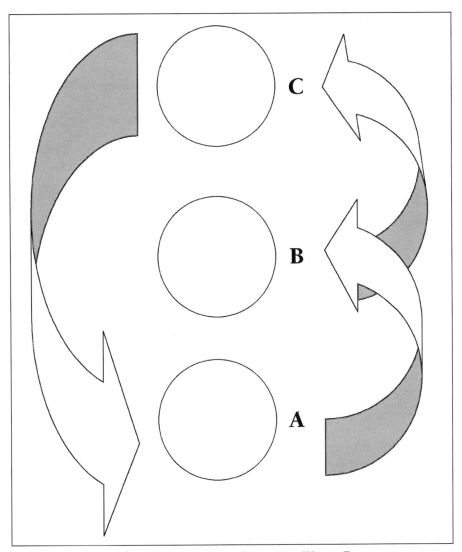

Figure 1. Movement of Test Papers During a Cooperative Written Exam

other's answers. In essence, the students must reprocess the test papers anew each time they receive them because even though the questions are static, the answers are continually changing. The test papers are transformed into a living and evolving work. Students are encouraged to correct each other's mistakes by crossing them out and writing corrections. Some of the answers may be changed as many as three or four times. Students grappling with their answers is clear evidence that intense thinking is taking place. The fact that they cannot erase their mistakes is valuable in that everyone can trace the thought paths that were taken, which can have a definite impact on future study and test-taking habits, teaching, and test design. Occasionally a student will cross out a correct answer and substitute an incorrect one that the other members accept, sacrificing points for the group. Although they may lose the points, they will not be likely to make the same mistake should the question be recycled in a future exam. Students are also encouraged to be as accurate as possible.

Because each student uses a different color pen, many of these group-constructed sentences and changed answers cause the test papers to look like multicolored, abstract-expressionist works of art. Aside from the subliminal effect that all this color may have, the color-coding also permits the students and instructors to differentiate what each student has written.

For the instructor, there is the added benefit of having fewer papers to grade. This timesaving feature increases the feasibility of including more written-response questions and compensates for the extra time required for their evaluation.

Test Method: Scoring

Two grades are given to the students: a group grade and an individual grade. The group grade consists of a numerical score. It is arrived at in a traditional manner by counting correct responses. The individual grade is given in the form of + symbols, with a single + being the lowest score and +++ being the highest score. It is given to each student on the basis of holistic contribution to the group grade. The volume and quality of correct answers each student in the group writes compared to what an average student in the class writes determines the individual grade. If a group's test score was 40% consistently, all of which one student had contributed, that student would consistently receive an individual grade of +++, whereas the other two students would consistently receive +. All three would receive the same numerical grade of 40%. As a final grade, the student who contributed the most on the tests might receive A, B, or C depending on various other factors; the others would probably fail the course. The individual grade is norm referenced inasmuch as the students are being compared to one another. Its importance lies in the mitigating effect it has on the students' final grades.

❖ DISTINGUISHING FEATURES

Motivation to learn and to continue learning long after the course has finished is perhaps at the crux of the whole issue of education. What first comes to mind when one thinks of traditional forms of classroom motivation is educational achievement through quantification (i.e., tests, test scores, grades). Indeed, many students only study when there is a test coming up. Although not verbalized, some students may view traditional testing as being an unkind and impersonal form of coercion. On the other hand, this form of evaluative motivation often works well for those driven students who come to class predisposed to achieve. For many, however, tests are just a manifestation of what is thought of as the education game. In other words, they see getting a good or passing grade as their main educational goal and crowning achievement, not the learning itself (Leamnson, 1999). In this sense, the traditional evaluative method of motivating students through tests has utterly failed.

One purpose of the cooperative tests is to get feedback to see if learning is taking place. In this sense, all forms of assessment are a kind of feedback for teachers. Likewise, test grades and comments that teachers write are feedback for the students. During the cooperative written test, each student gives feedback to his or her group members, showing understanding of the test questions by answering them.

Feedback is in fact multidirectional amongst students, groups, and the instructor, and its ultimate purpose is to develop teaching and improve learning. However, the test instrument itself as feedback is limited in its scope, and a variety of formats are needed to get a well-rounded picture of what is taking place in the classroom.

There are two basic types of feedback: (a) formal, which is elicited; and (b) informal, which is based on observation. Informal feedback is generally less informative because it is easily misread. Examples are facial expressions and body language, which vary from student to student and culture to culture. Eliciting verbal or written feedback is more useful for the instructor because it is more objective and can be gathered via impromptu or planned questions, interviews, or surveys. It can be multiple choice, sliding scale, or an open format that requires longer responses. It can be done individually or cooperatively and in class or at home.

Feedback from the students regarding the cooperative tests shows that most students prefer them because it is felt that, although rigorous, they are easier than individual tests. Many express a preference for cooperative learning and testing, because it enables them to develop close friendships with their classmates.

One important bit of feedback from the students provoked a major developmental change in the tests. When the cooperative tests were first designed, there was only a group grade. In feedback, comments by a number of students who viewed themselves to be more advanced expressed dissatisfaction with the cooperative tests. These students felt they were doing most of the work in their groups. Why then should they get the same grade? This feedback was the impetus for the addition of individual scores and the use of color-coding to differentiate the students' answers on the test papers. It illustrates the importance student feedback can have as a guide to teaching and materials design.

In this course, formal written feedback is done several times a year on such subjects as class activities, the instructor's teaching style, course materials, tests, other group members, the school, the students' likes and habits with regard to computers, and, most important, the students' learning. Sometimes names are left optional to give students, who are reluctant to give negative feedback, the chance to do so anonymously.

Student participation in real time is another element of feedback that may be used for assessment purposes. In this context, participation is defined as an interactive exchange of ideas as when volunteering, asking questions, or responding in English during class. Responding includes utterances such as " I don't understand" or "please speak more slowly" as opposed to a lack of response. The continuous nature of ongoing assessment creates a situation that challenges students to think, pay attention, and perform, not only on the day of a test but every day. Data on student participation is collected through observation and by putting marks next to the students' names when they participate during class.

◈ PRACTICAL IDEAS

Assess in a Variety of Ways

One interesting observation regarding the results of the assessment methods described is that some students, who were below average at test taking, excelled in class participation or using the word-processing software. There is a need for variety in assessment to get a total view of a student's learning. It therefore helps to include tests, projects, interviews, written reports, and role-plays when doing assessment.

Utilize a Variety of Formats

There is no magic panacea with regard to assessment or learning. Although cooperative assessment is a wonderful approach, it may not be suited to all cultures. High-stakes situations, where large numbers of students must be classified according to level, usually demand individual assessment. In such cases, computer scoring of individual assessment instruments may be more appropriate and economical. However, this does not preclude using cooperative assessment as a preparatory step toward norm-referenced standardized testing or lessen its usefulness as a tool for motivating students.

Use Criterion-, Domain-, and Objectives-Referenced Scoring Whenever Possible

Unless ranking students for program placement or norm-referencing purposes, teachers should assess their students on the basis of the content or skills that were focused on in class. To do otherwise is quite simply unfair and illogical. Teachers should concentrate on the overall scope of the topic learned, as well as specific points and skills.

Be Creative in Developing New Forms of Assessment and Class Activities

This is really what a teacher's job is all about: creating an environment where learning can take place and students can demonstrate what they have learned. It means taking risks and making adjustments when things do not go smoothly. Students are generally happy to give input and aid in this development.

Elicit Formal Feedback Regularly

Feedback informs teachers about what and how their students are learning and, therefore, how effective their teaching is. It also permits students to express their feelings and thoughts about the course content and materials. Teachers can then apply this feedback selectively to course improvement.

Include an Interaction Focus as a Major Constituent of Assessment Design

The more variety of interaction, the more learning can occur. The need for it is even more pronounced in a language course, where the language is to be used as a mode of communication. It should ideally include the four skills of speaking, listening, reading and writing and involve the students in social and academic interaction. Academic interaction occurs among individual learners, their peers, and instructors. It also encompasses the course material and can further involve the use of technology, visuals, movement, and music.

◈ CONCLUSION

Perhaps the aspects that most distinguish the methods described in this case study are the creative and interactive elements. It is the teachers' responsibility to make their assessments interesting and motivating, which means experimenting with new ideas. Like any experiential experiment, it must be carefully planned, the results have to be reflected upon and analyzed, and then adjustments must be made (Kolb, 1984). It then has to undergo further trial, error, and revision, and things will not always go smoothly. However, incorporating creative and interactive elements into assessments is one way to make them more interesting and motivating. It seems obvious that assessment is part of the learning process. Unfortunately, it is easy to overlook the learner and neglect the learning that should be taking place during the assessment process. If one believes that learning is a natural and continuous human condition, then infusing a memorable learning element into the assessment experience should be a primary concern. Otherwise, what will students be able to make of assessment? If a memorable learning element is not built into an assessment, then it serves only the short-term goal of evaluation. Learning should be at the heart of the assessment process and not the other way around. Assessment should serve the long-term goal of learning first, and the instructor's evaluation requirements second. Teachers certainly want their instruction to be creative, motivating, educational, exciting, and memorable. The same attitude should be taken toward assessment.

◈ CONTRIBUTOR

Mitchell Goodman has been teaching English in Japan for 15 years and is currently affiliated with several universities, including Seikei, Rikkyo, Gakushuin, Saitama, Tsuda, and Takachiho. His interests include assessment and the use of dramatic role-play in the classroom.

PART 3

In-Program Assessment

CHAPTER 5

Linking Assessments With Instruction in a Multilingual Elementary School

Nancy Frey and Douglas Fisher

◈ INTRODUCTION

The results of standardized tests are currently used around the world to allocate resources, determine teacher pay, award school vouchers to students attending unsuccessful schools, and decide whether a student may graduate from high school. In this climate of accountability, testing is assuming an increasingly important role in the structure of the curriculum and in the amount of instructional time dedicated to it. Yet the efficacy of any single assessment to determine such a wide scope of variables seems unlikely. Although there may be a tendency to overgeneralize what test scores can reveal, evaluation research has become an increasingly sophisticated assessment tool that goes beyond simply testing large numbers of students to provide broad measures of group achievement (Lipson & Wixson, 1997).

Far more than standardized test results, which often do not arrive until the following school year, teacher-based assessments are the tools educators rely on as they design reading language arts instruction. Teacher-based assessments are those selected and administered by the classroom teacher in order to determine what instruction needs to occur next. Astute classroom teachers possess a wealth of information about their students' knowledge of literacy and evaluate literacy events such as book talks and oral readings to gauge students' progress and drive future instruction. Wise practitioners recognize the value of such assessments as a rich source of data. Examples of teacher-based literacy assessments in this discussion include interactive writing charts, running records, KWL (what do we <u>k</u>now/what do we <u>w</u>ant to know/what have we <u>l</u>earned) charts, and reader response logs.

◈ CONTEXT

The classrooms in which we examined the link between assessment and instruction are located in a large, urban elementary school in southern California. More than 1,500 students from the most densely populated community in the city attend this school. They bring with them the richness of 39 languages, and many of them experienced their early childhood years in locations far removed from their present home—the rainforests of Vietnam, war-torn Somalia, large cities and tiny villages in Philippines, rural Mexico, and the mountains of Cambodia. A large tile mosaic on the front of the school building celebrates this diversity—"We have many faces, we come from different places."

The wide range of experiences and languages present at this elementary school provides many challenges to effective assessment and instruction. Traditional testing alone is not appropriate for many of the learners at this school because language and cultural differences may present barriers to a student's ability to demonstrate what they know (Alexander & Parsons, 1991; Shohamy, 1997b). Informal classroom assessments are also problematic if not designed, delivered, and interpreted in a sensitive manner. The teachers at this school have consistently worked toward a model of assessment and instruction that rejects the deficit theory of schooling for students from diverse backgrounds (Powell (Eller), 1998). Deficit theory suggests that socioeconomic status is equated with an impoverished set of language experiences and serves as a predictor of diminished achievement. To avoid this, these educators use a variety of authentic assessments to measure their students' literacy growth.

❖ DESCRIPTION

Mr. Klein, a kindergarten teacher, uses a daily teaching event to gather evidence of his students' understanding of writing. Second-grade teacher Ms. Antonio uses guided reading to assess her learners. And Mrs. Ying, a fifth-grade teacher, examines her students' work in science to determine to what extent they are utilizing their literacy strategies. As with all good teachers, they gather information, interpret it, and then act upon it. Their view of teaching as a recursive process has been influenced by their work in a master's degree program that focuses on action research in the classroom (Stringer, 1999). As with action research, these teachers use assessments to set goals and purposes, collect data, and interpret results for the purpose of informing instruction. Although separating these dynamic phases from one another in the classroom is virtually impossible, examples of their application are discussed below. Looking inside these three classrooms and observing how teachers link assessment and instruction can reveal useful data for guiding instructional decisions.

Classroom 1: Writing in Kindergarten

The students in Mr. Klein's kindergarten classroom scurry to the carpeted area to take their places. The teacher has just directed them to meet in the Writer's Corner. The children know that this daily event is an opportunity to discuss and write about their lives. It is also a chance to participate, for Mr. Klein rarely misses a chance to involve all his students in the activity. Hakly and Marcos gather the markers, whiteboards, and wipes that their classmates will share. Margarita gets the pointer, translucent tape, and clothespin Mr. Klein will need. Soon, they are all seated, anxiously awaiting the first question. Mr. Klein takes his seat next to the chart stand, looks around at each of the students, and in a conspiratorial tone announces, "I have a secret to share. . . ."

This kindergarten teacher uses his daily classroom instructional activities to gather important assessment data on his students. Mr. Klein's Writer's Corner is more commonly known as interactive writing (McCarrier, Pinnell, & Fountas, 2000). This instructional tool calls for teacher and students to "share the pen" by first discussing the purpose and content of what is to be written. The teacher then facilitates the group's writing on a chart paper by assisting them in letter formation; letter-sound relationships; cumulative word analysis; and concepts about print, syntax, and semantics. Mr. Klein views this time as an opportunity to witness the evolving skills of his young writers, and he keeps a clipboard of student observation sheets nearby to record important data for later analysis (see Figure 1).

On this day, Mr. Klein has identified four students for observational data collection. He will be noting the progress of Luis, Vu, Kelly, and Mubarek in three areas: (a) oral language development, (b) print conventions, and (c) letter formation. He will note evidence of the extent of their oral language skills during the group discussion of Mr. Klein's secret: A surprise guest will be arriving the next day to answer questions about the new aquarium in the classroom. The teacher's goal for this activity is to capture the students' questions about the fish in the tank, as well as the care and feeding of their fish. They will use this class chart to guide their discussion the following day. As Mr. Klein leads this interactive writing session, he notes whether Vu's contributions to the discussion are on topic. When Kelly is called to the chart to write, the teacher observes her use of spacing and other print conventions. Mr. Klein requires all the children to write the message on their whiteboards at the same time it is being recorded on the chart. Not only does this keep the students engaged, but it allows Mr. Klein to assess Luis's letter formations when he proudly holds up his whiteboard. Mubarek, who arrived from Somalia only 2 weeks earlier, is just now beginning to participate in the routines of the classroom.

Student Name: _____ Date: _____

Writing Topic: _____

	Proficient	Attempted	Not Evidenced	Not Available
Letter Formations (Record letters)				
Concepts of Print				
Spacing				
Directionality				
Capitals				
Oral Language				
Uses language to represent ideas				
Grammatically correct				
Predicts and recalls				
Uses accurate vocabulary				
Interacts with peers				
On topic				
Inquires				

FIGURE 1. Interactive Writing Observation Guide

Mr. Klein notes Mubarek's use of language to negotiate the sharing of the marker and whiteboard with his partner.

Classroom 2: Guided Reading in Second Grade

"Hector, Eduardo, Carmelita, and Mercedes, please join me at the reading table," asks Ms. Antonio. It is a Tuesday morning in Ms. Antonio's second-grade biliteracy class, and four students are about to participate in a guided reading lesson. Importantly, each child is leaving a different center activity. Ms. Antonio believes in heterogeneously grouping students for most instruction, while reserving homogeneous grouping for specific teacher-directed activities like guided reading. "It just didn't make any sense to me to limit the number of children each student gets to work with. I used to rotate them all through the centers in their reading groups, but I noticed that some students just didn't progress like I thought they would," notes Ms. Antonio.

This teacher uses the Center Activity Rotation System (Flood & Lapp, 2000), commonly known as CARS, to organize her literacy block. This classroom organizational system was first introduced to her through the ongoing professional development available at her school, when teachers had identified through a needs assessment that they would like more information on grouping and management. Because she regroups her students frequently, she needs to assess them often.

The four second-graders take their seats at the reading table. Ms. Antonio distributes copies of *Alexander, Que Era Rico el Domingo Pasado* [Alexander, Who Used to Be Rich Last Sunday] (Viorst, 1991). The students eagerly reach for the now familiar book, which they have read before in both English and Spanish. "Please begin reading softly to yourself, and I'll listen. Remember that you're not reading together, just at your own pace," says Ms. Antonio. She leans in to listen to Mercedes, and asks her to read just a little bit louder. As the student reads, Ms. Antonio completes a running record to document her reading behaviors (see Figure 2).

Later, when she analyzes the record, she realizes that Mercedes is self-correcting more frequently. She also completed a running record on Hector, and he read the entire text correctly.

Ms. Antonio relies on running records to analyze the strategies her learners are applying to their reading (Fountas & Pinnell, 1996). She completes a running record on each student in 4-week intervals and then regroups readers based on their instructional level and their need for instruction in the use of specific strategies.

After listening to the students read, Ms. Antonio lays out fifteen 3x5-vocabulary cards in English and Spanish, featuring words from the story. The teacher and her students begin arranging the words in a variety of open sorts, using categories the students have determined. Words are variously sorted according to word families as well as to words with similar conceptual values. Ms. Antonio writes anecdotal observations about each child's knowledge of the various ways that words can be manipulated.

Classroom 3: Literacy Across Content Areas

Mrs. Ying circles the classroom, listening in on the excited conversations of fifth graders in the process of being stumped, amazed, and otherwise dumbfounded. "Look at this one!" says Orian as she holds up a "magic eye" painting for her group

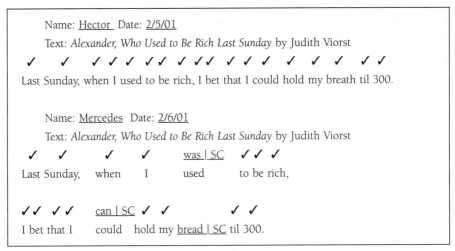

FIGURE 2. Excerpt From Two Running Records

Key. SC = self-correcting

members. "The Statue of Liberty's in there—can you see it?" she asks. At another learning center, four students are trying to beat "Poggendorf's Illusion," a visual puzzle first created by Johann Poggendorf in 1860 and now featured on the Sandlot Science Web site (http://www.sandlotscience.com). Another small group of students are using *Hello, Red Fox* (Carle, 1998) to test the theory of color reversal by gazing at the seemingly miscolored images in the book and then shifting their focus to a blank white sheet of paper, where a correct image appears before their eyes. "Cool!" whistles Miguel. Mrs. Ying smiles to herself. The introduction to her new science unit on illusions and perception is already a success.

After the students have explored many of the illusions set out by Mrs. Ying, she signals an end to exploration and moves to the next task. "I'm very curious about your conversations. We're going to begin a science unit called 'More Than Meets the Eye.' Let's write your thoughts and questions down so we can begin to discover the answers to them," she says. She then moves to the large KWL chart posted at the front of the classroom (Figure 3).

Mrs. Ying has created an observational event in order to elicit student responses for the purposes of informing future instruction. Known as a KWL chart (Ogle, 1986), it serves a dual purpose in this science classroom: It assists students in organizing their prior knowledge and wonderings as well as serving as an assessment tool to determine prior knowledge and areas of future instruction.

"What do you already know about illusions?" prompts Mrs. Ying. "Those magic eye paintings are illusions!" calls out Orian, gesturing to the posters on the table at the back of the room. Patrick chimes in, "Magicians perform illusions! I saw them on TV!" Naushad wrinkles his forehead and asks, "But do they work on everyone? Does everyone get tricked?" Mrs. Ying, who had been recording student responses in the first column, turns to face the class and replies, "That sounds like a question to me. I'm going to write that in the 'want to know' column."

Mrs. Ying used the information on the KWL chart to plan her instruction for the unit. She was surprised that some of the students were familiar with the phrase

What do we know about illusions?	What do we want to know?	What have we learned?
• Magic eye paintings are illusions. • Magicians do them. • They play tricks on your brain. • They are very fun. • There are optical illusions. • Some illusions are used in art. • Animals use illusion to hide (camouflage).	• Do they work on everybody? • Could we invent new ones? • What happens in your brain when you see an illusion? • Do your eyes get mixed up or does your brain? • Are there other illusions? • Why do some animals use camouflage and others don't? • Why don't humans use camouflage?	

FIGURE 3. KWL Chart for "More Than Meets the Eye" Unit

optical illusions and pleased to hear of their curiosity regarding the biological basis of these visual puzzles. Her unit of instruction extended over 2 weeks and included a detailed look at the relationship between the eye and the brain. Students researched optical illusions and constructed their favorites for a "More Than Meets the Eye" gallery walk at the end of the unit. However, the KWL chart was not finished yet. Further assessment information was also collected at the end of this unit using this KWL chart. The last phase ("what we learned") was done first in small groups and then completed in a classwide discussion. Mrs. Ying recognized that this instructional event served the multiple purposes of reinforcing new knowledge and providing her with a window on the progress of the class.

❖ DISTINGUISHING FEATURES

The distinguishing features of this elementary school are twofold. First, the teachers and university faculty created a unique professional development system designed to improve student achievement. This includes both preservice and in-service teachers and focuses on providing quality literacy instruction. Second, the teachers and we, as university faculty, have adopted a model of assessment based on the work of Calfee and Hiebert (1988, 1991). Not only have we adopted the model, but we have implemented it with real students in real classrooms. As a result, we have found that we can impact student achievement and ensure that more and more students leave us as readers.

Professional Development System

Much of the development of the school's strengthened commitment to authentic assessment stems from the staff's participation in a sophisticated model of professional development. More than half of the school's staff is enrolled in a unique on-site master's degree program in elementary curriculum and instruction at a local university. This program was designed by the professional development school (PDS) committee, which included school personnel and university faculty. This initiative is sponsored by the City Heights K-16 Educational Pilot. Begun in 1998, this 6-year partnership between San Diego State University, the San Diego Unified School District, the San Diego Education Association, and Price Charities seeks to enhance the student outcomes in an elementary, middle, and high school while improving preservice and in-service professional development. In this model, professional development is viewed as a continuum that ranges from student teachers to teachers who are new to the profession to master teachers. At each of these points in their careers, teachers require customized avenues to professional development. In addition to the on-site master's degree program, the PDS committee has created multilevel staff development opportunities that include professional reading clubs, workshops, coaching and demonstration lessons, and mentoring.

Current trends in teacher education emphasize collaboration between schools and universities in an effort to support the continued growth of preservice personnel. Although much of the literature focuses on preservice teacher education and development (e.g., Darling-Hammond, 2000; Levine, 1992), there is a smaller but growing body of research on PDS committee collaborations for the purpose of in-service teacher professional development and student outcomes. Groulx and Thomas (2000) found that a PDS partnership positively influenced the multicultural perspectives of teachers. A study conducted by Knight, Wiseman, and Cooner (2000) demonstrated that PDS activities had a positive impact on elementary students' writing and mathematical skills. Abdal-Haaq (1998) reports that there are more than 600 school-university partnerships in the United States, with the PDS becoming a widely used vehicle for the educational and professional development of teachers.

Thus, the teachers at this urban, diverse elementary school have a number of resources available to them. As a group, they have decided to focus on improving literacy instruction through professional development. As a learning community, we examined current literature on literacy improvement and noted the need to begin with assessment practices. Clearly, instruction must be based on assessment. The challenge at this school was to ensure that teachers could collect assessment information that was useful in instructional planning.

Teacher-Based Assessment

Calfee and Hiebert (1988, 1991) have proposed that teachers participate in three phases of teacher-based assessment: (a) setting goals and purposes, (b) collecting data, and (c) interpreting data. These activities closely parallel effective instructional principles (Bereiter & Scardamalia, 1996). In this model, instruction is infused with assessment rather than being seen as something separate from the instructional flow of the classroom (Frey & Hiebert, 2002). These three phases of teacher-based assessment are further described in the sections that follow.

Setting Goals and Purposes

The goals and purposes of gathering assessment data are influenced by the teacher's beliefs about what constitutes literacy, the frequency and timing of their administration, and the type of information needed by the teacher. When these goals and purposes closely match those of the students, the link between assessment and instruction becomes clear-cut and definitive. It is when the goals and purposes do not complement the classroom that both educators and learners struggle to find meaning in these time-consuming practices. In fact, when a teacher protests that he or she does not have time to assess, the cause may actually be a poor match of assessments to students.

One of the strongest predictors of teachers' choices of assessment tools is in the way they define literacy. In other words, teachers' beliefs about the fundamentals of literacy directly influence their choice of assessment instruments. In a classroom where responses to literature are highly valued, it can be expected that much of the assessment will focus on reflection and literature circle discussions. If fluency and automaticity are emphasized in another classroom, measures of words read per minute would be frequently used. Educators often have an easier time linking assessment to instruction when there is a menu of instruments available to match their classroom practice.

When and where an assessment is given also reflects the teacher's goals and purposes. For example, even the most carefully designed assessments are squandered if they are used infrequently and erratically. To avoid this, many teachers collect informal assessment information at regular intervals to make grouping decisions that respond to continually changing student needs. Wise practitioners recognize the value of flexible grouping patterns as a way to build community and increase learning (Flood, Lapp, Flood, & Nagel, 1992). The results of these assessments are then used to group students in a number of ways, including interest, skills, and for social development. This mix of heterogeneous and homogeneous grouping ensures that students have many opportunities to work along side one another. Like frequency, the timing of the assessment also reveals teachers' goals. Some choose an anticipatory activity at the beginning of a unit to provide information about the content to be taught. One example of this is the KWL chart (Ogle, 1986). Analysis of student responses on a KWL chart can alert teachers to specific points that need to be taught as well as those that only require a brief review.

As with teacher beliefs, frequency, and timing, the type of information needed by the teacher also influences the selection of assessments. Teachers of emergent readers may choose assessments that yield a current analysis of each student's literacy skills so they can effectively instruct on problem-solving strategies such as chunking smaller word parts and using context. They may analyze running records to identify the strategies each reader is using but confusing. Teachers of more fluent readers may be concerned with their students' comprehension strategies. Vocabulary assessments, information webs, and extended writing responses are likely to be more common in these classrooms.

Collecting Data

After determining the goals and purposes of teacher-based assessments, teachers collect the information they are seeking about their students. A running record (Clay,

1979) is an important tool because it allows the teachers to monitor progress in reading and to strategically group students for focused instruction in a skill. When Ms. Antonio discovered that three of her students were consistently having difficulty with the *th* sounds during the reading of *And to Think We Thought We'd Never Be Friends* (Hoberman, 1999), she grouped the students for reteaching. She then led them through a word study of the problem vocabulary in the story: *that, think, thwacked, thirsty, thought, they, together, there, then, thin, them, their,* and *the*. Clearly her data collection resulted in an instructional opportunity.

Mrs. Ying enjoys introducing students to quality literature and facilitating their love of literature. She values the transactional nature of reading as well and understands that talking and writing about books is very important. Thus, this becomes one of her goals for assessment. She uses reading response logs that are completed by students as they finish their books. In addition to the title and author, the reading response log provides three sentence starters that students complete in their journals:

- I chose this book . . .
- I thought that . . .
- I want to read . . . (Dewsbury, 1994)

After reading their books and completing their reading response logs, students then conference with the teacher and discuss their responses. The teacher asks questions about the characters, plot, and setting but also makes certain to ask inferential questions as well, such as inquiring about character motivation. Finally, the interview ends with questions about students' aesthetic responses to the book (e.g., How did the story make you feel?). When asked this question after reading *A Long Way From Chicago* (Peck, 1998), Akemi cried out, "Oh! I felt so sad that those kids had to live in the country! Their grandma really took good care of them, maybe better than their momma. My grandma takes care of me all year, but we don't have chickens and pigs and stuff. We still do cooking together and make things and take walks, just like Mary Alice and her grandma." Only through this interview was Mrs. Ying able to determine that Akemi truly understood the message of this book and that she had made a personal connection to the text. Mrs. Ying knows that an aesthetic response to text promotes a lifelong love of reading (Sebesta, Monson, & Senn, 1995).

The methods used to collect data in these classrooms can be categorized into three activities: (a) observing, (b) interviewing, and (c) sampling student work (Frey & Hiebert, 2002). By relying on a multifaceted approach to data collection, these teachers ensure a more complete portrait of each student's progress.

Interpreting Data

As stated earlier, it is virtually impossible to separate the phases of teacher-based assessment when they are done effectively, because their recursive nature propels assessment in a fluid fashion from setting goals to collecting data to interpretation and instruction and then back again to new goals. There are, however, critical features of interpretation to consider.

One is the reliability of the information gathered. On any given day, a child may be able to perform (or fail to perform) a discrete skill or task. A single performance may not indicate whether the skill has been mastered. To assure that his assessments are reliable, Mr. Klein administers assessments on several occasions. For instance, the interactive writing assessments he uses are given approximately once every 6 weeks. This increases his confidence, for example, that Javier, a student whose performance may have been depressed because of a conflict earlier in the cafeteria, still has an opportunity to demonstrate what he knows of letter formation. As a wise practitioner, he knows the value of analyzing the context of an assessment event, not just the end product.

Validity, like reliability, must be considered with all forms of assessment. A way to increase validity in teacher-based assessment is to take care that the assessments reflect the daily instructional climate (Mabry, 1999) and do not require the student to perform an artificial task. Ms. Antonio accounts for this when she uses running records because the assessment is directly tied to authentic instructional activities during her guided reading groups. The story read by the student is one used for instructional purposes and has been viewed once or twice before (Fountas & Pinnell, 1996). A criticism of standardized testing for reading is that it often does not reflect the daily instructional activities that take place in a classroom (Murphy, 1995).

❖ PRACTICAL IDEAS

Use Daily Teaching Events

Assessments are often criticized because they replace instructional time in a classroom. Teachers who understand the use of assessments as instructional tools are not taking away valuable time to conduct assessments. Instead, they use their daily teaching events to collect data. For example, Mr. Klein used his interactive writing time to collect information about four students. Ms. Antonio used her guided reading group time to collect information. The key is understanding which students will be the focus of assessment data collection for the day and which tools will produce the best, or most useful, information.

Match Assessments to Instructional Practices

As noted above, teachers must select tools that provide them with useful information. It would not have been helpful for Mr. Klein to use a KWL chart during his interactive writing time. It would have been equally useless for Mrs. Ying to focus on the print conventions while introducing the whole class to a unit on illusions. Different assessment tools have different purposes and yield different information. The teachers in this school favor interactive writing charts, running records, KWL charts, and reader response logs. However, there are many other types of assessment tools including those outlined in the assessment book by Mariotti and Homan (2001).

Use a Variety of Tools

As we have noted, no one assessment tool can provide the information that teachers need to plan instruction (or make placement decisions or determine the success of a school, for that matter). The teachers at this school use a variety of assessment tools to plan their instruction. The composite view provided by these various assessment tools allows teachers to make generalizations about student learning and required teaching. Storing this assessment information can be a challenge (e.g., Courtney & Abodeeb, 1999). In response, several teachers in this school have created showcase portfolios in which specific pieces of student works are maintained. For example, in Mrs. Ying's class, students each maintain their own showcase portfolio. There are required entries such as a beginning of the year writing sample, book logs, and KWL charts from each science unit and optional (student choice) entries such as journal entries, reading assessments, and informal inventories.

Plan Instruction After Assessments

All too often teachers plan their instructional units and then determine the assessments they will use to gauge student success and determine student progress. For the teachers in this school, that is backward planning. Mr. Klein, Ms. Antonio, and Mrs. Ying use the assessment information they have about their students to plan instruction. They know what each of their students needs to be taught next and consider instructional units that will allow them to accomplish that task. As they plan their instruction, they are also aware of opportunities to gather additional assessment information about students to make midcourse corrections. These teachers focus on what students already know and can do as the basis for instructional planning. Although they acknowledge that this can be more time-consuming, they believe it is an important shift: Students come first in planning.

Make Assessments Recursive

The most important lesson we have learned from this case study is that the link between assessment and instruction is not linear. The teachers at this school understand the recursive nature of setting goals and purposes, collecting data, and interpreting data. They know that this interpretation will result in the establishment of future goals and purposes and direct new data collection that requires interpretation. This case study illustrates how teaching and learning form a continuous process in which teachers use information to plan instructional interventions.

◈ CONCLUSION

The link between assessment and instruction is a central feature of effective teacher-based assessment. Policy centers (e.g., International Reading Association, 2000; National Association of Secondary School Principals, 2000) cite the importance of a recursive process of assessment and instruction in the effort to achieve critical goals of literacy. Mr. Klein, Ms. Antonio, and Mrs. Ying demonstrate Calfee's (1994) statement that classroom teachers can apply research methods in a unique fashion, not only to measure current status but also to inform practice. They pinpoint their instruction through the use of informal and ongoing assessments.

A challenge to school districts, staff developers, and university teacher preparation personnel is to clearly link assessments with instruction. This linkage has sometimes been an afterthought in the rush to quantify students and teachers. When this occurs, assessments are perceived as separate from daily classroom life.

Thoughtful practitioners, such as the teachers profiled here, view assessment as an intentional and strategic process to engage students and facilitate learning.

◈ CONTRIBUTORS

Nancy Frey is a faculty member of literacy at San Diego State University, School of Teacher Education. She has authored books and articles on literacy education and is interested in ensuring that all students have access to quality literacy instruction based on sound assessments.

Douglas Fisher is a faculty member of language development at San Diego State University, School of Teacher Education. He is the author of books and articles on literacy instruction and is interested in assisting struggling readers in urban schools.

CHAPTER 6

From Paper and Pencil to the Web: A Testing and Technology Partnership

Greta J. Gorsuch and Katherine A. Austin

◈ INTRODUCTION

Administering large-scale tests via computer is a topic of increasing interest among teachers and administrators in English as a second language/English as a foreign language (ESL/EFL) and foreign language programs. This case study describes an innovation in program-level testing in which we adapted an existing paper-and-pencil English language proficiency test (popularly known as the Michigan Test) to a Web-based computer format and then administered the test to 86 graduate and undergraduate international students entering a major U.S. university. The paper-and-pencil form of the test had been purchased many years previously and was being used to decide whether international students should be required to take courses in the university's academic English program.

The test was converted to a Web-based format for three reasons. First, administering tests by computer would reduce potential errors made in calculating examinees' test scores. Computer-based scoring yields a higher degree of accuracy (Bahr & Bahr, 1997). Previously, examinees' answer sheets had been scored by hand and their scores manually calculated. Second, with computerized tests, examinees' responses can be analyzed at the item level without the time-consuming step of inputting by hand all the responses on every item into a spreadsheet program. Lastly, in terms of language testing at the university, this innovation was an important first step toward the eventual use of computerized test administration procedures.

Adapting conventional tests to a Web-based format alerted us to issues inherent in computerized test administration. One issue was whether examinees' level of experience with computers might affect their test performance. We were also concerned with what computer test tutorial formats would most effectively help examinees. Additionally, we were interested in working with our test proctors and technical staff on proofreading and test rehearsal procedures. We wanted the Web-based version of the test to be accurate, and we wanted the examinees to feel comfortable and confident in reading and scrolling the texts on the computer screen and then using the mouse to indicate their responses. Finally, we wanted to identify the sorts of problems with computerized test administration that are site specific and sometimes hard to anticipate. In this case study, we use specific insights from our experience to illuminate the issues mentioned above and to suggest a procedural blueprint for readers who are interested in administering computerized tests.

No test administration of this magnitude can be planned and carried out by one person. In our case, our partnership included a language program/test administrator, a technologist interested in computerized test administration, technicians, and test proctors.

◈ CONTEXT

Exemption and Retention Testing for Language Programs

ESL program administrators are often charged with testing large numbers of newly arrived international students at the beginning of a school year or semester. The most immediate concern for the university is whether the students' English abilities are sufficient for academic study. A test can be administered to the students before the new semester begins. The program administrator may then set a cut score, and students who receive scores above the cut score are exempted from taking additional ESL courses. Students who receive test scores below the cut score, however, are retained, meaning they must take additional oral or written ESL courses for at least a semester.

Local Test Validation

Validating a proficiency test (even if it is commercially produced) for use with a specific group of examinees minimally involves using examinees' responses on the test to calculate statistics such as item facility, item discrimination, mean, standard deviation, internal consistency reliability, and standard error of measurement. Computerized test administration is particularly suited to calculating item facility and discrimination, as examinees' responses are downloaded into a computer file that can then be put into a spreadsheet or statistical program for analysis. Any patterns of missing data can also be noted. If one particular item is missing a lot of data, it may mean that either the item is too difficult or confusing or that the item did not appear on the computer screen in a way that examinees could understand or answer it. The item should be checked on both the paper-and-pencil and computerized versions. Brown (1996b) lists many factors that may reduce the reliability of a test, such as a noisy room, poor test directions, examinee health or mental state, errors in scoring, and item quality. He also mentions "equipment," which could mean malfunctioning computers during a computerized test administration, and names "limited screen size" and "computer anxiety" as potential threats to computerized test reliability (1997, p. 50). All of these factors should be examined, and, if possible, controlled by the test administrator and proctors. This means keeping the test room quiet, using properly operating computers with large screens, giving clear directions, and so on. Finally, all tests should be accompanied by a questionnaire that asks examinees about their test-taking experience. Examinees should be asked the degree to which they are familiar with computers. See Appendix A for a sample questionnaire.

Computerized Test Administration

The application of computer technology in academia has dramatically increased in the last 20 years (Zandvliet & Farragher, 1997). Two different models of computerized testing have been developed and empirically evaluated. Computer-based testing refers to the simple transformation from a paper-based test to a computerized version. A second genre involves computer adaptive tests, which present questions to the test taker based on his or her performance on the previous question (Brown, 1997; Overton, Harms, & Taylor, 1997). Because we wanted to compare the computerized version of the Michigan Test with the paper-and-pencil version, we elected to use the computer-based testing model.

Computer-based testing offers test administrators significant advantages compared to paper-and-pencil test administration (Bugbee, 1996). To begin with, computers dramatically improve test administration and evaluation (Jacobs, 1998; Perkins, 1995–1996). Computers automatically record, store, and report examinee responses. This allows the test administrator to focus on testing and score analysis, not data gathering and data integrity. Secondly, we hypothesized that computerized testing would create a more flexible and positive environment for students and administrators. Because the computer test was easier to administer and manage, proctors could spend more time interacting with the examinees. Our team approach allowed the technologists to monitor the technology and the proctors and test administrator to focus on the well-being of the examinees. Lastly, the efficiency of the process would benefit examinees in terms of timely and accurate feedback on their performance. With the computer analyzing and collecting much of the data, the test administrator was able to analyze the test validity as well as examinee performance.

However, in the context of computer-based test administration, the direct advantages need further investigation (Bugbee, 1996). Our first concern was that computer anxiety might negatively impact student performance (Bowers & Bowers, 1996; Heinssen, Glass, & Knight, 1987). A second concern involved examinees' prior experience with computers. Because computer experience and exposure can affect comfort, attitude, satisfaction, and performance, we needed to measure examinees' experience level (Taylor, Kirsch, & Eignor, 1999). Although we had a survey that would indicate students' level of experience, we created a tutorial and an on-site information-gathering process that allowed us to address differing levels of experience.

Web-Based Testing

In the last few years, scholars have concluded that the Web further enhances computer-based testing. A hypertext environment creates a nonlinear and multidimensional environment for information organization and collection (Olaniran, Stalcup, & Jensen, 2000; Smith & Stalcup, 2001). Hypertext environments are flexible and conducive to active exploration (Bonham, Beichner, & Titus, 2000; Zammit, 2000). Given the international popularity of the Web, we hypothesized that students would be comfortable with the medium. Three types of student Web users have been identified (Neiderhauser, Reynolds, Salmen, & Skolmoski, 2000):

- *Knowledge seekers* are very directed and diligent as they interact with the interface.

- *Feature explorers* tend to be less directed and more adventurous.

- *Apathetic users* are the most difficult to assist as they are unwilling to embrace the technology.

In our testing situation, we address the needs of each type of student in the tutorial and through private, friendly talks with examinees before the test.

A second area relevant to assessment conducted over the Web concerns the computer screen display design, which can have a significant impact on student performance. For instance, an inconsistent interface increases student errors and causes confusion (Ozok & Salvendy, 2000) and increases the knowledge demands on examinees (Wright, Fields, & Harris, 2000). An increased cognitive load diminishes student performance and satisfaction. Obviously, an interface that increases cognitive load would be a source of significant measurement error in a testing situation. To address these issues, we agreed to select a uniform management tool that would address the issues of consistency, navigation, and organization (Goldberg, 1997).

Although the Web is generally accepted as an effective medium for testing, many technologists have warned of potential problems. Two common failures occur during testing. First, the number of server requests created by the students logging onto the server simultaneously may exceed the memory capacity of the Web server. In that case, students would receive error messages and would be unable to take the exam. A more common problem is that the simultaneous requests may not overwhelm the server, but the server may not able to process them efficiently. In this case, students experience delays in logging in, saving answers, and returning to unanswered questions. This potential problem was our greatest concern as our planned tests were timed.

In examining the Teaching, Learning, and Technology Center (TLTC) servers and client computers, we determined that the resources were sufficient. We rehearsed the test before the regular semester began, at a time when the server had significantly less activity. Additionally, we carefully tested each client machine and browser to ensure that the client systems were reliable and stable. We determined that, in this situation, the potential benefits of testing via the Web outweighed the associated risks.

Texas Tech University

The university at which the computerized test administration took place enrolls 18,700 undergraduate and 3,400 graduate students each year in 186 different undergraduate and graduate degree programs (Institutional Research and Information Management, 2000). Currently, there are 161 international students in undergraduate programs and 766 in graduate programs. Each academic year, approximately 350 new international students arrive on the campus (S. Murphy, personal communication, October 14, 2001). In this case study, 86 examinees took the computerized tests. In a program-related survey, 8 reported they were undergraduates, 72 reported they were graduates, 59 reported they were male, and 27 reported they were female. Some examinees did not report undergraduate/graduate status or gender. The examinees represented 22 different nationalities, including Estonian, Chinese, Jordanian, Singaporean, and Indian. The examinees were enrolled in more than 20 different academic majors.

Academic English Program (AEP) and the Michigan Test

The AEP is intended to serve graduate and undergraduate students enrolled at the university "to improve their English proficiency so that they can take good advantage of their education at Texas Tech" (Academic English Program, 1998). A three-part battery of tests is administered to incoming international students. For the purposes of this case study, only two will be described. The first is the Michigan Test of English Language Proficiency (MTELP) (English Language Institute, 1962), a multiple-form, 100-item test with three subtests: grammar, vocabulary, and reading comprehension. The second is the English Language Institute Listening Comprehension Test (ELILCT), a multiple-form, 45-item "aural grammar test" (English Language Institute, 1986, p. 1). These two tests are multiple choice and objectively scored. Historically, examinees had a test book and a separate answer sheet on which they marked their answers. Examinees' answer sheets were individually hand scored by test proctors. Examinees' raw scores on each of the two tests were converted to equated scores using a chart provided by the test maker.

The AEP offers two courses that are related to this case study. ESL 1301, Oral Skills for International Students, assists international students in developing fluency and accuracy in spoken English, and provides instruction and practice in listening comprehension and in the rhetorical conventions of academic English and sentence-level English grammar. ESL 1302, English Grammar and Composition for International Students, assists international students in developing English writing skills and fluency needed to be successful in academic subjects at the university level (Academic English Program, 1998).

Examinees who receive an equated score of 84 or less on the listening comprehension test (ELILCT) are required to take ESL 1301. Examinees who receive an average equated score of 84 or less on the grammar, vocabulary, and reading comprehension test (MTELP) and an impromptu written essay are required to take ESL 1302.

❖ DESCRIPTION

Selecting WebCT

Once we decided that computer-based testing was an ideal format for the test administration, our next task was to select and customize an appropriate interface. The team selected WebCT for five reasons:

1. WebCT has a consistent interface design throughout the program. Each screen has navigation buttons and task-representation icons to aid the student (Goldberg, 1997).

2. The built-in quizzing module provides individual visual representations of the examinees' progress as they take the test. The program also allows students to skip and return to questions whenever they want.

3. WebCT provides a built-in timing mechanism that could be used to simulate timings for paper-and-pencil versions of the tests. During the exam, examinees could see the time remaining on their screen.

4. In any test administration, the logistics of student management and security is always an administrative hurdle. WebCT requires each examinee to have a unique account and password.

5. WebCT has a sophisticated, highly reliable data collection and management system that facilitated our viewing examinees' responses,

determining item facility and item discrimination statistics, and identifying missing data immediately after the test was administered.

Putting the MTELP and ELILCT on WebCT

The makers of the MTELP and ELILCT were contacted to get permission to create a Web-based version of the MTELP and the ELILCT. We detailed our plans for ensuring test security and fidelity to the suggested norms of test administration. Once we selected WebCT, the team constructed the on-line version of the Michigan Test. The first task was to enter the questions into the WebCT database to exactly match the paper-and-pencil version of the test. The MTELP only required text questions, but the ELILCT required a more creative approach. The ELILCT requires students to listen to recorded prompts and then answer questions immediately after hearing the information. After reviewing the technological alternatives, we decided that we would allow all students to listen to the test from a tape recorder piped into the sound system of the examination rooms but then register their responses to the prompts on the computer.

Developing Visual and Aural Computer Testing Tutorials

We created a visual computer-based tutorial with complementary aural instructions to address several student needs. We could not predict student technology experience and comfort levels beforehand. Therefore, we developed a tutorial that helped students learn the fundamental skills required to navigate the interface and take the examination. We felt that a hands-on tutorial would reduce anxiety and increase familiarity and comfort. We included an instructor with the tutorial so that students could interact with both the instructor and the computer.

The tutorial taught and reinforced three skill sets. First, the tutorial reinforced general browser skills such as using the navigation buttons and entering the address location. Second, the tutorial introduced students to the specific WebCT testing interface. A last skill set involved general technology dexterity. The TLTC staff monitored the students and watched for mouse control problems and hand-eye coordination problems. When we identified struggling students, we provided assistance and suggestions to improve their accuracy.

An unexpected problem was that the technologist who delivered the tutorial was inexperienced with international students. We realized that her speed, cadence, and word choice would be a barrier in teaching the technology skills because her rapid speech and relaxed enunciation would be difficult for those who do not speak English as a primary language to understand. Our solution was to script the entire tutorial and explain the issues to the technology instructors. In this way, we were able to dramatically improve the quality and efficacy of the aural tutorial.

Cheating

The tests were administered in the university's TLTC. The TLTC is a multipurpose facility, so the computers in the rooms used for the test had no special testing security hoods. We took several measures to reduce cheating. First, we assigned examinees to the laptop computer room because the laptop screens were liquid crystal and, therefore, it was difficult for candidates to view other computer screens in the room.

The second idea for reducing cheating came from the test proctors who suggested seating arrangements to inhibit cheating. Tom Cox, one of the proctors, came up with a third idea: have examinees read and sign a "Michigan Test Academic Integrity Contract" before beginning the test.[1] In addition, we planned to have the proctors tell the examinees that if they had any problems during this test, they should ask a proctor for help, not another student. Finally, test proctors were asked to watch examinees for any unusual eye movements.

Proofreading

We wanted the Web-based version of the MTELP and the ELILCT to be true to the paper-and-pencil versions. The authors, a TLTC staffer, and the test proctors proofread the Web-based test versions against the test booklets. We gave the test proctors temporary account numbers and passwords to access the tests on the Web so they could proofread at home.

Rehearsing

We rehearsed taking the Web-based versions of the MTELP and ELILCT. One of the authors and a TLTC staffer administered the test to four proctors. After going through the tutorials and the tests, the proctors offered the following suggestions (actions we took are noted in italics):

> Provide three to four on-screen sample questions from the tests for the tutorials so that the tutor can physically demonstrate answering questions and saving responses onto the server. *A TLTC staffer integrated sample questions from the paper-and-pencil test instruction sections into the on-line tutorial.*

> Do not identify the test form on the computer screen. *A TLTC staffer removed the information from the Web-based tests.*

> Remove number of points that appear after each item. *A TLTC staffer was able to remove this visual distraction, a WebCT feature, from the Web-based tests.*

> Take the time limit off the ELILCT, as the audiotape the students will listen to may extend beyond the specified WebCT time limit. *A TLTC staffer removed the time limit from the Web-based ELILCT.*

In addition, the proctors, in taking the tests, discovered potential on-screen distractions for examinees. On some computers, for example, the window for the Web-based tests initially was small. The proctors figured out how to maximize the window, which was incorporated into the tutorials. In general, however, the Web-based version of the tests received high marks from the proctors. They especially liked the features that candidates could see that their answers were registered and that the on-screen displays were clear and easily navigable. The proctors also raised useful questions. For example, what if an examinee's computer screen freezes or an examinee accidentally logs off WebCT? Our response was to have the TLTC staffer help the examinee immediately reset or log back on and assure the student that whatever items he or she has already answered has been saved by the server.

---

[1] This contract is available upon request from Greta Gorsuch at greta.gorsuch@ttu.edu.

Administering the Test

Like any day on which a test is administered to a large number of people, there were things that went well and things that did not go so well. On the positive side, we accomplished our goal of getting everyone tested in ordered and relaxed surroundings. WebCT worked well, and there were no server failures. The examinees seemed to confidently apply themselves to the task of taking the tests on computer. We did not observe any examinees having difficulty scrolling up and down the screen, and they seemed to choose and then save their responses with ease. Only one examinee claimed to have no computer experience at all. We quietly placed the examinee in a front row and assigned a test proctor to discreetly help her. She completed the tests without any observable difficulty. All examinees' data were saved in perfect order, and we were able to get their total scores on the MTELP and ELILCT and all of the item statistics on all items immediately after both tests were over. As soon as the tests were completed, a TLTC staffer took the tests off the Web. There were no breaches in test security. Finally, there were no incidents of cheating that we could observe.

There were some glitches, and these can be separated into problems with scheduling and facilities and problems with technology. Only the technology problems will be reported here. To begin with, our Web server did experience sluggish response with both the MTELP and ELILCT as the students started the examination simultaneously. This seemed to make the examinees nervous, and students feared that their responses were not being registered. Because the proctors were comfortable with the interface, they quickly responded with positive reinforcement when we encountered slow response time. Once all the examinees were logged in and started the test, server response time quickly recovered. A TLTC professional monitored the processing capacity and the memory allocation and confirmed that the student responses were being registered in the WebCT database.

A second problem concerned the perceived accuracy of the time and progress display on the screen. Given that students were keenly focused on questions and relying on the right panel for a map of their progress, we quickly realized that the computers were not refreshing the screen every minute. In fact, the computer screen would only refresh when a student saved an answer. Some students noticed that the time remaining display was not changing and became concerned. With the click of a simple icon, the screen would refresh immediately. By the second test administration, we incorporated this oversight into the tutorial.

A related third technical problem arose with the ELILCT. As with all listening comprehension tests, the audiotape proceeds in a fixed period of time. Students were perplexed when the time remaining display fell behind the audiotape. In the MTELP this was not an issue, but with the ELILCT all students were dependent on one audio device for their item prompts. Lastly, we experienced technical problems with a few of the laptop client computers. During the MTELP, two examinees apparently dislodged the power cables under the table accidentally and caused their computers to turn off (they were logged back on immediately). One of the positive features of WebCT is that student answers are saved in the event of inadvertent exit, and the time remaining at the point of exit is also remembered.

◈ DISTINGUISHING FEATURES

Local Test Validation

Administering the tests using WebCT helped us to establish a number of things. For instance, we were able to investigate the examinees' responses at an item level, something that could never be done on a paper-and-pencil test with 145 items and 86 examinees. We found patterns in missing data that suggested that one item type in the vocabulary section presented problems for a few of the examinees. We also discovered that both tests had many items with high-item facility, whereas the ELILCT contained many items with low-item discrimination.

Knowledge of Computerized Language Testing

Through our partnership, we were able to mutually construct a local body of experience and knowledge on computerized language testing. For instance, we learned that test administration always takes longer than expected and that extra time for computer tutorials should be scheduled. We also know that the server becomes sluggish when 30 or more examinees try to register their responses at the same time. We learned that test fatigue is a potentially serious issue with the kind of schedule we used. We need to create a testing schedule that will make life easier for the examinees and reduce measurement error. Finally, we now know that examinee eye fatigue may be a threat to test reliability and that we need to this investigate this matter further.

Future Development of Computerized Test Administration in Languages

We believe that administering the MTELP and ELILCT on computers was an important first step for future development of computerized language testing at the university. We showed that it can be done and, with further investigation of scheduling alternatives and control of measurement error, that we can get reliable, useful, and timely information on examinees' language abilities. This has three main implications. First, we can begin to gather hard evidence that may aid future decisions on whether to continue using the Michigan Test battery and in what form. Second, using computerized testing we can begin to save and store items from the various forms of the MTELP and ELILCT with item facility and discrimination information. This will enable us to choose a balanced variety of easy, moderate, and difficult items that discriminate between high- and low-ability examinees effectively. Third, these items can then be put into a new test, which could be a conventional computer-based test or a computer-adaptive test in which items are administered according to examinees' responses on items of varying levels of difficulties.

Computer Experience and Attitude Questionnaire

This was an important feature of this innovation for three reasons. First, we feel it is necessary to get feedback from examinees on their experiences with the tutorials. For example, we found that examinees felt that both the on-screen and oral tutorials were helpful. Examinees reported that they felt they were able to change their answers, save their responses for individual items, and save their answers on the test with relative ease.

The questionnaire also focused on the examinees' feelings of confidence using the mouse and scrolling functions necessary for taking the exams. Examinees indicated they were confident that they had the skills to navigate and use the mouse appropriately. A final reason why the questionnaire was important concerned whether examinees' level of computer use and experience had an effect on their test scores. In general, we found that the examinees had far more computer experience than we had anticipated. Through statistical analyses, we found that examinees with limited computer experience still did as well on the MTELP and ELILCT as examinees with more experience.

Academic Integrity Contract

Having examinees read and sign an academic integrity contract was an effective measure against cheating. This contract, based on the university's student handbook, provided an important introduction for the examinees into the standards expected of students at Texas Tech.

Creation of Partnerships

We formed a unique partnership between the AEP and the TLTC. The test administrator could not have computerized and administered the MTELP and ELILCT without the technology professional's expertise and the resources the TLTC had to offer. We hope that other language program administrators will identify individuals and technology centers for helpful partnerships with their computerized testing.

◈ PRACTICAL IDEAS

Plan Ahead

Converting a paper-and-pencil test to a computerized format takes a lot of planning. Do not underestimate the time it takes to put the test into a computer, proofread the test items, and then conduct some sort of rehearsal—at least a month is needed. Also, do not underestimate the time it takes to complete a computer tutorial on the test day itself. It may be advisable to offer the tutorials on a continuous walk-in basis on the day before the test.

Recognize That Computerized Testing Is Not a Panacea

The advantages of computerized test administration are enormous, but computerized testing brings with it its own challenges and problems. These include new threats to test reliability, such as examinee computer familiarity, eye fatigue, and sluggish servers. Language testers will have to get used to the fact that computerized testing does not reduce measurement error; it simply keeps some of the old sources and introduces some new sources. Program administrators must remain ever vigilant and continuously investigate how well the test scores are serving the purpose of making decisions about examinees' lives. In fact, changing the medium of tests (from paper and pencil to computer) might have systematic effects on test takers' performances that in turn will necessitate additional analysis and caution in interpreting test takers' scores on computerized tests. See American Educational Research Association, 1999; Chou, 2000; and Fulcher, 1999 for additional information.

❖ CONCLUSION

We learned a great deal from converting paper-and-pencil tests to computerized versions. We learned that the computerized versions were just as good as the older, paper-and-pencil versions. In fact, there were significant advantages to computerizing the test that outweighed the efforts we undertook with this innovation. We also learned the importance of examinee training and how to create comprehensive yet easy-to-understand computerized test-taking tutorials. Most important, we learned we needed to follow an overall strategic plan to implementing the innovation. Fortunately, we were able to determine ahead of time most of the issues of concern and created strategies for addressing these concerns. For instance, we knew that proctor involvement in proofreading and test rehearsal would help us find answers to our concerns about equivalence of the paper-and-pencil and computerized versions of the test and to our worries about cheating and student confusion with the computer interface. We recommend this innovation to interested program administrators and hope that our case study offers sufficient support and raises the necessary issues.

❖ ACKNOWLEDGMENTS

The authors would like to thank Tom Cox, Karla Konrad, Dale Griffee, Sherri Brouillette, Kathy Stevens, and David Smallwood, the proctors; Carla Castle, the AEP secretary; and Jennifer Castleberry and Anthony Oden, the TLTC staff. Their assistance was absolutely necessary in undertaking this innovation.

❖ CONTRIBUTORS

Greta J. Gorsuch teaches applied linguistics and ESL courses, and directs international teaching assistant training at Texas Tech University. An author of articles on testing, educational cultures, and teacher development, she is interested in helping teachers and administrators develop appropriate and reasonable local testing practices.

Katherine A. Austin manages the technology programs at the Teaching, Learning, and Technology Center at Texas Tech. An author of articles on computer-based interaction and instructional technology, she is interested in the instruction and technological issues involved in computer-based test design and implementation.

◈ APPENDIX A: MICHIGAN TEST QUESTIONNAIRE (MAIN TEST AND LISTENING TEST) VERSION 3

(This questionnaire is adapted from Stalcup, 1999.)

Part 1

Circle the best answer for you.

How often do you use a computer in a month?

| 0–10 | 11–50 | 51–100 | 101–200 | 201+ |

How often do you access the Internet in a month?

| 0–10 | 11–50 | 51–100 | 101–200 | 201+ |

I can easily control a computer keyboard and mouse.

5	4	3	2	1
agree strongly	agree	do not know	disagree	disagree strongly

I can easily scroll the content displayed on a computer screen using a keyboard and mouse.

5	4	3	2	1
agree strongly	agree	do not know	disagree	disagree strongly

Part 2

Circle the best answer for you.

I enjoy using computers.

5	4	3	2	1
agree strongly	agree	do not know	disagree	disagree strongly

The Internet offers me useful information.

5	4	3	2	1
agree strongly	agree	do not know	disagree	disagree strongly

I believe that having computer skills will benefit my future career.

5	4	3	2	1
agree strongly	agree	do not know	disagree	disagree strongly

Computers are useful tools for measuring my language capabilities.

5	4	3	2	1
agree strongly	agree	do not know	disagree	disagree strongly

Computer skills are necessary for me to function in this world.

5	4	3	2	1
agree strongly	agree	do not know	disagree	disagree strongly

I am anxious about using computers.

5	4	3	2	1
agree strongly	agree	do not know	disagree	disagree strongly

Part 3

Circle the best answer for you.

How many times have you taken tests on a computer?

| 0 | 1–3 | 4–6 | 7–9 | 10 or more |

How many times have you taken foreign language tests on a computer?

| 0 | 1–3 | 4–6 | 7–9 | 10 or more |

I am comfortable taking tests on computers.

5	4	3	2	1
agree strongly	agree	do not know	disagree	disagree strongly

I am comfortable taking foreign language tests on computers.

5	4	3	2	1
agree strongly	agree	do not know	disagree	disagree strongly

I am comfortable taking foreign language tests using a test book, answer sheet, and pencil.

5	4	3	2	1
agree strongly	agree	do not know	disagree	disagree strongly

Part 4

Please read the statements below and indicate the level of your agreement with them by circling the best answer for you.

The training session before the grammar, vocabulary, and reading test was helpful.

5	4	3	2	1
agree strongly	agree	do not know	disagree	disagree strongly

The directions on the computer screen for the grammar, vocabulary, and reading tests were helpful.

5	4	3	2	1
agree strongly	agree	do not know	disagree	disagree strongly

The training session before the listening test was helpful.

5	4	3	2	1
agree strongly	agree	do not know	disagree	disagree strongly

The directions on the computer screen for the listening test were helpful.

5	4	3	2	1
agree strongly	agree	do not know	disagree	disagree strongly

I was able to change my answers if I wanted to change them.

5	4	3	2	1
agree strongly	agree	do not know	disagree	disagree strongly

I knew how to save my answers after each question.

5	4	3	2	1
agree strongly	agree	do not know	disagree	disagree strongly

I knew how to save all my answers at the end of the test.

5	4	3	2	1
agree strongly	agree	do not know	disagree	disagree strongly

On the listening test, I could hear the tape well enough.

5	4	3	2	1
agree strongly	agree	do not know	disagree	disagree strongly

Part 5

I think taking the Michigan Test on computer is a good idea. (Circle the best answer for you.)

5	4	3	2	1
agree strongly	agree	do not know	disagree	disagree strongly

I have the following suggestions for future tests (please write your answer):

_____

_____

_____

The good points of taking the test today were (please write your answer):

_____

_____

_____

The bad points of taking the test today were (please write your answer):

_____

_____

_____

Demographic Questions

We would appreciate you taking some extra time to answer the questions below.

Are you male or female? (Circle one.)

      male   female

How many years have you been learning English? (Circle one.)

     0–4   5–10   11–15   15 or more

What is your age? (Circle one.)

   17–20   21–24   25–28   29–32   33–36   37–40   40+

I went to a high school or college where most school subjects were taught in English. (Circle one.)

     yes   no

In what country did you attend high school? (Please write your answer).

_____

How many years have you been using computers? (Circle one.)

    0–2   3–5   6–8   9–11   12+

Is there a computer in your family home? (Circle one.)

     yes   no

What is your first language (the language you grew up speaking)? (Please write your answer.)

_____

Are you an undergraduate or graduate? (Circle one.)

What is your major (specialized area of study)? (Please write your answer.)

_____

CHAPTER 7

Beyond the Individual Speaker in New Zealand

Helen Basturkmen

◈ INTRODUCTION

Speaking in presentations is a form of discourse that is relatively monologic and planned. Assessment procedures in English language teaching (ELT) are fairly well established for this form of discourse. Speaking in discussions is dialogic and spontaneous. This poses a challenge for assessment, and procedures for assessing this type of discourse are less well developed. This case study reports on the approach to assessment developed in an academic speaking course for nonnative speakers of English at Auckland University, New Zealand. Our aim was to move beyond assessing the presentation skills of the individual speaker to assessing the discussion skills of the interlocutor as well.

◈ CONTEXT

The academic speaking course is part of Auckland University's English Language Program. The program aims to support nonnative-speaking students already enrolled and taking courses in their subject areas. The program focuses on the general academic writing, listening, and speaking needs of students studying a range of subjects (e.g., commerce, computer science, Asian languages and literatures, science). Students earn credits from participating in courses in the program.

A needs analysis study at the university (Gravatt, Richards, & Lewis, 1998) found that students reported experiencing difficulties in speaking in class discussions, participating in seminars, and giving presentations. The difficulties included asking questions, planning presentations, and participating in whole-class and small-group discussions.

The academic speaking course was set up with the goal of helping students with the problems identified by the needs analysis. It aims to foster the development of both presentation and discussion skills. The objectives of the course are for students to improve their ability to give presentations (i.e., speaking skills) and their ability to participate in university-type discussions (i.e., interlocutor skills).

This one-semester course includes 48 hours of instruction over a 12-week period. As many as seven language instructors and 12 classes of between 14 and 20 students are involved in this course at any point. The course has been running for more than eight semesters.

The majority of students in the course are undergraduates in their 1st and 2nd years of university study. The students come from a number of countries, with most students from Asian countries, especially Korea, China (mainland and Hong Kong), and Taiwan. There are also some students from Eastern European countries and Sweden. Most permanently reside in New Zealand, although they vary in the length of time they have lived here. Some have lived in New Zealand for a number of years and completed some secondary school education in the country. Others are fairly new arrivals in the country and have been resident for only a few months or even weeks. Around 20% of the students are in New Zealand for study purposes only and will return to their native countries on completion of their degree programs. Although student ages range from 18 to 50, most students are around 20 years old.

The students vary also in their English language proficiency levels. Entry to the course is based on student self-selection. A few students have near-native proficiency in English whereas others are considerably weaker. Generally, the minimum requirement for nonnative speakers who are not residents in New Zealand is Band 6 (a generally good command of English but with some inaccuracies) on the International English Language Testing System (IELTS) for most undergraduate degree courses at the university.

From this brief description, it should be clear that there is enormous diversity among the students in terms of their English language ability, their subjects of study, their length of time in New Zealand, and their experience of English-medium education. This diversity of student intake makes the course an interesting one to teach in terms of the rich mix of students, but, at the same time, the diversity also poses a number of challenges in terms of design and planning as there is no one group or subject area that can be targeted.

◈ DESCRIPTION

One challenge in the development of assessment for the academic speaking course was to find a means to assess students with a range of proficiency levels. Students with higher proficiency levels of general English may find such a course not demanding and do little work. This is because they feel that they already have good speaking skills and are thus likely to get a good grade anyway. Students with a lower proficiency level may find the task daunting. These students can too easily feel that they will not be able to get good grades whatever they do. These are very reasonable thoughts on the part of students. After all, the students often have a background of many years of studying English as a second or foreign language. It has taken them years to reach their current proficiency level at the outset of the speaking course. It is clear that a 48-hour course of instruction will not result in a great improvement in the students' general level of speaking proficiency.

In light of the above situation, we wanted to devise a course and assessment that would target the type of speaking and discussion skills that students need for study purposes that could also be improved in a short period of time. We also needed to develop an approach that would even the playing field, an approach that would not reward students for simply having prior, good linguistic proficiency. In response to this challenge, we developed an assessment plan that aims to assess students on achievement of task outcomes and specific discussion skills and strategies taught in the speaking course.

A second challenge was to devise ways to actually assess discussion skills. Conventional approaches to assessment of speaking focus largely on the individual speaker. Such approaches attempt to isolate the skills of the speaker in conveying information and ideas, organizing talk, and signaling content. They work well for assessment of planned speaking (e.g., presentations, long turns at talk) but are less relevant for unplanned speaking (e.g., short turns in two- or multiparty discussion).

Forms of speaking exist on a continuum between highly planned and spontaneous. Planned forms of speaking are largely scripted and organized in advance of delivery. Ideas and information are carefully organized and articulated ahead of time to achieve maximum effectiveness. These forms of speaking are basically monologic. Some forms of talk are in the middle of the continuum (e.g., impromptu talks). At the other end of the continuum are forms of talk that are unplanned or only marginally planned before delivery. There are a number of features of planned language use that set it apart from unplanned language use (Hatch, 1992). For example, there is typically use of a wider range of cohesive devices in planned language than in unplanned language. The latter typically uses a narrow range of devices, namely, *and, or, but,* and *so.*

Unplanned forms of talk are basically dialogic and come about when two or more people are jointly responsible for the talk. Examples are debates, brainstorming, and convergent and divergent discussions. More spontaneous forms of talk are characterized by the emergence of information and ideas in-flight rather than advance planning. Information and ideas develop during talk and are often co-constructed by two or more interlocutors. Because of this, information and ideas are often less well polished in terms of linguistic expression and grammatical accuracy than would be the case in planned forms of talk.

ELT has developed approaches to the assessment of monologic, planned speaking rather than spontaneous and dialogic forms of talk. Assessment of the former often involves checklists of fairly well-known assessment criteria. These criteria usually work well when applied to the assessment of prepared talks because they are based on a view of speaking as an individual activity, one in which ideas and viewpoints are preformed and are presented in talk. ELT has less well-developed ways of assessing discussion. The discussion task in the Test in English for Educational Purposes is as follows: "Candidates have to imagine they are in a small discussion group. They listen to a discussion and at certain points they have to answer questions or give their opinions" (Weir, 1990, p. 111). This task is problematic. Although it is situated in a discussion, candidates are not interlocutors but simply respondents. They are not required to lead discussion, control the topic, or initiate exchanges—characteristics of interlocutors. The assessment criteria for this task, which include adequacy of vocabulary, grammatical accuracy, intelligibility, fluency, and relevance and adequacy of content, are also problematic. These criteria arguably apply better to planned and monologic speaking than to spontaneous and dialogic talk. In short, neither assessment task nor criteria target the ability to engage in discussion.

A third challenge for developing an approach to assessment was our wish to introduce some form of self-assessment by students of their performances. We believed that students would participate better in the assessment process if they had some say in interpreting events and were not just passive in it.

Research shows self-assessment is limited when used as an alternative to conventional language testing. Brown and Hudson (1998) argue that the accuracy of self-assessment varies according to the linguistic skills and materials involved in the assessment. In a study of self-assessment methods in language ability, Yamashita (1996) found that the more proficient students were, the more they tended to underestimate their language abilities. Students tended to evaluate themselves in line with how they perceived that others evaluated them (e.g., past academic records, parental expectations). Nevertheless, it is generally accepted that self-assessment is likely to be successful when used for low stakes rather than higher stakes purposes such as placement (Brown & Hudson, 1998; Dickenson, 1987). Because of these considerations, we wanted to introduce self-assessment not as an alternative to teacher assessment but as a complement to it, a low-stakes form of self-assessment.

The approach to assessment developed for the academic speaking course was based on three considerations:

- the realization that conventional assessment of speaking can fail to capture the interactive and spontaneous nature of discussion

- the need for a system that would not reward students simply for already having good, general linguistic proficiency

- our desire to include some form of self-assessment into the assessment process.

These considerations led us to develop our own individual approach to assessment, an approach with a number of distinctive features.

◈ DISTINGUISHING FEATURES

Designing Task-Based Assessment

Task-based assessment allows students with more limited proficiency to do well alongside students with higher linguistic proficiency because the evaluation criteria are not defined purely in linguistic terms (see Table 1). Students are assessed on their attainment of task outcomes as well as on presentation and interlocutor skills. Part of the grade is given to content (see Appendix A). To get good grades for content on Task 3, the student needs to have read the article reporting the innovation carefully and done further research on the subject (e.g., reading and often consulting with an expert such as a faculty member from the school of engineering or a family doctor if the innovation is health related). In addition, the student needs to have thought through how to explain the innovation (e.g., using visuals, realia) and anticipated the type of queries that will be raised. Students with high linguistic proficiency need to do the reading, researching, and planning alongside students with lower levels of linguistic proficiency. High linguistic proficiency in itself does not ensure a good grade.

One principle underlying the design of the assessment tasks was that the tasks would place students in the role of an expert. Task 1 requires students to talk on concepts from their own subject area. Task 2 requires them to report findings from a study they themselves designed and conducted, and Task 3 requires them to report on a recent innovation (i.e., a topic others in the group are unlikely to know about). The idea behind this is that being the expert eases students' apprehension about speaking in public.

TABLE 1. INSTRUCTION AND ASSESSMENT ON THREE SPEAKING TASKS

Task	Task specification	Expected task outcome	Individual, pair work, or group work	Grade
1. Short talk of definition	Students give a short talk to define two concepts from their own subject of study (e.g., a student of computer science might choose the terms *Internet* and *intranet*). Students respond to requests for clarification on the terms.	The meanings of the two terms are clear.	Individual talk followed by group discussion	20%
2. Presentation of findings of a survey study	Students design a survey (e.g., student opinions on the parking facilities at the university), develop an interview protocol, and conduct interviews. They analyze and report on their findings.	The main findings of the study and the evidence for them are clear.	Pair work survey, individual reports of findings leading to group discussion	30%
3. Explanation of an innovation	In a small group setting, students give an explanation of a recent technological innovation (e.g., a new method of keeping roads in Japan ice-free) and lead a discussion in the group on it.	The objective for the innovation and its design or operation are clear. The merits and implications of the innovation are debated.	Individual explanation and group discussion	30%

A further principle underlying the design of the assessment tasks was that the tasks would result in discussion following the prepared talk or presentation. Following Douglas (2000), we drew up task specifications. These specifications were that the tasks should lead to two-way discussion, engage students in extended exchanges of interaction, and place students in the role of interlocutors. Task 1 requires students to engage in exchanges to clarify the meaning of the defined terms. Task 2 requires students to query and answer queries about the findings and conclusions of the survey. Task 3 requires students to lead and participate in debate on the merits and implications of the innovations.

Basing Assessment on Research Into Discussion Skills

We wanted to assess discussion skills as well as presentation skills. However, we could find very little in the way of preexisting checklists and criteria dealing with this aspect of talk. Thus, we needed to construct assessment criteria from scratch. Our first step was to consult research-based literature. We consulted literature about the skill of speaking (Richards, 1990), features of conversation (Hoey, 1991; Tsui, 1994), classroom interaction (Boulima, 1999; Tapper, 1996; Tsui, 1995) and the features of academic speaking in discussion (Basturkmen, 1999, 2000; Furneaux, Locke, Robinson, & Tonkyn, 1991; Jordan, 1997; Lynch & Anderson, 1991; Micheau & Billmyer, 1987; Weissberg, 1993). From these sources we identified characteristics of the discourse. We also identified skills involved in discussion such as the abilities to:

- take part in short and extended exchanges
- elicit and proffer information and ideas
- confirm information and ideas
- manage communication breakdowns and interturn repair sequences
- extend exchanges until a satisfactory outcome is achieved
- enter and leave discussions
- initiate and change topics
- draw others into discussions
- respond to the contributions of others
- revise ideas in light of feedback from others

We then set about transforming the information about spoken discourse and speaking skills into assessment criteria. We did this by adding sections to assessment checklists we had developed for evaluating presentation skills. Appendix A shows the assessment checklist for Task 3.

The assessment checklist, which is used for both assessment and feedback purposes, comprises five sections. The first four are used to assess the student's ability to introduce the innovation to the group (which students do in groups) and the final section is used to assess the student's performance as a group member when the others explain their innovations.

The first section, labeled content, contains criteria whereby task outcomes are assessed. These outcomes are that the function of the new device is clear to the others in the group, that the design or operation is conveyed, and that the benefits and implications are conveyed. The second and third sections, labeled organization and delivery, consist of criteria concerned with planning and presentation skills, such as logical grouping of ideas and voice quality.

The fourth and fifth sections consist of criteria for assessing interlocutor skills. The fourth section, *communicative quality*, is concerned with how the participant introducing the innovation to the group works toward making the event interactive and not just a one-way transformation of information. For example, students may use strategies for engaging audience interest (e.g., asking them questions, finding out about the state of their knowledge on this topic, visually demonstrating how the device works). The students are also evaluated on their ability to express and elicit opinions (e.g., about the sales potential and uses of this innovation) and on their ability to facilitate and lead discussion (e.g., to draw others into the discussion, to respond to contributions from others, to get group members to respond to each others' contributions). The final section, labeled *seminar participant*, consists of items concerned with the discussion skills of the student in responding to the explanations of innovation given by the others in the group. The criteria refer to the ability to ask questions and make comments showing a critical appreciation of the information given by others and the ability to take an active role in discussion (e.g., by initiating exchanges, challenging initial responses, and driving exchanges until satisfactory outcomes are achieved).

Students are awarded either a good, satisfactory, or unsatisfactory score for each of the criteria. Our experiences of assessing groups in real time led us to realize that a range of three grades was as much as the assessor could realistically cope with.

A band system of grading was developed to accompany each task. For example, for Task 3 (introducing and leading a discussion on an innovation), A grades (A+, A, or A–) are awarded to students who have scored *good* for content criteria, a number of *goods* for presentation skills, and *good* for seminar participation criteria.

Instructors found that they needed to make a record of events in discussion on which to base their grading of individuals. They make records of participation in discussion by drawing up a seating plan at the outset of the task. On this, they write in the names of the students involved. During the task, the instructor records types of participation by each name. Each instructor has developed his or her own system of symbols for the characteristics of discussion and interlocutor skills identified from the literature and research and discussed in our meetings. See Table 2 for an example of symbols used.

Linking Assessment and Teacher Development

Generally speaking, the instructors teaching the academic speaking course were knowledgeable about speaking skills in presentations and the criteria by which they can be judged. Most of them, at some time, had used or been exposed to the type of checklists and criteria developed in ELT to evaluate speaking and presentation skills. However, they were generally less aware of the features of interlocutor skills. This was not surprising given the relative lack of information about these in the literature.

A number of instructors were teaching (and assessing) this course at any one time, so it was important to develop a system for standardizing grading. We also needed a way to familiarize the teachers with the nature of discourse and interlocutor skills in academic discussion. We combined these two needs and decided to use standardization sessions to raise the teachers' awareness of the features of interactive speaking.

A standardization session is held before each of the three task assessments. In these sessions, a tentative grade sheet and criteria are distributed. Together we

TABLE 2. CODING SYMBOLS FOR INTERLOCUTOR SKILLS

Symbol	Meaning
?	Asks information-seeking question
?!	Asks question involving critical appreciation of information provided in previous discourse
? ++	Asks question and then pursues the topic over several turns until a satisfactory outcome is achieved
>	Draws another student into the discussion

discuss our understanding of the criteria and their relationship to the research-based literature. We then review sample video recordings of past student performances on the tasks. By a process of comparing the grades we would individually give to each student and discussing our reasons for doing so, we negotiate a common grade. We also continually refine the criteria themselves by incorporating suggestions from the instructors. Over time, we have developed a shared mind-set of both our expectations for students' performance and what an A, B, or C grade level means. Standardization and development of the checklists have been gradual procedures.

Incorporating Self-Assessment

Speaking and discussions take place in real time and naturally offer no record with which students can reflect on their own performance. Therefore, we felt it important to offer students some opportunities for self-reflection. We developed a form of self-assessment based on reflection tasks. Students used these tasks in conjunction with video or audio recordings of their performances in assessment and some classroom teaching tasks. The reflection tasks give students an opportunity to revisit and retrospectively reflect on their performances.

There are two main reasons why we wanted to include some self-assessment in our assessment program. First, self-assessment provides an opportunity for students to participate in the assessment process and this, we believe, helps alleviate victim-like thinking about testing. Second, self-assessment offers opportunities for learning. Self-assessment or monitoring has been referred to as a "systematic approach to the observation, evaluation and management of one's own behaviors for the purposes of achieving a better understanding and control of one's behavior" (Richards, 1990, p. 118). Self-assessment can help narrow the gap between students' imagined view of their own speaking and interaction and the reality. It can help students better understand their own strategies in interaction. Reviewing video or audio recordings of performance in speaking and discussion allows the students to gain a perspective on how they function in interaction otherwise unavailable to them (e.g., they may see how active they are in discussion, or they may see how they may stop others completing their turns at talk). We believe self-observation for the students is a catalyst for change and complements feedback from the teacher about their interlocutor skills.

The procedure we use involves video or audio recording students during task performance. We then distribute reflection task sheets requiring students to make observations of these recordings. On the basis of their observations and their recall of events, students write up reflection notes commenting on their strengths and weaknesses. These reflection tasks are graded for depth of treatment, level of awareness, and the suitability of remedial strategies suggested. They are not graded for language. Twenty percent of the overall grade is given to the reflection tasks.

Appendix B shows two of the reflection tasks used. One accompanies the second assessed task (reporting the results of a survey). The other is used following class instruction focusing on discussion skills and strategies.

In short, the approach developed to assess academic speaking attempts to focus on interlocutor skills as well as speaker skills, assess task outcomes as well as linguistic performance, and encourage students to participate in the process of assessment through self-evaluation.

◈ PRACTICAL IDEAS

Integrate Assessment Into Instruction

Often the assessment of speaking skills is neglected as teachers feel that assessing these skills poses insurmountable problems, especially that it will be too time-consuming and thus impractical. One of the lessons we learned is that some of these problems can be overcome by a judicious use of class time for assessment. We are able to do all our assessment of the students during normal class instruction time. We use 3 teaching weeks during the 12-week course for assessment. This assessment time we feel is justified. We do not see it as time away from instruction because the students are still getting presentation and discussion practice during assessment tasks. They also are able to work toward the assessment tasks in the preceding weeks and receive feedback on their performances in the assessment tasks during this time. In short, we integrate assessment and instruction. We do not see assessment as time lost from instruction but as a different use of class time.

Consult the Literature on Language Descriptions and Research

If teachers are developing language tests on new skill areas or aspects of language use that are relatively little known in testing practice, they might find it helpful to consult the literature on language skills and language descriptions and analyze sample language extracts in reference to concepts from this literature. We found that developing assessment criteria for interlocutor skills was new territory. We consulted language descriptions of academic speaking in the literature reporting research in discourse and conversation analysis. We also used recordings of students on task to discuss and develop criteria for our checklists. These are practical ways teachers can develop assessment criteria for the areas of language use they wish to target.

Work With Teachers to Develop Assessment Checklists and Procedures

It is often the teachers who carry out assessment in ELT. It is therefore important for test developers to listen to the teachers' thoughts on the assessment scheme. Teachers are often the best placed to judge whether something is likely to work out in practice. For example, we found the teachers were able to tell us if assessment criteria would be easy to use or whether a task would be appropriate to the students' interests and level. It is, therefore, preferable for teachers to be involved in at least some stages in the process of test development.

When developing our approach to assessing academic speaking, we needed to develop checklists. We consulted with the teachers on the checklists by having standardization sessions in which we together piloted tentative checklists with video recordings of students on task or engaged in tasks similar to the assessment tasks. In this way, we not only worked toward standardization of grading but were able to share information about discussion skills and discourse with the teachers and, more importantly, the teachers contributed their ideas on how to transform this information into easy-to-use checklists and criteria. The teachers have made numerous suggestions for fine-tuning the checklists and assessment procedures themselves.

Involving teachers cooperatively in at least some stages of the process of developing assessments can work better than simply presenting teachers with preformed instruments and requiring them to implement them.

Involve Students in Assessment

Teachers in other assessment situations may wish to consider using some form of student self-assessment. Self-assessment can enable students to become participants in assessment that can help reduce some of the tension that normally surrounds assessment.

Reflection tasks, such as the ones we have used and that involve students in reviewing their work guided by a few open questions, could offer students opportunities to become involved and to voice their opinions. Reflection tasks are not particularly difficult to devise. We found through a process of trial and error which items worked well (i.e., elicited the most thoughtful information from the students) and which worked less well. Thus, we have been able to fine-tune these self-assessment tasks over time.

◈ CONCLUSION

The approach to assessment developed on the academic speaking course was driven mainly by the wish to move beyond assessing the individual speaker and to assess interlocutor skills as well. By including discussion skills in our assessment scheme, we hoped to encourage students to use fully the opportunities offered in the course to improve their discussion skills. If discussion skills were not assessed, we knew that students might not actively seek out ways to improve them.

The attempt to assess discussion skills led us to examine the literature on interaction and discourse in conversation. From this, we identified the elements of discussion skills that informed the development of assessment criteria and tasks. The approach was also driven by the wish to incorporate an element of student self-assessment into the scheme. This led us to develop reflection tasks for students to use in conjunction with recordings of their assessment task performances.

Despite our feeling of satisfaction with the approach, there is still work to be done. There is a continual need to follow the research findings into language use in spoken discourse and the skills of speaking and discussion. Information from such sources will enable us to more finely tune the criteria by which we evaluate students. We also need to investigate students' perceptions and use of self-assessment and find out in what ways the students find self-assessment useful and in what ways they do not. We would like to interview students and study students longitudinally to see to what extent the opportunities for self-assessment lead to actual change in behaviors and strategies for interaction.

◈ CONTRIBUTOR

Helen Basturkmen is a lecturer in the Department of Applied Language Studies and Linguistics at the University of Auckland, New Zealand, where she lectures in the master's degree program in language education and teaches academic speaking in the language acquisition program. Previously she taught English for academic purposes and worked as a teacher trainer in Turkey and Kuwait.

◈ APPENDIX A: CHECKLIST FOR ASSESSMENT OF TASK 3

Student Name: _____ Student ID: _____

Article Name: _____ Date: _____

Seminar Leader	Comments		
	Good	Satisfactory	Unsatisfactory
Content			
—clarity of function of the innovation			
—clarity of design explanation			
—clarity of advantages, applications, and so on			
Organization			
—signaling of topics/topic change			
—meaningful grouping of ideas			
Delivery			
—speed and pitch			
—pronunciation of key words			
—eye contact and expression			
Communicative quality			
—engages audience interest			
—ability to express and elicit opinions			
—facilitates and leads discussion			
Seminar Participant			
—questions and comments showing a critical appreciation of others' talks			
—active role in discussion			

Additional Comments   Grade _____

◈ APPENDIX B: SELF-ASSESSMENT TASKS

Task 2: Making a Presentation and Responding to Questions

Date: _____ Name: _____

Complete the following as fully as possible.

1. What do you think the survey task was trying to achieve?
2. What aspects of the task did you find most challenging and why?
3. What about working in a pair surprised you?
4. The most effective survey report I saw was . . . .
5. It was effective because . . . .
6. What did you observe that made some reports ineffective?

Before completing this section, review the video recording of your report available in the audiovisual library.

7.   What was the best aspect of your presentation?

8.   What were one or two aspects of your presentation that you were not happy with? What were they and why were you not happy with them?

9.   If you could do the presentation again, how would you change it, if at all?

Task 3: Taking Part in Discussions

1.   How successfully do you feel you contributed to discussions in class this week?

2.   What are your strengths and weaknesses in discussion in English? (If you wish, refer to the checklist of discussion skills in the course handbook.)

3.   What can you do to improve your contributions to discussions?

4.   Did the group in your last discussion activity in class manage the discussion effectively?

5.   What could the group have done to improve discussion?

CHAPTER 8

A Quest for the
Perfect Portfolio

Barbara Dogger, Jeff Moy, and Manny Nogami

◈ INTRODUCTION

It started with some misgivings. A business expert came into town with a new acronym: CQI, (continuous quality improvement), a bottom-up, egalitarian approach to solving institutional problems. Meetings were held to assess needs and identify problems. Everyone was able to participate and be part of the process. Administrators, advisors, faculty members, adjunct faculty, and even students were allowed to contribute to the new vision of success.

With all stakeholders included, any problem could be discussed and any solution could be put forward for discussion. It was brainstorming beyond the classroom. With the help of yellow sticky pads, problems could be recognized, sorted, and assigned to CQI teams. In this far-reaching climate of hope and change, a solution to deal with the problem of misplaced, wavering English for speakers of other languages (ESOL) students was put forward: portfolio assessment. After lengthy deliberations a pilot ensued, and soon Richland College in Dallas, Texas, developed a customized system of portfolio assessment.

This case study will describe the broad context that created the need for an alternative system of assessment for determining an ESOL student's readiness for the next ESOL writing class and, ultimately, for freshman (i.e., first-year) composition. Also, we will report on the various pilots that we launched including what aspects succeeded and what failed. In addition, we will detail why we chose to forego focused holistic scoring in favor of multiple-trait scoring paired with double-blind scoring. This case study will also refer to how we developed exit criteria, scoring rubrics, and descriptors as well as how we provided rater training. Moreover, we will refer to literature that had a significant impact on our assessment decisions.

◈ CONTEXT

In the 1980s many ESOL programs across the country experienced phenomenal growth. Like any educational institution encountering unprecedented growth, there were problems that needed to be addressed in Richland's ESOL department. For instance, some of the students who had been placed into the first semester of freshman composition were performing poorly. During this period, the ESOL department relied solely on teacher recommendations for a student's readiness for freshman composition. Although many of the ESOL students were successfully completing college-level writing courses, others were just not ready for the challenging demands of freshman composition. As one English teacher remarked, ESOL students were writing essays with many *stoppers*, sentences that make the reader pause and ask, "What does that mean?"

As a stopgap measure, some of the ESOL students who were not ready for freshman English were placed into the developmental writing program that was designed principally for native speakers who needed remediation in basic writing skills. However, the developmental writing curriculum was not designed to address the special needs of speakers of other languages. Despite various institutional reforms, a lack of consensus about college-level entrance criteria prevailed, which allowed many ESOL students to exit the ESOL program before they were ready for college-level courses.

Meanwhile, Texas established a state-mandated test of basic skills called the Texas Academic Skills Program (TASP) test (National Evaluation Systems, 1993). The state test mandated that students had to pass the TASP test to avoid ESOL or remediation courses. Not surprisingly, many ESOL students as well as native English speakers failed the TASP test. As a result, a significant number of ESOL students who failed were forced by state law to take, and in many cases retake, ESOL writing and grammar courses. Thus, the TASP test raised the standards of proficiency for ESOL students to take college-level courses.

As a result of the high number of ESOL TASP failures, it became clear that the ESOL department had to rethink its standards for exiting students out of the program and into college-level writing classes. Before long, the ESOL department began to develop more stringent exit procedures for the writing and grammar classes. It was during this period that the portfolio process of assessment was piloted.

◈ DESCRIPTION

Richland's ESOL writing program emphasizes process writing. In other words, students go through the steps of inventing, drafting, revising, and editing. This process allows students to work collaboratively with fellow students at each step of the writing process, from inventing strategies to peer review. Throughout the semester, the students write essays covering a variety of rhetorical patterns.

Level 1 focuses on basic grammar and writing sentences. Level 2 focuses on narration, description, explanation, process, and summary at the paragraph level. Level 3 emphasizes narration, description, explanation, comparison/contrast, and cause/effect at the essay level by writing essays from three to five paragraphs in length. Level 4 has a greater emphasis on academic writing and focuses on expository, summary, classification, explanation, comparison/contrast, cause/effect, and argumentative papers by requiring students to write essays from four to five paragraphs in length. In addition, to prepare for college-level writing courses and the TASP writing test, students in Levels 2 through 4 are given opportunities to practice in-class writings immediately after completing an out-of-class essay in the same mode.

An emphasis on process writing allows and encourages students to become aware of themselves and each other as writers. Developing an awareness of one's strengths and weaknesses in writing is variously referred to as metacognition or self-awareness. Portfolio assessment helps students understand the importance of self-assessment because each student must critically evaluate his or her own essays and select the best ones to be placed into the portfolio for evaluation. Because of the natural fit with our philosophy of process writing, portfolio assessment was chosen as an alternative system of assessment (Elbow & Belanoff, 1991a; Roemer, Schultz, & Durst, 1991).

The conviction that there should be a constructive relationship between instruction and evaluation greatly influenced the type of assessment we chose. This "set of beliefs about the relationship between testing and teaching and learning" is referred to as *washback*, which can be positive or negative (Hamp-Lyons, 1997, p. 295). Testing should and does have consequences for instruction. Invariably, teachers tend to teach to the test. Therefore, we wanted to design a system of assessment so that teaching to the test means teaching to the curriculum. Hamp-Lyons (1997) describes this positive washback as "congruence between tests and educational goals" (p. 296). In other words, performing well on a test should reflect mastery of a specific curriculum. This concern for an overlap between how writing is taught and how essays are evaluated further supported the decision to adopt a portfolio system of assessment.

Initial Committee Work and Pilot (January 1995–September 1996)

In the spring of 1995, the CQI Exit Criteria Task Team began its work to develop an alternative system of assessment. Its members first completed an initial review of the literature in portfolio assessment, in particular, *Assessing Second Language Writing in Academic Contexts* (Hamp-Lyons, 1991a) and *Portfolios: Process and Product* (Belanoff & Dickson, 1991). Also, the team visited other community college campuses to look at various exit procedures and how they were being implemented. In addition, team members applied for and received an instructional development grant from the college to conduct a pilot study during the 1995–1996 academic year. Following an in-depth review of the literature by six team members during the summer, the first pilot study was conducted in the fall of 1995. The exit criteria team included ESOL writing instructors teaching at Levels 1 through 4. Moreover, the team divided into subteams of two individuals, both of whom were teaching at the same level.

Because the pilot's initial purpose was to explore various ways of conducting portfolio assessment, each sub-team was allowed to design its own rating sheet. Issues addressed by the team included questions such as:

- Should all students be evaluated or should just borderline students be evaluated?
- How detailed should each rating sheet be?
- What criteria should be included at each level?

These are only a few of the myriad questions that were asked during this initial pilot. At the end of the semester, each subteam reported its results: what worked and what did not work. From this initial pilot, the group developed a plan about how a second pilot (conducted during the spring of 1996) should take place. The group developed some basic assumptions including:

- A streamlined portfolio will only include one direct writing sample, one out-of-class essay, and a metacognitive cover sheet, if desired.

- The portfolios of all students will be evaluated.
- The class instructor plus another instructor from the same level will evaluate a class's portfolios.
- A focused holistic rating sheet will be used at each level.
- All teams will complete the second portfolio simulation by the 10th or 11th weeks of the 16-week semester.
- Level 1 students will not submit portfolios for evaluation.

During the spring semester, each subteam met weekly to work on revising the rating sheets, refining course objectives, and developing teaching materials. The exit criteria team met monthly to share progress from each level and to begin work on the training manual and final report. Both of these documents were completed during the summer of 1996, and the first portfolio exit procedure was implemented across the entire ESOL writing and grammar program in the fall of 1996.

Model 1 (September 1996–December 1997)

This first model of portfolio assessment was successfully implemented for three semesters. It included the parameters listed above as basic assumptions.

Model 2 (January 1998–Present)

As we began implementing the second model of our streamlined portfolio, we stumbled upon areas that needed tinkering. During the first implementation of the process, we realized that our interrater reliability was very shaky. We knew we were in trouble when one rater gave an essay a score of 55 and the second rater gave it a score of 80. As we debriefed following this first round, we resolved that we would work tirelessly as a portfolio committee to identify ways in which we could tighten up the process to establish a reasonable amount of consistency among our raters. In addition, we realized that we needed more in-depth guidelines for our instructors to aid them in the reading and rating process. Therefore, we selected a set of anchor essays and descriptors.

During this time period, a major reorganization in the college occurred in which the ESOL program joined forces with Foreign Languages to form the World Languages Division. As a result of all of these institutional and curricular changes, a major paradigm shift took place in the ESOL writing program. The model that will now be analyzed in this case study is a result of this paradigm shift.

◈ DISTINGUISHING FEATURES

Multiple-Trait Scoring

The feature that most distinguishes Richland's system of portfolio assessment from others is its departure from using a holistic method of assessment. Focused holistic assessment is a type of assessment that evaluates whole texts based on some guidelines such as a list of criteria or benchmark essays. All of the criteria are used to give the writing sample a single composite score (e.g., 1, 2, 3, 4). At first, focused holistic assessment appealed to us primarily because of our familiarity with it as the form of assessment used for evaluating essays on the TASP test. However, after attempting to use various versions of a holistic method of assessment, it increasingly became apparent that some raters preferred or even needed a more detailed approach for evaluating a portfolio (Cumming, 1990; Elbow, 1993). Therefore, we chose to adopt a more analytical system of assessment: multiple-trait scoring.

Multiple-trait scoring is an analytical form of assessment that involves the scoring of essays based on numerous scales in which each scale focuses on a defined and described facet of writing. Multiple-trait scoring is not a holistic approach but a multidimensional approach. It does not "claim to assess every element of writing ability that may be manifested" in a writing sample (Hamp-Lyons, 1991b, p. 248). Rather, multiple-trait scoring focuses "only on the most salient criteria or traits as established through careful test development" (p. 248). Instead of a single score based on a set of criteria as in focused holistic scoring, multiple-trait scoring is used to assess specific features of an essay to obtain a set of scores. To obtain the final score each criterion is given a score, and then the scores are calculated based on a formula.

Richland's system of portfolio assessment uses five criteria to evaluate a portfolio's essays:

- purpose and audience
- focus and development
- organization
- sentence structure
- edited American usage

Purpose refers to the purpose or mode utilized in the essay. Audience is the reader to whom the writer is writing the paragraph or essay. Focus and development, the broadest category, refers to unity, focus, and support or content. Organization refers to the structure of an essay as well as its coherence and cohesion. Sentence structure encompasses global errors that tend to significantly interfere with the meaning of the essay (e.g., word choice, word order, verb tense), whereas edited American usage refers to local errors that are usually considered merely distracting (e.g., subject-verb agreement, spelling, capitalization).

One of the most dynamic features of multiple-trait scoring is that certain criteria can be given more weight or importance than others can. For instance, we assign more weight to the development of ideas than to grammatical accuracy. In addition, some of the criteria are weighted differently for each class level (see Table 1). Focus and development makes up 30% of the score in the Level 2 writing class, 40% of the score in Level 3, and 50% of the score in Level 4. Focus and development gets more weight as the courses become more advanced because we expect our advanced students to demonstrate more sophisticated ideas and more in-depth content than students in lower level courses.

The score of an essay is determined by evaluating each criterion based on a 10-point scale that is labeled on the rating sheets as excellent, good, average, needs improvement, and unacceptable. (See Appendix A for a sample rating sheet.) After each criterion has been evaluated, the score is calculated by multiplying it by the appropriate weighting. Then, the scores for each criterion are added together. The

TABLE 1. WEIGHTING OF CRITERIA FOR EACH CLASS LEVEL

Criteria	Weighting for each class level		
	0052 (Level 2)	0053 (Level 3)	0054 (Level 4)
Purpose and audience	5%	5%	5%
Focus and development	30%	40%	50%
Organization	30%	25%	15%
Sentence structure	20%	20%	20%
Edited American usage	15%	10%	10%

sum of the scores is divided by two to get the final score.[1] If the score is 75 or higher, the portfolio passes. The pass mark of 75 was painstakingly reached by comparing portfolio scores with acceptable and unacceptable benchmark essays.

Double-Blind Scoring

Another feature of the portfolio system of assessment at Richland is the use of double-blind scoring and its system of providing feedback. Double-blind scoring is a common method of evaluating essays in which two raters independently, without collaborating, evaluate a portfolio. If the raters agree on passing or failing the portfolio, the score stands. If the raters disagree, it goes to a third reader who also evaluates the portfolio and breaks the tie. After the final result is determined, the instructor receives the student's score and a copy of the rating sheets that contain diagnostic information about the student's strengths and weaknesses in writing. The instructor shares the results and diagnostic information with the students on the last day of class.

Portfolio Content Selection

In practical terms, Richland's portfolio assessment process involves two portfolios. The first one is called the *working portfolio*. This portfolio is a folder in which students keep all of their writing assignments throughout the semester. The working portfolio includes out-of-class writings, in-class essays, and a self-assessment. The second portfolio is called the *evaluative portfolio*. Because students are taught and encouraged to critique and improve their own writing, it is a natural step for them to select one out-of-class essay and one in-class essay for evaluation. After selecting these two best writings, the student places them in the evaluative portfolio and turns them in to the instructor.

To maintain impartiality, submitted portfolios do not contain a student's name. Portfolios are submitted in a folder that is labeled with the ESOL class and section number, the student's class number (from the roll sheet), and the student's

---

[1] The final score is divided by two to make the math easier during the scoring process; otherwise, the criteria would have to be multiplied by fractions.

identification number. Computers are used to generate labels so that student information can be put on folders more easily. Also, essays in the portfolios must not contain any grades or teacher comments.

To maintain fairness and reliability, all students were given common writing prompts for the evaluative in-class writings. Four prompts were given each semester. Students were allowed to write an impromptu essay in response to one of the two prompts without the aid of a dictionary. Students selected one of the two in-class writings to include in the evaluative portfolio. Limiting the number of rhetorical patterns also increased reliability. The following rhetorical purposes were chosen:

- Level 2: description, evaluation
- Level 3: compare/contrast, cause/effect
- Level 4: cause/effect, argumentative

Students were also required to write out-of-class essays based on the same required rhetorical patterns as the in-class essays. Throughout the semester, instructors were asked to grade the out-of-class essays by using a grading sheet that was very similar to the rating sheets. These common grading forms, which we termed *working portfolio rating sheets*, contributed to increased interrater reliability. Furthermore, the rating sheets provided diagnostic feedback to students as well as a grading guideline for instructors. As a result, throughout the semester, students were gaining skills in writing both the out-of-class paper and the in-class paper.

Another distinguishing feature of Richland's system of portfolio assessment came about from the portfolio committee addressing the problematic issue of the relationship of the in-class essay to the out-of-class essay. In some writing programs, essays are evaluated separately and then the scores are averaged or assigned a percentage (e.g., 60% for the in-class essay and 40% for the out-of-class essay). We decided to take a more streamlined approach and assign an overall score for both essays. Both pieces of writing are considered as a part of the evaluation and are evaluated on one form. However, the in-class essay is evaluated first in order to establish authorship. Next, the out-of-class essay is reviewed as corroborating evidence. We instruct raters to concentrate primarily on assessing the in-class essay and use the out-of-class essay to gain a wider perspective of a student's writing ability. Sometimes, students receive so much help from other sources that the out-of-class essay is no longer a valid representation of their writing ability. Thus, if the raters consider an in-class essay to be drastically different from an out-of-class essay, the portfolio must be resubmitted or the out-of-class essay is ignored. Needless to say, it behooves students to submit an out-of-class paper that accurately reflects their writing.

While developing our system of portfolio assessment, there were many lengthy discussions about how to describe a portfolio that met the minimum standards of proficiency. These negotiations and adjustments led to a consensus about what kind of writing is acceptable and what is unacceptable. One of our goals was to describe how many grammatical errors were allowed without resorting to error counting. The easiest way to relate this information to other instructors was to point to anchor essays that represented our commonly agreed-upon standards. Anchor essays are essays that have been given an agreed-upon score by a group of experienced raters. In other words, anchor essays are examples of acceptable and unacceptable essays that reflect the consensus of our common writing standards. Also, anchor essays contain a rating sheet that has been marked so that other instructors can see examples of average organization or good grammar.

Putting together a collection of portfolios with anchor essays was, in hindsight, the relatively easy part. The harder task was writing sentences that explain what is good grammar or grammar that needs improvement. These descriptions of each criterion along a range from excellent to unacceptable are called descriptors (see Appendix B). Writing the descriptors and selecting the first set of anchor essays was one of the most difficult tasks of setting up our system of assessment, yet the breakthrough enabled us to proceed to the even more daunting task of finding a way to achieve interrater reliability.

Assessment Training and Rater Reliability

Training and training materials are necessary for developing a reliable system of assessment. Instructors are given a portfolio handbook that contains background information, an overview of Richland's system of portfolio assessment, guidelines, procedures, suggestions, teaching materials, rating sheets, anchor essays, descriptors, and an annotated bibliography. This information is provided at the beginning of the semester during orientation. The handbook and other materials help to standardize the entire assessment process so that everyone can adhere to the same plan.

To achieve interrater reliability, calibration sessions are held during the middle of the semester. The calibration training sessions occur 1 month before the students' portfolios are to be evaluated. Calibration is the process whereby raters make mental adjustments in order to move closer toward "commonality of standards" (Elbow & Belanoff, 1991b, p. 21). Our calibration sessions are organized as follows. First, instructors are grouped by levels. Then, each group reviews the anchor essays and their scored rating sheets. When clarification of the standards is needed, the groups also review the descriptors. Next, each instructor evaluates sample portfolios. The sample essays include one clear (or unambiguous) pass, one clear repeat, and two borderline samples. The borderline samples are right at the edge between passing and failing and seem to elicit the most interesting and productive discussions. During the process of rating and discussing the sample portfolios, the instructors' scores are anonymously displayed for comparison. Then, everyone discusses their reasons for their judgments about various features of an essay and how they translated those judgments into scores for each criterion. In this way, instructors can compare their scores with other instructors. Ideally, all instructors should score within 10 points of each other on a particular essay. However, the most important point of agreement is on whether or not a portfolio passes or fails.

The process of calibration helps everyone achieve a consensus as raters make adjustments for being too strict or too lenient (Lumley & McNamara, 1995; Weigle, 1994). The fact that we employ multiple-trait scoring also makes the calibration process different from and more in-depth than other calibration processes. In comparing scores, instructors are able to identify specific areas for review. For example, one instructor may discover that he or she is too lenient in grammar whereas his or her standards for focus and development are too high. This process of sharing opinions and making adjustments to the group enables instructors to adjust their own standards to those of the entire program.

Multiple Sources of Information

Recently, Richland's system of assessment has evolved into a new form. Instead of the portfolio being the sole arbiter of a student's chances of moving into the next level, now the portfolio and the course grade are used together to evaluate a student's proficiency. We have come to the conclusion that "multiple sources of information" are preferable for making important assessment decisions (Brown & Hudson, 1998, p. 670). Or, as White (1995) claims, "multiple measures are always better than single measures" (p. 38). Using multiple measures has helped to achieve a better balance between two overarching constants: the need to maintain academic standards while respecting the academic freedom of teachers. In short, the new system is a shift back to giving more control to the teacher in determining a student's grade. However, keeping the portfolio system of assessment provides a vehicle for maintaining consensus of standards while striving toward interrater reliability.

◈ PRACTICAL IDEAS

Select Members for the Portfolio Committee

Because of the magnitude of any programwide exit procedure, especially one involved with writing, it is crucial to take a team approach. Hence, a portfolio committee should be established. In the case of Richland, the exit criteria team, which had originated as a subteam of CQI, evolved into the portfolio committee.

The membership should include instructors at each level who are implementing the committee's decisions on a daily basis. This collaborative process allows for a greater sharing of ideas and responsibilities and also provides input from those who are affected by the decisions.

Determine a Needs Assessment Strategy

When first implementing a program, it is necessary to assess the current needs of students as well as the constraints posed by the institution. For example, at Richland, the high failure rate among ESOL students on the TASP writing subtest triggered the initial need for an exit procedure. At the same time, no exit writing procedure existed as a standardized gatekeeper for students wanting to qualify for freshman English. These two realities prompted the original exit criteria team to explore assessment options that would address these two issues.

This needs assessment may be done formally through a questionnaire or more informally by means of brainstorming sessions conducted with key players dealing with ESOL students. A combination of these two methods would most adequately achieve a profile of student needs and institutional constraints.

Review Literature and Research Programs With Existing Procedures

A review of the literature on assessment pilots and portfolio exit packages is a crucial step in getting started. This review will provide some of the background information needed to be familiar with the major issues that are a natural part of any exit assessment procedure. In addition, researching ESOL writing programs at other institutions will help to gain practical background information about the implementation of exit procedures for ESOL students wanting to meet college/university admission requirements for participation in freshman English or other college coursework.

Conduct a Pilot Study

Because pilot studies allow for field testing of procedures with a limited number of students, they are extremely useful when developing a new exit procedure. In the case of Richland, the 10-month pilot study took place in two phases (the first in the fall; the second in the spring). This two-step process allowed for trial and error and for making revisions for the second phase that greatly strengthened the process when it was implemented across the program.

Implement the Portfolio Exit Procedure

Following the needs assessment, literature and program review, and pilot study (all of which can easily take 15–18 months), implement your new portfolio exit procedure. The implementation will require active participation by the members of the portfolio committee as well as administrative support. At Richland, a faculty coordinator and an administrative assistant provide this administrative support. Together, they establish and publish the semester timelines and syllabi; put together the packets for the calibration training session each semester; assemble, distribute, and collect common prompt packets during the 8th and 10th weeks; sort and record the portfolio results following the reading/rating sessions; return these results along with a set of advisement forms and a course spreadsheet to instructors during the 15th week of the semester; and, finally, provide a computerized list of student results and advisement recommendations to the ESOL student advisors for use in registering students for the next semester. All of these procedures help to standardize the portfolio process to provide a more reliable system of assessment (Hughes, 1989). Any program that deals in-depth with a portfolio exit procedure will require commitment and follow-through on the part of each instructor involved, the portfolio committee, and the administrative team.

Plan for Ongoing Revision

As with all programs seeking to meet student needs, it is necessary to self-evaluate and monitor the success of the exit procedure. At Richland, this self-monitoring and revision has been ongoing since the program's first implementation in the fall of 1996. With each semester of implementation, new issues are discovered and dealt with by the portfolio committee. Any institution that chooses to implement this form of exit testing will need to be prepared to self-monitor and to proceed with a spirit of openness in order to adapt and refine the procedures involved. Indeed, the quest for the perfect portfolio will be an ongoing endeavor.

◈ CONCLUSION

The most challenging task that continues to reappear is maintaining interrater reliability in the assessment of writing. Interrater reliability is based on the assumption that everyone is familiar with the common standards of the ESOL writing program. However, instructors come and go, and like knowledge of anything else, it tends to fade. Therefore, calibration sessions are held each semester in an effort to maintain the benefits of portfolio assessment. Obviously, calibration sessions are costly and time consuming, but without them, we believe that our sense of being a community of writing teachers who share common standards and practices would surely be diminished.

As the portfolio system at Richland continues to become more standardized, other initiatives are developing. Currently, a prompt handbook has been developed that provides some clear guidelines for the ongoing task of developing fresh writing prompts. Perhaps the next step is improving our rater training and interrater reliability through the use of computers and statistical information. We may need to do some evaluating across the curriculum and consult the computer and math departments for their expertise.

The entire process of evaluating portfolios has changed in the past and probably will continue to change in the future. These changes and refinements are an attempt to achieve an equitable and reliable system for exiting students from the ESOL writing and grammar program into college-level courses.

At this point in the history of portfolio assessment for the ESOL writing program at Richland, the members of the portfolio committee who have been involved since its beginning stand back and marvel at the evolution of this alternative assessment procedure on our campus. Little did we know as we embarked on this project that we would be helping some 600 writing students each semester to develop their language and writing skills. Furthermore, we could not have predicted the far-reaching implications that a new form of assessment would ultimately have on the development of a stronger writing curriculum. Finally, we also failed to realize at the time that our quest for an adequate writing assessment tool would lead us on a never-ending journey of self-evaluation, both of our process of exit assessment and of our writing program in general. However, unlike Don Quixote, our results have reaped tangible and positive rewards—the joy of seeing increased student success.

◈ CONTRIBUTORS

Barbara Dogger is an ESOL lead faculty member at Richland College in Dallas, Texas. She is past president of TEXTESOL V.

Jeff Moy is an ESOL instructional specialist for the American English and Culture Institute at Richland College and Dallas County Community College.

Manny Nogami is an instructor at Spring International Language Center in Denver, Colorado.

◈ APPENDIX A: ESOL 0053 EVALUATIVE PORTFOLIO RATING SHEET

Course Number: _____   Section Number: _____

Portfolio Number: _____   SS Number: _____

Rater Code: _____   Date: _____

Score

☐   PURPOSE AND AUDIENCE (multiply rating by 1 point)
Why are you writing and who will read it?

Excellent	Good	Average	Needs Improvement	Unacceptable
10	9–8	7	6–4	3–0

Score

☐   FOCUS/DEVELOPMENT (multiply rating by 8 points)
Do the topic sentences support the thesis statement? Do the sentences in each paragraph support the topic sentence?

Excellent	Good	Average	Needs Improvement	Unacceptable
10	9–8	7	6–4	3–0

	OK	Not OK
Introduction		
Funnel Support	_____	_____
Thesis Statement	_____	_____
Body		
Topic Sentences	_____	_____
Supporting Detail	_____	_____
Conclusion		
Restatement of Main Points	_____	_____
Concluding Sentence	_____	_____
Unity of Supporting Detail	_____	_____
Content	_____	_____

Score

☐   ORGANIZATION (multiply rating by 5 points)
Do you have both a logical order and a flow of ideas in your essay?

Excellent	Good	Average	Needs Improvement	Unacceptable
10	9–8	7	6–4	3–0

	OK	Not OK
Coherence (logical order)	_____	_____
Cohesion	_____	_____
Parallel Structure	_____	_____
Pronoun Reference	_____	_____
Transitional Words	_____	_____

Score

	SENTENCE STRUCTURE (multiply rating by 4 points)

Are your sentences complete and correct?

Excellent	Good	Average	Needs Improvement	Unacceptable
10	9–8	7	6–4	3–0

	OK	Not OK		OK	Not OK
awk/unc = awkward/unclear	____	____	vb tns = verb tense	____	____
cs = comma splice	____	____	wc = word choice	____	____
frag = fragment	____	____	wf = word form	____	____
mm = misplaced modifier	____	____	wm = word missing	____	____
ros = run-on sentence	____	____	wo = word order	____	____

Score

	EDITED AMERICAN USAGE (multiply rating by 2 points)

Do you use correct formal English?

Excellent	Good	Average	Needs Improvement	Unacceptable
10	9–8	7	6–4	3–0

	OK	Not OK		OK	Not OK
adj/adv=adj/adv forms	____	____	plf=plural form	____	____
apos=apostrophe	____	____	pos=possessive	____	____
art=article	____	____	prep=preposition	____	____
cap/lc=capital/lowercase	____	____	pro=pronoun	____	____
div=word division	____	____	sn/pl=singular/plural	____	____
form=format	____	____	sp=spelling	____	____
neg=negative	____	____	sva=subject-verb	
p( )=punctuation	____	____	agreement	____	____

	TOTAL	**Process paper supports in-class paper yes___ no___**

◈ APPENDIX B: DESCRIPTORS FOR 0053 PORTFOLIO FORM

Purpose and Audience

Excellent	The essay has a clear and sustained purpose and is written for the appropriate audience.
Good	The essay has an overall clear purpose and is written for the appropriate audience.
Average	Sometimes the essay's purpose is unclear. The essay is written for the appropriate audience.
Needs Improvement	The essay has an unclear purpose. Word choice and style are not appropriate for the purpose and audience.
Unacceptable	The essay contains shifts in purpose or conflicts of purpose. The essay is written for an inappropriate audience. The essay is written in the wrong mode or with an inappropriate purpose.

Focus and Development

Excellent	The thesis statement or main idea and supporting points of the essay are clear. The essay is fully developed. The essay is unified and focused. The introduction and conclusion are complete and effective.
Good	The thesis statement or main idea and supporting points of the essay are clear. The essay is adequately developed. The essay is unified and focused. The introduction and conclusion are complete and effective.
Average	The thesis statement or main idea of the essay is clear. Some aspects of the supporting points are unclear. The essay is supported but needs more development. The essay is unified for the most part. The introduction and conclusion are somewhat effective.
Needs Improvement	The thesis statement or main idea is difficult to understand. One of the supporting points is unclear. The essay is supported but needs more development. The essay lacks unity, and the focus is unclear. The introduction is only partially effective at establishing the purpose and stating a topic. The conclusion is only partially effective.
Unacceptable	There is no thesis statement, or the thesis statement is inappropriate or confusing. The supporting points are unclear. The essay lacks unity and focus. The support is irrelevant, or it is insufficient to explain the supporting points. The introduction and conclusion are either ineffective or absent.

Organization

Excellent	The essay is organized and logical. The writer demonstrates the effective use of cohesive devises such as transitional words and pronoun-antecedent agreement.
Good	The essay is organized and logical. The writer demonstrates a limited use of cohesive devices.
Average	Although the essay is organized and logical for the most part, some relationships among ideas are illogical. The writer makes little use of cohesive devises.
Needs Improvement	The essay lacks organization. The writer demonstrates very little use of cohesive devices.
Unacceptable	The essay is unorganized, incoherent, and not cohesive.

Sentence Structure

Excellent	The essay demonstrates effective use of complex constructions. The essay contains few errors in verb tense and word order. There are almost no awkward or unclear sentences.
Good	The essay demonstrates effective use of simple constructions, but complex constructions have minor errors. The essay

	contains some errors in verb tense and word order. The meaning of the essay is not obscured by grammatical errors.
Average	The essay contains some problems in simple and complex constructions. There are frequent errors in verb tense and word order as well as fragments, comma splices, and run-ons. The meaning of the essay is somewhat obscured by grammatical errors.
Needs Improvement	The essay contains major problems in simple and complex constructions. There are frequent, repeated errors in verb tense and word order as well as fragments, comma splices, and run-ons. The meaning of the essay is frequently obscured by grammatical errors.
Unacceptable	The essay demonstrates virtually no mastery of sentence construction rules. Grammatical errors dominate the text. The meaning of the essay is obscured.

Edited American Usage

Excellent	There are very few errors in spelling, mechanics, and usage.
Good	There are few errors in spelling, mechanics, and usage.
Average	There are occasional errors in spelling, mechanics, and usage.
Needs Improvement	There are frequent or reoccurring errors in spelling, mechanics, and usage.
Unacceptable	The essay is dominated by errors in spelling, punctuation, and usage. There is no paragraphing.

PART 4

End-of-Program Assessment

CHAPTER 9

Multiple-Measures Assessment: Using Visas to Assess Students' Achievement of Learning Outcomes

Peter Davidson and David Dalton

◈ INTRODUCTION

This case study describes an outcomes-based approach to curriculum development and the accompanying assessment protocols that are used to determine students' readiness to enter academic study at Zayed University (ZU) in the United Arab Emirates (UAE). After providing a context for the case study, we explain the academic model and the outcomes-based approach taken by ZU. We briefly outline the role of ZU's English Language Center and describe the preuniversity Readiness Program. We then give an explanation of the assessment methods that are used to gauge students' progress within the Readiness Program. This is followed by a description of the multiple-measures assessment tasks, called *visas*, that are used to assess students' readiness to engage in baccalaureate study. The visas are essentially multidimensional assessment tasks designed to measure students' achievement of the Readiness Program's learning outcomes. In the chapter's final sections, we raise a number of issues and offer practical suggestions on how similar assessment protocols might be set up and utilized in different educational contexts.

◈ CONTEXT

The UAE and ZU

The UAE as a modern state is less than 30 years old. In that short time, development and modernization have moved at a rapid pace. Hand in hand with this structural development has come the evolution of a higher education system that is proving to be equally impressive. To facilitate continued development, ZU was founded in 1998 with two campuses, one in Abu Dhabi and the other in Dubai. The aim of the university is to prepare leaders who will play a significant role in the future of the country. This mission has led to some unique features to help produce students who will function competently in a multicultural and information technology-oriented environment. Each student has a personal laptop computer that is used as a learning tool for research, problem solving, independent learning, and language development.

Students and Faculty

The students, all UAE women, come from a wide range of backgrounds, general academic levels, and language proficiency levels. Many of them are unfamiliar with the concept of a Western-style university and need to be supported in constructing their own schemata about the nature and purpose of the institution. Their needs are therefore complex and varied, from pastoral to academic. Many have a passive knowledge of English but little experience with its application and use. Many have internalized dependency on teachers, and being responsible for time management and self-directed study is often a new concept.

The faculty is multicultural and multinational with some 32 nationalities represented. In addition to teaching, many faculty members are involved in task groups that are putting the new academic model into practice. This involves participation in learning communities, task groups working on refining our learning outcomes, curriculum development work such as course design and validation, assessment development, and review of our program delivery methods.

The Academic Model

The university's new academic model has been founded on the principles of outcomes-based education. In an outcomes-based system for teaching and learning, the planning and structure of the curriculum are driven by learning outcomes as opposed to content (Brady, 1997). The academic model provides the framework for coordinating and integrating the academic program. Rather than functioning as disciplinary enclaves that focus on teaching content, academic departments work together as learning communities to align students' educational experience (Zayed University, 2001). As Fitzpatrick (1995) states:

> Outcomes for student learning are based on a shared vision of the well-educated graduate and are defined in terms of interdisciplinary learnings, such as problem-solving and communication skills, and essential discipline-based learnings in specific content areas. (p. 13)

Learning outcomes are the higher order intellectual capacities and key competencies that students will need to develop to succeed in the 21st century. The six macro-level ZU learning outcomes that have been identified and prioritized in the academic model are:

1. information literacy and communication
2. information technology
3. critical thinking and reasoning
4. teamwork
5. globalism
6. leadership

In addition to these six macro-level learning outcomes, there are five general education (GE) learning outcomes that are the main focus of student learning for the first 2 years of the 4-year program. The GE learning outcomes ensure an appropriate breadth and depth of educational experience for all students and help guide faculty in the development of the curriculum. The GE learning outcomes were developed in the following five domains: (a) creative expression; (b) culture and society; (c) humanities; (d) language and communication; and (e) science, mathematics, and technology (Zayed University, 2001).

All graduating students, regardless of their major, will have demonstrated competence in all these learning outcomes. Criteria and standards for each of these learning outcomes are being developed. The ZU learning outcomes are assessed through portfolios and a major project in which students are expected to demonstrate their ability to synthesize, integrate, and apply their knowledge and skills by conducting research in an area related to their major. In addition to the ZU and GE learning outcomes, there are learning outcomes for each content course in the majors and for all the courses in the Readiness Program.

◈ DESCRIPTION

The English Language Center

The main role of the English Language Center (ELC) is to prepare learners for successful participation in the academic program. Upon arrival, the majority of students are placed into the Readiness Program in which they develop their language, information technology, and academic skills. Once students meet the exit criteria of the program, they progress to the academic program that consists, on average, of 2 years of GE followed by 2 years of study in the students' selected major. The ELC also offers three academic skills courses and an introductory research course in GE, a range of content-based GE courses, and support for students who use English for specific purposes (ESP) in their major fields of study.

The Readiness Program

During the 1999–2000 year, an ELC task group was set up to develop the English program in terms of learning outcomes, resulting in the new Readiness Program. Each course in the program has an overall course learning outcome (CLO) based on a clear understanding of the knowledge, abilities, skills, competencies, and attitudes required by learners in the academic program. The CLOs are further refined through the use of performance indicators (PIs), which are specific statements of what the student can do at any stage of the program.

Currently the Readiness Program contains eight 10-week modules that meet 20 hours each week. Each module is divided into core language input courses and a range of noncore courses that together recycle skills and competencies in an increasingly complex fashion as learners proceed through the program. Lower level courses provide support in specific areas of linguistic weakness, whereas higher level modules move increasingly toward content. Thus students build language skills and then apply them in more content-oriented environments. In an English for publishing course, for example, students use language with the necessary information technology and journalistic and desktop publishing skills to produce an electronic magazine. Independent learning skills and strategies are also taught, as our students are expected to work without teacher supervision, set targets, define work, and meet deadlines.

Materials and Support

Materials are drawn from a wide range of sources and increasingly are being generated by faculty members as they become more familiar with learner needs and abilities. We have a range of textbooks that the faculty can use as resources. As long as learning outcomes are being met and the students show mastery of the indicators, the professional judgment of the faculty determines the materials that are used. Faculty members work in teams at modular level, which facilitate the identification and use of appropriate and effective materials. Our concern is to teach learners effective strategies to use to solve particular problems. The teachers therefore engage in one-on-one conferences with learners where problems are identified and possible solutions are agreed upon.

An important aspect of the program is the provision of frequent and formative feedback given by the teacher. We further attempt to provide extra support and be flexible to individual learner needs by referring students to ZU's Writing Center, directing them to focused independent learning in ZU's Learning Enhancement Center, and meeting their specific needs more directly by having a safety net of ancillary classes. Diagnostic information is given by the core teacher to a team member designated as an ancillary teacher who works with the students in small groups around shared areas of more discrete needs. Students, therefore, in the same class may be working on different skill areas at different levels of text according to their individual needs in these areas. Progress and development is then communicated to all team members so there is a shared understanding of each learner's profile.

Level Assessment

The assessment protocols that we have devised to measure students' achievement are based on common outcomes-based practices. We recognize, for example, that the main purpose of testing is to facilitate learning. The CLOs are clearly articulated so that the learners know what they are required to do to meet the learning outcomes of a particular course. Teachers employ both traditional and alternative assessment methods to decide whether a student has met the learning outcomes of a particular module and is therefore ready to progress to the next module. Traditional assessment consisting of an end-of-course examination, written by an assessment team, constitutes 50% of a student's grade. The remaining 50% is derived from what is commonly called *alternative assessment.*

However, Weir (2000) notes that negative connotations are often associated with this term. He also expresses concern that alternative assessment methods increasingly are being used as an alternative to traditional assessments. Weir proposes, therefore, using the term *additional assessment* to describe those assessment methods that can be used in conjunction with, rather than as an alternative to, the more traditional assessments. To ensure the additional assessment techniques that we use are reliable and valid, they are subjected to the same rigorous processes of piloting, calibrating, and reliable marking that more traditional tests undergo.

The use of portfolios is one of the most common additional assessment methods that teachers in the Readiness Program utilize. Students use portfolios to demonstrate to their teachers how their writing is progressing by including self-selected writing samples that show measured improvement over a period of time. Teachers also administer and rate weekly timed writings. Students compile self-selected portfolios to demonstrate their achievement of learning outcomes in reading, listening, speaking, grammar, and vocabulary. An effective but often underutilized method of assessment is the use of direct classroom observation. Teachers observe and note what the learners are achieving on a daily basis. Students' performance on a range of language learning software programs and a self-tracking reading system is also kept and contributes to the overall perception of student progress. Descriptive banding scales for writing and speaking are being devised to assist teachers when they are deciding if a learner has met specific learning outcomes.

◈ DISTINGUISHING FEATURES

Assessment Through Visas

The overarching learning outcome of the Readiness Program is to prepare students to participate effectively in the ZU academic program. This entails learners acquiring the necessary linguistic, information technology, and academic study skills to cope with the demands of baccalaureate study. Assessing students' achievement of the program's learning outcomes is accomplished by using assessment protocols called *visas*. The visas are, in effect, the program's exit requirements. Each of the five visas is a multidimensional task derived from the learning outcomes. Rather than receiving a percentage score, a student receives an S if the completed task is satisfactory or a U if the task is unsatisfactory. In the same way that someone must complete certain formalities to gain a visa before being permitted to enter another country, students must meet the program's exit requirements (the visa) by demonstrating their achievement of certain learning outcomes before they are granted entry into the baccalaureate program.

The starting point for the development of the visas was a set of higher order learning outcomes that reflect the kind of knowledge and skills that students need to engage in academic study. The needs analysis that the Readiness Program is based on established that students in the academic program would require competence in the following six basic academic skills: (a) listening to lectures and taking notes, (b) reading academic texts and taking notes, (c) participating in academic discussions, (d) conducting basic research, (e) giving oral presentations, and (f) writing academic essays. Once these constructs were established, a task group developed them into the five multidimensional tasks that are outlined below.

Visa 1: TOEFL

We felt that the Readiness Program should utilize an international English examination to establish a benchmark and help the program gain international recognition and standing. Detailed evaluation of both the International English Language Testing System (IELTS) and the Test of English as a Foreign Language (TOEFL) led us to the conclusion that neither of them would provide us with sufficient information as to whether a learner was ready to enter the academic program. What the results of these examinations would tell us, however, was that a student had reached a certain degree of language proficiency. Other assessment tasks would be needed to assess whether a student was ready to study in the academic program. The use of other visas also contributes to what Hughes (1989) refers to as *beneficial washback* as teachers not only focus on getting students through the TOEFL but also ensure students achieve all of the CLOs.

For logistical reasons, we decided to use the TOEFL. To complete Visa 1, therefore, learners must achieve at least a 500 on the paper-based TOEFL or at least a 173 on the computer-based TOEFL.

Visa 2: Listening and Summary Writing

To obtain Visa 2, learners must listen to a lecture, take notes, and write a summary based on their notes. The lecture, delivered on a videocassette, lasts 20–25 minutes and is of a similar level to a lecture given at the beginning of a GE course. During the lecture students are required to take unguided notes, and, at the end of the lecture, they are encouraged to ask a teacher questions about the content of the lecture. Students then use their notes to write a summary of the lecture. The summary should, therefore, include the majority of the main ideas and sufficient supporting detail from the initial lecture.

This visa contrasts markedly with the listening component of the TOEFL that only provides learners and teachers with a general idea of learners' listening ability. Visa 2 reflects more closely the type of listening activity that students will actually experience in the baccalaureate program and is therefore a more informative measure on whether a learner will be able to cope with the type of listening tasks she will encounter. The written summary provides evidence that a learner not only understands a much longer piece of discourse than in the TOEFL but also can identify main and supporting ideas, take useful notes, possibly seek clarification on parts of the lecture not understood, and use her notes to reconstruct the lecture. It is worth noting that the listening component of the new TOEFL will utilize integrated tasks similar to Visa 2, where students listen to a lecture and respond both orally and in written form.

Visa 3: Reading and Writing

This visa encompasses a range of CLOs and assesses the level of competence a learner has reached according to performance indicators related to reading, note-taking, synthesizing information, and academic writing. Learners are required to read three or four short texts from a range of sources (e.g., GE textbooks, academic journals, magazines, newspapers, the Internet), take notes, and then write an academic essay based on these notes. The texts, which students receive 4 days before they write their essay, may include some graphic information such as graphs, diagrams, charts, and tables. Students read the texts in their own time and are encouraged to take notes. Four days after receiving the texts, they are given 90 minutes to write, or preferably type, a 500–600 word academic essay. The rhetorical structure of the academic essay is either solving a problem or supporting an argument. Students are allowed to bring the articles and their notes into the writing room, but they cannot bring in any prewritten essays or parts of an essay. Students are allowed to refer to dictionaries (either hard copy or electronic) and can use spelling and grammar checks. Plagiarism is unacceptable; therefore, when using ideas from the texts, students must give full citations.

Visa 3 also contrasts dramatically with the TOEFL. Given that texts in the reading section of the TOEFL contain only one or two paragraphs and that students must read the texts very quickly and answer multiple-choice questions, such a test can only generally indicate a learner's reading ability. Visa 3, on the other hand, provides us with information about a student's ability to read a variety of relatively long academic texts, take notes, paraphrase, and synthesize information.

Visa 4: Information Literacy

For this visa students must write a research paper in which they support an argument through independent research and then defend this research orally. Students are required to independently decide on a topic and write a research proposal. They must then identify and select a total of 5–10 electronic and print sources and take notes on these sources. After conducting research using questionnaires, surveys, and interviews, the students must paraphrase, summarize, and synthesize all the information they have gathered into a 1,200–1,500-word research paper. Students research and prepare the paper during class time in the last few weeks of the course. Finally, students must discuss, defend, and elaborate on the research they have conducted in a viva, an oral defense that lasts between 10 and 15 minutes. This visa is different from the other visas in that it is related to a course in which students are taught where to obtain information using the library, the Internet, and databases and to evaluate the merits of the sources they find. This is obviously a crucial skill and one that students need if they are to participate successfully in the baccalaureate program.

Visa 5: Academic Discussion

The final English visa entails students participating in a 15–20 minute academic discussion with three to five other students on a topic that they have previously studied. In some institutions this is referred to as a seminar discussion. We felt that students needed to master this type of speaking activity rather than oral presentations, which are dealt with early on in a GE course. Four days before the discussion, the teacher gives the students four to six relatively short articles on an academic theme. The articles typically present arguments for or against a particular topic. On the day of the discussion, 10 minutes before the discussion begins, the teacher assigns each candidate a point of view to argue. A facilitator, who starts and concludes the session and directs the discussion or its participants when needed, supervises the discussion. The academic discussions are audiotaped in case they need to be reviewed.

❧ PRACTICAL IDEAS

Ensure That Multiple Measures Are Used to Assess Students

Some educators, especially those without English as a foreign language (EFL) or testing experience, would argue that a single-measure assessment such as the TOEFL provides sufficient evidence to decide if a student is ready for academic study. However, it should be noted that a high level of language proficiency on its own is not a reasonable predictor of academic success. For example, consider native speakers of English, who would presumably attain very high scores on a proficiency exam such as the TOEFL but would not be guaranteed of academic success at university. Educational Testing Service (ETS), the organization that writes the TOEFL, advises institutions to "base the evaluation of an applicant's readiness to begin academic work on all available information, not solely on test scores"

(Educational Testing Service, 1997, p. 26). ETS quotes numerous studies that "have shown that correlations between TOEFL test scores and grade-point averages are often too low to be of any practical significance" (p. 27). There are obviously other cognitive, affective, and personal factors that interact to determine academic success.

Furthermore, if all a student needed to succeed at university was a certain level of proficiency, then preuniversity English programs would focus solely on teaching language. The fact that the majority of preuniversity English programs worldwide focus on academic study skills, critical thinking, and learner independence in addition to teaching language demonstrates that language proficiency on its own is not a sufficient indicator of success in university programs. If a single measure assessment such as the TOEFL is used as the sole measure to determine students' readiness to engage in academic study, it is likely that the teaching and learning will focus on passing that single assessment measure to the detriment of other key learning outcomes. In addition to language proficiency, the multiple-measures assessment protocols that we have developed attempt to measure students' competence in a range of academic and critical thinking skills, as well as affective factors such as motivation, attitude, and learner independence. By adopting multiple-measures assessment, we are ensuring that we are more informed when making decisions on students' readiness for academic study.

Ensure That Your Assessment Protocols Are Valid

The need for validity is important in any type of assessment and perhaps more so when implementing new and innovative assessment protocols. Specifically you need to ensure that your assessment tasks have construct validity (i.e., that they accurately measure the particular skills and proficiencies you set out to measure). You need to articulate the constructs that you are attempting to assess and then evaluate how effective you were at measuring them. We accomplished this by showing the visas to a group of teachers and then asking them to determine what they thought the constructs were that we were measuring. We compared the list of constructs that the teachers developed to the list of constructs that we were attempting to measure. As both lists were identical, we were confident that the visas had a high degree of construct validity.

You also need to ensure that your assessment protocols have content validity (i.e., that the assessment you give is based on a good coverage of what students have learned). Content validity can be increased by ensuring that the specifications for the assessment protocols are derived from the course objectives or learning outcomes. In the Readiness Program, the assessment protocols and the learning outcomes have become interrelated to such an extent as a result of the washback effect that the visas essentially have become the learning outcomes of the program, hence the high degree of content validity.

Face validity also needs to be considered when setting up a new assessment package such as the visas. You need to ensure that your assessments look and feel like other traditional assessments, even though the process may be different. For Visas 3 and 5, for example, we send students articles that have clear titles and footers indicating that they are visa assessments. Clear procedures have been established and recorded for faculty regarding the scheduling, proctoring, and rating of the visas. Students receive a visa booklet outlining what they can and cannot do before and during the visa assessment. This has resulted in the students acknowledging that the visas are a valid assessment method.

Ensure That Your Assessment Protocols Are Reliable

Reliability of assessment protocols is an equally important consideration. In essence, you need to ensure that the implementation of your assessments will yield consistent results. To this end, you need to develop criteria, set standards, and write calibration documents for use in calibrating or standardizing raters. This needs to be an ongoing process with numerous opportunities for revision and fine-tuning. With the assessment protocols, we have developed criteria for each of the visas (see Appendix A). The visas are rated by an assessment team made up of teachers. The raters regularly attend calibration sessions to ensure that they are rating reliably. Two members of faculty rate each visa task. If these two raters disagree, a third rater rates the visa. Interrater reliability is calculated to ensure consistency of rating.

It could be argued that assessment protocols such as the visas are not a reliable measure of students' ability because all students are subject to different input (e.g., in Visa 2, students are permitted to ask questions after the lecture). In addition, because the questions asked and answered on the two campuses would be different, students would be getting different input and therefore the task lacked reliability. Similarly, with Visas 3 and 5 students receive numerous texts 4 days before they are required to write an academic essay or participate in an academic discussion. It was argued that students would treat the texts differently (i.e., some students would read them only once, whereas others would read them twice or more). Some students may translate the texts or get others to translate the texts for them, whereas others might discuss the texts with their friends. The lack of control over the input, it could be argued, may result in unreliable assessment. However, Brindley (2001) has noted that assessment tasks such as the visas need not be subjected to the same psychometric measures of validity and reliability as traditional tests. Such reliability and validity checks are more applicable to tests that focus on the discrete measurement of a candidate's competency in the four skills and various subskills and their knowledge of the language system. As the visas are multidimensional tasks that assess a broad range of learning outcomes, different methods of determining validity and reliability need to be applied.

As with all outcomes-based assessment, the emphasis is on assessing performance: how well a learner is able to accomplish a task, rather than how well a student has mastered a number of discrete objectives. In essence, the visas establish whether or not a student will be able to effectively participate in the academic program. This cannot be effectively determined by how well students answer questions after listening to a lecture or reading a text, or how well they write an essay on an unfamiliar topic in a limited amount of time, as these are not activities that students are required to do in an academic program. Rather, students need to demonstrate that they can complete realistic and meaningful tasks that they are likely to encounter when taking academic courses. When using an outcomes-based approach, Fitzpatrick (1995) notes:

> The criteria for designing assessment strategies calls for developing authentic measures of student achievement of the intended learning outcomes, not simply testing what is easy to measure. (p. 13)

Whether or not each student receives the same input on the visas is not an issue, as students in the academic program do not all receive the same input either. Moreover, readiness to study in an academic program is not dependent on having competence in certain discrete skills: It is dependent on possessing a certain degree of language proficiency; reasonable competency in academic study skills; and a range of other cognitive and affective factors such as motivation, attitude, learner autonomy, problem-solving ability, interpersonal skills, communication skills, and the ability to work as part of a team. One of the major innovations of the visas is that they indirectly measure the extent to which a learner possesses these cognitive and affective factors.

Create a Learner Profile for Each Student

Data obtained from the additional assessment methods and traditional tests are summarized in an electronic learner profile (see Appendix B). The profile is a record of what overall learning outcomes, and specifically what CLOs, each learner has achieved. The CLOs in the learner profile are expressed as "can do" statements. Based on the modular assessments, teachers complete the profile, which helps them to decide if a learner has sufficiently met the learning outcomes of that particular module and is ready to progress to the next module. The teacher comments section of the profile directs the learner to areas of perceived weakness and suggests repair and development strategies. As the main purpose of any type of assessment is to improve teaching and learning, the visas also have a diagnostic purpose as they help to identify what the student can and cannot do and this, in turn, informs decisions about the type of learning experiences the student engages in. Furthermore, at the beginning of each course, teachers can analyze the learner profiles of their new students and identify their strengths and weaknesses even before they have met the students. It is envisaged that the learner profile will continue when the student is in GE and her major field so that by graduation a complete profile of each learner will be available.

Establish and Maintain Transparency

It is important to ensure that the whole assessment process is transparent. At the beginning of each module, students need to know precisely what learning outcomes they are expected to achieve and how these will be assessed. In the Readiness Program, for example, both students and teachers receive handbooks that explain in detail what is assessed, what criteria are used, what the standards are, and how the visas are rated. When a student unsuccessfully challenges for a visa, she receives a copy of the completed assessment criteria and additional diagnostic information from the teacher on why the task completed was unsatisfactory. Non-ELC faculty members attend a session to inform them about the visas. A Web site currently is under construction that aims to provide comprehensive information on the visas. The Web site will include the student handbook, a video lecture description of each visa, examples of actual visa tasks, samples of students' work, and visa practice materials that learners can work on independently. There will also be a video reenactment of students engaged in Visas 2 and 5 and the oral defense section of Visa 4 to increase students' awareness of what is expected in these tasks. Finally, the Web site will also have interviews with students who have successfully completed all the visas and will include advice on how to go about preparing for particular visas.

Engage in Rigorous, Ongoing Evaluation

Ongoing informal evaluation of the visas has revealed that faculty and students generally regard the visas as a positive means of assessment. Anecdotal evidence also suggests that those students who have gone through the Readiness Program and successfully completed all the visas are functioning at a higher standard in the baccalaureate program than those students who entered the program directly. Currently, the visas are undergoing a more thorough formal evaluation that will entail obtaining students' perceptions of the visas as well as the opinions of faculty in the ELC and those who teach GE courses. We need to track the performance of students in the GE and major programs to establish that the students who completed all the visas were in fact ready to enter the academic program. We also need to know the strengths and weaknesses of the students in the academic program so we might fine-tune visa tasks, criteria, and standards accordingly. Ongoing evaluation of the program and the assessment protocols is essential to identify and meet the continually changing needs of the key stakeholders of the university.

❖ CONCLUSION

Despite the challenges inherent in setting up and implementing an outcomes-based program, the benefits to the learner and broader community are far-reaching and substantial. An outcomes-based academic strategy provides a framework that aligns and integrates the efforts of faculty and ensures students receive focused and coherent learning experiences. The learning outcomes-based curriculum that has been developed at ZU provides students with educational experiences that are focused on achieving higher order intellectual capacities and key competencies. Students are being equipped with the appropriate knowledge and skills in order to develop their full potential and to enable them to prepare to take on leadership roles in society. Before a student enters the baccalaureate program we need to know with certainty that she has met the learning outcomes of the Readiness Program and will be able to cope with the demands of tertiary study. This case study has suggested that existing assessment tools did not provide us with sufficient information on student readiness for baccalaureate study because they lacked completeness and authenticity. Multiple-measure assessment protocols, such as the visas, are needed to comprehensively gauge a student's preparedness for effective participation in a baccalaureate-level program.

❖ CONTRIBUTORS

David Dalton is an academic supervisor at Zayed University in Dubai, UAE. He has previously taught in Spain, Mexico, the United Kingdom, and Greece. He is specifically interested in first language (L1) interference in second language (L2) orthography.

Peter Davidson is the assessment supervisor at Zayed University. He has previously taught in New Zealand, Japan, the United Kingdom, and Turkey. He is specifically interested in performance evaluation and assessment.

◈ APPENDIX A: VISA 2 ASSESSMENT CRITERIA

Name: _____ ID No.: _____

Date: _____ Rater: _____ Overall Rating: _____

1. Content

1.1 Coverage of main ideas (x 2)
Satisfactory (S) / Unsatisfactory (U)
Covers all the main ideas from the lecture.

1.2 Coverage of supporting points (x 2)
S / U
Covers the majority of the supporting points from the lecture.

1.3 Coverage of explanatory detail
S / U
Covers sufficient explanatory detail to exemplify main ideas and supporting points.

1.4 Communicative quality
S / U
Consistently communicates overall meaning with clarity.

1.5 Relevance
S / U
Retell is completely relevant with no unnecessary repetition.

2. Organization

2.1 Text structure
S / U
Organization of the retell demonstrates good understanding of the lecture.

2.2 Coherence
S / U
Consistent thematic development between and within paragraphs.

3. Language

3.1 Grammatical range and accuracy
S / U
An appropriate range of target grammatical structures used with only few inaccuracies.

3.2 Lexical range and accuracy
S / U
An appropriate range of lexical items used with only few inaccuracies.

3.3 Mechanics
S / U
Very few inaccuracies in spelling and punctuation—meaning is not impeded.

◈ APPENDIX B: READINESS PROGRAM LEARNER PROFILE

Name: _____ ID No.: _____

Instructors: _____ Advisor: _____

Date: _____

Reading	Satisfactory	Unsatisfactory	Comments
Can understand general and basic academic texts at preintermediate level and take semiguided notes.			
Can understand main points.			
Can understand some detail.			
Can note key words.			
Can use abbreviations, etc.			
Can note supporting information.			
Can paraphrase.			
Can ascertain word meaning from context.			
Can read nonlinear information.			
Can identify titles, legends, and axis.			
Can understand main ideas.			
Can understand specific information.			
Can detect trends.			
Writing			
Can write multiple paragraph descriptive and narrative texts of 200–350 words.			
Can plan.			
Can draft.			
Can evaluate.			
Can rewrite.			
Can develop ideas.			
Can organize appropriately.			
Can use cohesive devices.			
Can use appropriate language features.			
Can complete a guided summary.			
Can plan, draft, evaluate, and rewrite and use nonlinear information.			

Listening	Satisfactory	Unsatisfactory	Comments
Can understand and take semiguided notes while listening to adapted academic texts up to 8 minutes.			
Can identify main ideas.			
Can identify specific information.			
Can understand some details.			
Can use abbreviations, etc.			
Can note key words, main ideas, and supporting information.			
Can answer questions about spoken text.			
Speaking			
Can orally express thoughtful opinions including conversations, discussions of academic topics, and interviews.			
Can interact socially.			
Can use appropriate lexis.			
Can use correct phonology.			
Can interview and be interviewed.			
Can use appropriate language.			
Can use some oral presentation skills.			

CHAPTER 10

Assessing English for Employment in Hong Kong

Tom Lumley and David Qian

◈ INTRODUCTION

The English language plays a central role in the everyday life of Hong Kong as an international center of finance, business, trade, and tourism. The demand for high levels of English proficiency among local employees has not declined since Hong Kong's change of sovereignty in 1997. One group, university graduates, receives special attention when levels of English proficiency are discussed. Employers complain constantly about the English level of their employees. Perceptions of declining standards of English among recent university graduates are so widespread that the Chief Executive of Hong Kong explicitly raised this as an issue in his first policy address in October 1997. One response to complaints of declining levels of English proficiency has been to propose an exit test that students should take shortly before graduation. This case study introduces that test, the Graduating Students' Language Proficiency Assessment (GSLPA), developed in Hong Kong for use with students graduating from university. The case study considers the history and purpose of the GSLPA and reports on its development and implementation, which, to date, has taken place largely within one university, the Hong Kong Polytechnic University (PolyU).

The GSLPA was introduced formally in 1999–2000, following a 6-year development process (Hong Kong Polytechnic University, 1996, 1997). Probably no language test in Hong Kong has been the subject of such a careful research and development process.

The GSLPA is a performance test of writing and speaking. The content focuses on the professional workplace communication needs of recent graduates. In this way it looks forward to employment, rather than backwards at the academic context of university study. This is consistent with its major stated aim of providing information to prospective employers about the English language proficiency of new graduates.

◈ CONTEXT

The sociopolitical context in which the GSLPA has been developed is somewhat complicated, with many views operating within and across the various institutions involved (Hamp-Lyons & Lumley, 1998, 2000; Lumley, 1999). In 1994 the English Department of PolyU was awarded a research grant to develop a GSLPA for use as an exit test for graduates from PolyU as well as other tertiary institutions across the territory. It became apparent fairly soon that the use of a single English language exit test across all tertiary institutions was not feasible at that time. A major reason for this was the desire of institutions to maintain their autonomy, and the fear that a "league table" of performance (i.e., a table showing the comparative standing of all universities) on such a test would be developed. A second reason was the difficulty of developing a test that was suitable for students in all disciplines. A further reason was the desire to avoid the negative washback of a shrinking curriculum often associated with standardized tests, a dominant feature of Hong Kong education. Nevertheless, work continued on the GSLPA within PolyU, resulting in the development and trialling of successive versions of a test instrument.

In June 1996 the senate of PolyU decided to introduce mandatory language assessment of its language major students. The university decided to capitalize on the work done during the research project in developing the GSLPA and adopted this test as the instrument.[1]

Nonlanguage-major students, whose department heads determined the test should be mandatory, were also required to take it. The test was to remain voluntary for other students. The GSLPA thereby gained an official status, even if of a slightly ambiguous nature (Hamp-Lyons & Lumley, 1998, 2000; Lumley, 1999). The GSLPA moved from a research project to an operational test. PolyU has used its own funds for the test's development and administration since 1997.

More recently, there has been wider debate on how English language proficiency of graduating students across Hong Kong can be reported. The stated purpose of the GSLPA is to report to prospective employers on students' English proficiency around the time of graduation. To some extent, then, it is intended to address one aspect of the concerns about falling standards of English in the territory. In itself, no test will improve learning or standards; nevertheless, there is clearly a feeling among those responsible for language education policy that the introduction of a test would signal to students that English language proficiency is to be taken seriously.

Another potential purpose of the test, less clearly articulated but equally powerful, is to meet the need for accountability on the part of university funding bodies. The University Grants Committee (UGC), a government body, funds Hong Kong's eight tertiary institutions (seven universities and an institute of education). One part of this funding supports language enhancement courses, concurrent English language support provided to students during their university careers. The length and structure of these courses vary across institutions. Courses typically offered include English for academic purposes and English in the workplace. Students take one, two, or more courses, depending on the discipline in which they are studying, the type of course (e.g., higher diploma or degree), and the institution where they are studying. The UGC is keen to establish whether it obtains value for money in funding these courses and perceives a standardized test, allowing comparisons across universities, as one possible solution to this problem. Given the differences in levels of English among students when they commence their studies and the differences in provision among the institutions, it is not clear exactly how this would work, but the possibility of introducing a standardized test such as the

---

[1] A Chinese GSLPA was also developed. This case study discusses only the English GSLPA.

GSLPA appears to remain part of the agenda of the UGC, which funds the universities. An Inter-Institutional Task Force (I-ITF) was established in 1999 to consider possible formats for a common reporting framework for students' English language (see Berry & Lewkowicz, 2000) of which a standardized test might form one component.

The GSLPA therefore has the potential to be used for reporting on proficiency to employers as well as offering some kind of accountability mechanism for the UGC. The potential conflicts that arise when assessment serves multiple functions and audiences in other contexts are discussed in detail by Brindley (1998).

It is against this background that the GSLPA has been developed and implemented. This case study will focus on the situation at PolyU because this is where the GSLPA was developed and where it is principally used, although the test also has been piloted at Lingnan University (also in Hong Kong) and, in its early stages, at Hong Kong University.

The test development took as its focus the perceived English language needs of PolyU graduates in professional workplace contexts. As a former polytechnic, PolyU offers a range of technical and applied courses in six faculties.

In its early stages, the GSLPA project established that the potential target test population was both homogeneous and disparate (Hong Kong Polytechnic University, 1996). On the one hand, there are considerable similarities between potential test takers who are:

- (almost exclusively) speakers of Cantonese and literate in written Chinese

- students at universities in Hong Kong

- from similar education systems

- familiar with the cultural and geographical context of Hong Kong

On the other hand, there are a number of differences, many related to students' use of English:

- level of English with which they commenced university study

- level of exposure to English, both during school and at university

- motivation to use English

- amount of course time devoted to studying English

- importance placed upon English by the department in which they were studying

- subject area of study

- future professional and academic plans

More than 80% of employed students graduating from the university in 1995 obtained employment in industry, commerce, or professional firms or in government or utilities (Student Affairs Office, 1996), employment which may be assumed to have somewhat similar communication demands. Other groups, such as social work students, were excluded from the test population because the vast majority of their work required communication mostly in Cantonese within the local population. Separate assessments of language proficiency were developed for English teachers (Falvey & Coniam, 1997), making the GSLPA less relevant for them. The test therefore concentrated on the kinds of communication required for business, given the project's aim to provide employers information about the English language skills of their potential employees.

To allow students the opportunity of familiarizing themselves with the test's format and requirements, PolyU developed a learning package (Hong Kong Polytechnic University, 2000) that was available to students through the self-access unit of the PolyU English Language Centre. In addition to sample test materials and student responses, this package provided a range of teaching and learning activities designed to encourage students to take a broad view of possible approaches to improving their English language proficiency.

The trialling and revising of the GSLPA took place between 1996 and 1999, and the first operational administration was held in 1999–2000, with around 1,800 students taking part. Although the majority of students were required by their departments to take the test, significant numbers also chose to take it on a voluntary basis.

◈ DESCRIPTION

Needs Analysis

An early stage in designing the GSLPA involved conducting a needs analysis, based on perceptions of typical employers as well as previous studies. Relatively few studies have been conducted about the language needs of business in Hong Kong. Previous studies (Devereux, Cooper, & Ng, 1992) generally confirmed the need for English in both spoken and written communication. A study of the English language needs of Hong Kong accountants (Forey, 1996) found the main aspects of written language requiring improvement included structure and clarity of content, grammar, sentence structure, style, and tone. The main document types written by the accountants were listed as memos, faxes and formal and informal letters. In another survey of accountants and company administrators, Poon (1992) found that they used English for writing reports, business letters, memorandums, circulars and notices, agendas, minutes, budgets, job advertisements, and company regulations and contracts. Clearly, the content, structure, and type of writing contained in such documents as identified in these surveys will vary according to the purpose and content of the communication and the relationship between writer and reader. It appeared that, in broad terms, what employers require of graduates is flexibility: an ability to deal with different writing tasks in different ways, appropriate to the task and audience.

A survey of employers of PolyU graduates, postgraduate admissions officers, and undergraduate course leaders confirmed general impressions based on earlier studies (Hong Kong Polytechnic University, 1997). The survey respondents gave an overwhelming endorsement to the notion of an assessment of graduating students' English language proficiency. They also supported the reporting of language proficiency on a separate transcript from the academic transcript and expressed a desire for separate grades for proficiency in the speaking and writing components of the test with a description of the language proficiency attained.

Test Design

On the basis of the needs analysis, the model considered most appropriate for the GSLPA was a performance test, based on tasks that reflect real life settings, because performance tests are claimed to enable candidates to demonstrate what they "can do in their second language, rather than what they know about it" (Wesche, 1992, p. 104).

The GSLPA included writing and speaking components in response to the major stated requirements (as identified by employers in the needs analysis) and interests of employers. Listening skills were to be incorporated into the speaking component. Reading was not included because of the tremendous range of text types and content that new graduates might be expected to encounter in the workplace. Reading was not identified in any of the surveys of potential test users as a language skill of explicit critical concern. The framework of Bachman and Palmer (1996), and some of the examples they offer in the appendices to that volume, were helpful in developing the test specifications.

Writing

The writing subtest was intended to assess written communication with native and nonnative speakers from various professional backgrounds. Following a review of previous studies, supplemented by a survey of potential test users, it was determined that the writing component should aim to test the:

- ability to write coherent, well organised texts that satisfy the task requirements
- ability to write comprehensible messages
- ability to write in a register appropriate to the audience
- ability to use grammatically correct English, with a suitable range of vocabulary
- ability to produce a text conforming to a specified format

(Hong Kong Polytechnic University, 1996, p. 147)

The writing component of the test lasts a little under 2 hours and includes three tasks. The first two tasks require students to write a memo or professional letter. The first of these is designed to be straightforward, addressing a familiar audience and a relatively unproblematic situation, for which most of the information was essentially supplied. The second task, also a memo or professional letter, is intended to be more cognitively and linguistically challenging. It requires some kind of problem solving or argument, with careful attention to audience and register. It could take the form of a section of a report, presented as a memo, because report writing is a common requirement of employers. In both these tasks, the emphasis is placed strongly on quality rather than quantity, with students given sufficient time (90 minutes for both tasks) and space to produce a first draft and then present a final version for assessment. See Appendix A for a sample writing test task.

To allow an explicit assessment of grammatical knowledge, a third task is also included in the writing component. This takes the form of a proofreading and error correction task. This task is intended to consume relatively little time (15 minutes) and to contribute in a minor way to the final grade for writing. It also offers the possibility, as an objectively scored task, of a reliability check, of particular use in borderline score-reporting decisions.

Speaking

The speaking component of the test is tape based and lasts approximately 45 minutes. It includes five tasks, each with a different general function and purpose. Normal rates of speech are used throughout.

It is clear from O'Loughlin's (1995, 1997) work, that the types of discourse elicited in face-to-face and tape-mediated test situations vary somewhat. A tape-based speaking test format, administered in a language laboratory in which test takers respond to input provided through headphones and record their speech onto an audiotape, was selected after careful consideration of all factors involved.

The speaking tasks used are designed to reflect the professional communicative demands of a business setting. The speaker/candidate is assumed to be about to enter his or her first year of professional employment. The speaking tasks are well contextualized, allowing students to develop a sense of situation and audience. An attempt is made to provide a sense of contextual continuity from one task to the next throughout the test. For most of the tasks test takers are given planning time. Each time they speak, they are given sufficient time for an extended turn, ranging from 40 seconds to 3 minutes. This provides a substantial sample of spoken performance on which to base the speaking assessment, as shown in the following example of speaking tasks:

- *Task 1: Summarizing information from a radio interview.* Test takers listen to an interview that lasts 5–6 minutes, during which they take guided notes. They have some preparation time followed by 2 minutes of speaking time. The topic is chosen to be general and easily accessible. This task is intended to draw on the kind of underlying ability required in reporting the content of any extended piece of discourse involving more than one speaker, such as a professional meeting.

- *Task 2: Responding to a series of interview questions.* This is a situation that all students can expect to encounter. Test takers are presented with a wide variety of questions, which are categorized in terms of expected difficulty. Test takers have some preparation time and then are asked a series of questions to which they respond immediately.

- *Task 3: Presenting information from a written (graphic) source.* Test takers have time to prepare their presentation after which they have 3 minutes to speak. This task is presented to test takers as a rehearsal.

- *Task 4: Leaving a telephone message.* Again, test takers have time to prepare. This is one occasion where real life routinely requires speakers to make recordings of their speech.

- *Task 5: Providing information about an aspect of life in Hong Kong to a visitor.* Test takers are given time to plan a response and then have 3 minutes to speak. The ability to offer advice and speak in social situations with international visitors is considered by employers to be important. (Hong Kong Polytechnic University, 1997)

See Appendix B for a sample speaking task.

The test aims to model a range of varieties and speakers of English, both native and nonnative (e.g., British, Australian, American, Canadian, Indian, Hong Kong,

Malaysian, Mainland Chinese, German, Thai). All speakers used have a high level of English proficiency and are easily intelligible. Normal rates of speech are used throughout the test (Hong Kong Polytechnic University, 1997).

Assessment

Assessment is conducted using trained raters whose reliability is checked using a sample of test performances rated independently. All raters are first screened to ensure they possess both relevant English as a second language (ESL) teaching qualifications and experience.

The raters use analytic scales for rating both the writing and speaking components. The scoring categories for writing are task fulfillment and relevance, coherence and cohesion, register and vocabulary, and control of language.

The test takers' proficiency levels are reported on certificates given to all test takers, using abbreviated descriptions of performance based on the contents of the rating scale. Levels of proficiency are reported separately for writing and speaking, with six levels for each. Sample descriptors, from the GSLPA Reporting Scale, are as follows:

Descriptors of writing proficiency—levels 3–5

W5: Can produce well organised texts that communicate successfully and clearly on required tasks. Has generally good control of tone, style, vocabulary and sentence structure, despite some inaccuracies. A clearly competent writer.

W4: Can produce relevant, interpretable and generally well organised texts that address task requirements. Vocabulary is generally adequate, and grammatical errors do not obscure communication. A generally competent writer.

W3: Can produce generally relevant and interpretable texts that show basic ability to organise content appropriately. Vocabulary is adequate to convey basic meanings and grammatical errors rarely prevent communication. A basic writer.

Descriptors of speaking proficiency—levels 3–5

S5: Can communicate successfully, clearly and with confidence on a range of speaking tasks, generally using precise language. Sense is easy to follow throughout.

S4: Can convey meaning successfully on a range of speaking tasks, despite inaccuracies or limitations in vocabulary. Although organisation sometimes lacks clarity or fluency, message can be followed.

S3: Can convey meaning on a limited range of speaking tasks, but is sometimes hesitant. Despite inaccuracies, unevenness in pronunciation and/or limitations in vocabulary, message is mostly comprehensible.

(*GSLPA: English Scales for Reporting*, n.d.)

The test certificate also includes a brief description of the test and the tasks it includes to assist test users in interpreting the level descriptors.

Rating

Because the GSLPA is a subjective test almost entirely based on the test taker's performance on writing and speaking tasks, reliable rating of the performances is crucial in ensuring its effectiveness. For this reason, new raters go through strict selection and training processes, which include background screening and full-day rater training. Raters for the writing and speaking subtests are selected and trained separately. Final decisions on the accreditation of new raters are based on the results of multifaceted Rasch analysis and classical data analysis on the trainees' rating results on a large sample of writing or speaking performances. Every year, existing qualified raters are retrained when the testing season begins.

Each writing or speaking performance is rated by at least two accredited raters. A third rater rates a small portion of scripts and tapes when the test analysis suggests this is necessary.

For reporting purposes, Rasch analysis, using the software program FACETS (Linacre & Wright, 1992–1996), is used as the main procedure to produce final results of test takers' performances. This form of analysis, rather than merely being based on raw or averaged scores, estimates the difficulty of each task, as well as the inevitable differences among raters in terms of their harshness. It then builds these estimates into the calculation of the final score reported for each test taker, allowing the fairest possible calculation of reported scores. Finally, equating is conducted as an integral part of each year's analyses to ensure that all performances on GSLPA tasks are measured and reported on the same scale. The test population is large enough to allow this kind of analysis.

◈ DISTINGUISHING FEATURES

As a standardized English proficiency test, the GSLPA has a number of characteristics that distinguish it from some popular commercial English proficiency tests commonly associated with university students, such as the Test of English as a Foreign Language (TOEFL) and the International English Language Testing System (IELTS).

GSLPA as an Exit Test

In identifying an appropriate English proficiency test for graduating students at PolyU, a number of existing commercial tests (e.g., TOEFL, Test of Written English [TWE], Test of Spoken English [TSE], IELTS) were considered but rejected on the grounds that their focus was on university entry rather than exit. Predictions made by these tests relate primarily to courses of university study and not beyond them to the world of professional employment. This is perhaps the most important distinguishing feature of the GSLPA. To our knowledge it is the first such test explicitly designed for such a purpose.

GSLPA as a Task-Based, Workplace-Oriented Test

Other existing tests relevant to business English contexts, such as the Business English Certificate (BEC), administered by the University of Cambridge Local Examinations Syndicate, assume a certain amount of professional experience, sometimes in middle management. It was not considered reasonable to expect graduating students already to possess knowledge of such contexts. Another problem with this assessment is that it comes at three levels, each of which offers a pass/fail score. The GSLPA needed to cover a wider range of levels of proficiency than any one of the BEC levels. Both the writing and speaking components of the GSLPA are based on practical tasks, which are likely expected from entry-level professionals in the workplace. Although the test does not assume that the test takers possess prior knowledge of the workplace, the assessment tasks do provide situations in which the students would be able to demonstrate their English language proficiency in carrying out tasks as entry-level employees. The tasks were designed in such a way that any graduating university students with reasonable common sense would be able to understand and perform them without much difficulty.

GSLPA as a Performance-Based Test

As a performance test, the major components of the GSLPA are two productive parts, writing and speaking, both of which are based on real situations and require the test taker to provide appropriate input as needed by the situation. The GSLPA writing component is different from TWE in that the former requires the test taker to produce two pieces of work-related writing (e.g., memos, business letters, reports), whereas the latter generally expects the examinee to write an argumentative or analytical essay that usually is not situation based. Unlike a number of other standardized tests designed for workplace contexts (e.g., TOEIC), the GSLPA includes no multiple-choice component. Test takers are thus required to demonstrate what they can do in the language rather than what they can recognize. Taking into account employers' needs, this is considered to be a critical issue.

GSLPA as a Semidirect Speaking Test

Due to the concern of administering the speaking subtest to many thousands of test takers within a period of a few weeks, the speaking component has been run as a tape-mediated test in language laboratories. This mode of assessment has maximized the value and use of the limited resources available, including a team of trained and highly qualified examiners. Of course, two issues needing further investigation are the extent of differences in performance between direct and semidirect speaking tests and how the presence (or non-presence) of a human examiner affects the performance of the examinee.

Multiple Rating and Rasch Analysis

As described earlier, the GSLPA undergoes rigorous procedures of rating and data analysis to ensure fairness to all test takers and reliability of the test results. All performances on the GSLPA are rated by at least two trained and accredited raters who are guided by a rating scale. When there is a considerable gap between the judgements of the two raters, a third rating is called upon, in which case the final grade is derived based on the three ratings. Rasch analyses allow aspects of the data including differences in rater harshness and task difficulty to be taken into account in calculating the final score reported for each test taker. Classical analyses are also used to obtain general descriptive information. Equating is conducted on a regular basis to ensure that performances from different years are measured on the same scale of difficulty. These procedures enable the GSLPA to remain a suitably reliable measure for its original purpose.

◈ PRACTICAL IDEAS

Develop an In-House Exit Test

Develop an in-house exit test, but only if no suitable existing alternative exists. The GSLPA is an exit assessment of English proficiency that was developed in Hong Kong and designed specifically for use with graduating students at Hong Kong universities in response to demands from the community. The experience in the Hong Kong context may have parallels in other situations, where there may be increasing calls for accountability of various kinds. As a noncommercial, locally developed standardized test, the experience of GSLPA has demonstrated that, if properly researched, organized, and managed, it is feasible for a university to conduct by itself the complete process of a fairly large-scale standardized assessment. Nevertheless, the resources required are substantial, and if a suitable alternative exists, it is probably preferable to use it.

Analyze the Testing Situation

Consider stakeholders and their needs. These include the target test population, users of the results, course providers, and funding bodies. Issues to consider here are the language that should be assessed, the kinds of tasks that are appropriate to assess this, scoring criteria and level descriptors appropriate to these tasks, and the kinds of responses they elicit. Consider available resources including possible test methods and reasons for using them. Consult widely and be creative.

Ensure Assessment Quality

In addition to careful analysis of the test situation, ensuring test quality requires serious attention to the following:

- test specification
- design, editing, and trialling of test materials before operational use
- conditions of test administration
- selection, training, and monitoring of raters
- analysis and reporting of test results

The resources required include staff with suitable expertise in language assessment research, development, and validation. Without proper attention to test quality, the information obtained from the assessment will be unreliable and of dubious value.

Design an Informative Report Card

One useful aspect of the GSLPA is the reader-friendly, six-level set of proficiency descriptors contained in the certificate as described earlier in this case study. These descriptors go beyond a letter-grade ranking of students (such as those in academic transcripts) and offer a statement about the test taker's proficiency level of both

English speaking and writing. The plain language employed is intended to make the statements easily comprehensible to the users of the test results, in this case, employers in Hong Kong. This approach may be suitable in other educational contexts, including classroom English as a second language/English as a foreign language (ESL/EFL) assessments, for reporting on performance assessments. Naturally, descriptors should be based on the specific assessment procedures used and the types of performances elicited in these new contexts.

◈ CONCLUSION

This case study has described the history, development, and management of a new English language exit test for graduating university students in Hong Kong. It is a purpose-made, workplace-oriented, and task-based performance test. As the first of its type in Hong Kong, the GSLPA has provided a good example of how a test of this nature can be made useful and practical in an ESL context for relatively large-scale, standardized assessment. A number of aspects of this assessment, such as the development of assessment tasks and level descriptors, have the potential to be adapted to other educational contexts.

However, it is essential to remember that, as a new test that has only seen its 2nd year of formal implementation, continuous test development and validation are two important aspects of work for the GSLPA project. At present, the project team is conducting two concurrent validity studies with established international tests that share some similarity of purpose and plans to carry out a qualitative study with test takers and users to further examine some relevant issues in test validation and standardization, especially the vital issue of consequential validity. Another aspect that needs to be investigated is the desirability, feasibility, and practicality of delivering the GSLPA on-line as a computer-based test. This will be a topic for future research by the project team.

◈ CONTRIBUTORS

Tom Lumley was the associate director of the Asian Centre for Language Assessment Research (ACLAR) in the Department of English at the Hong Kong Polytechnic University (PolyU) until 2002, before returning to the Language Testing Centre at the University of Melbourne. He has had extensive experience and involvement in a wide range of language assessment research and development projects and consultancies, at school and university level, in Asia and Australia. He has taught language testing courses and led numerous professional development workshops on assessment-related issues for practicing teachers of children and adults.

David Qian is an assistant professor in the Department of English, associate of the ACLAR, and a member of the GSLPA project team at PolyU. Before joining PolyU, he was a TOEFL 2000 Postdoctoral Fellow at the Educational Testing Service, where he was principal investigator for two TOEFL 2000 research projects. His current interests are in large-scale performance testing and reading and vocabulary assessment in ESL.

◈ APPENDIX A: SAMPLE WRITING TASK

Task 1

Situation: You work for a large company with many sections and departments. Your section supervisor has sent out the following memo:

To:	*All Staff Members of Section 8*
From:	*Alvin Wong, Section Supervisor*
Date:	*July 5, 2000*

The company is planning to run a training course on effective communication. The course can be:

- *on weekday evenings from 6:30 to 9:30 p.m. **or** Sunday mornings from 9:30 am to 12:30 p.m.;*
- *internally in our office **or** externally at the Polytechnic University's campus;*
- *in English **or** in Cantonese.*

Please indicate if you would like to attend, stating your preferences for the options mentioned above and reasons for your choices. The company will organize the course to accommodate the most popular options.

You are very interested in attending this course.

Task:

Write an internal memo to your section supervisor

- stating that you would like to attend
- indicating your preferences
- explaining the reasons for your preferences

Spend no more than **35 minutes** on this task.

You will be assessed on your ability to organize your writing clearly and to complete the task using correct and appropriate language. Use complete sentences.

You should write approximately **150 words.**

(From *Graduating Students' Language Proficiency Assessment–English Learning Package (Stage A, Unit 2. Writing Task A. Learning & Practice)*, p. 9, by The Hong Kong Polytechnic University, 2000, Hong Kong: The Hong Kong Polytechnic University. Copyright © 2000 by The Hong Kong Polytechnic University. Adapted with permission.)

◈ APPENDIX B: SAMPLE SPEAKING TASK

Task 3: Oral Presentation

Well done. You got the scholarship, completed the course, and obtained a professional certificate! You now work for Dragon Company, a large international corporation.

Your company is going to hold a convention in 3 months' time with representatives from all over the world. You are part of a committee that has to select a suitable hotel for the convention. You have found three possible hotels, and you have summarized information about them in the table below. Tomorrow you are going to give a short presentation to members of other convention committees. Because you will only have 3 minutes to talk, today you need to practice what you are going to say. Your task is to talk to the other committee members about the three hotels.

In your presentation you should

- give a short introduction
- explain the variations in services, facilities, and costs
- encourage other committee members to consider all three options

Be sure to make it interesting!

You will have 2 minutes to prepare for the task and 3 minutes to make the presentation.

Begin your presentation when you are told to do so.

Table of Hotel Services

	Hotel International	Dragon Hotel	Hotel New Hong Kong
Free transportation to and from airport	☑	☑	☑
Room facilities	☐ phone/fax	☐ phone	☐ phone/fax ☐ minibar
Business center	☐ computers (with printer, e-mail, and Internet)	☒	☐ computers (with printer, e-mail, and Internet) ☐ videoconferencing
Convention room (size and facilities)	☐ up to 100 people ☐ overhead projector/video	☐ up to 80 people ☐ overhead projector	☐ up to 200 people ☐ multimedia facilities
Language translators	☐ on request ☐ charge $800 an hour	☒	☐ free of charge
Catering packages	☐ includes breakfast, morning and afternoon tea	☐ includes breakfast and morning tea	☐ includes breakfast, lunch, and unlimited refreshments during conference
Room price	☐ $850 per night	☐ $500 per night	☐ $1,150 per night

Key. ✓ = available; X = not available.
(From Graduating Students' Language Proficiency Assessment–English Learning Package (Stage A, Unit 6. Speaking Tasks. Practice Booklet), pp. 6–7, by The Hong Kong Polytechnic University, 2000, Hong Kong: The Hong Kong Polytechnic University. Copyright © 2000 by The Hong Kong Polytechnic University. Adapted with permission.)

PART 5

Program
Evaluation

CHAPTER 11

A Curriculum Review of an ESL Composition Program

Edwina S. Carreon

◈ INTRODUCTION

Many of us in language teaching have at some point in our professional life experienced being part of a program evaluation. The few who have not might consider themselves lucky. Although this process does not take place often, being involved in a review or evaluation of one's program is something one does not easily forget. Part of the reason is found in the nature of program evaluation. Evaluation as defined by Lynch (1996) is the systematic attempt to gather information in order to make judgments or decisions. To do an evaluation correctly requires planning, research, and a commitment of time and effort on the part of those involved. Another reason why the experience is difficult to forget is that program evaluations are often prompted by accountability or accreditation requirements. As such, they are seen as externally motivated and controlled, often resulting in their being perceived as threatening and ineffective by teachers, staff, and students who form the core of those involved in the undertaking.

But what if the investigation is internally motivated, involves only the teachers and staff of the program, and is a goal-free review or self-study rather than an evaluation (Long, 1984; Wintergerst & Kreidler, 1995)? Is such a self-study less threatening and more useful?

In the fall of 1999, our English as a Second Language (ESL) Composition Program at Ohio State University (OSU) began the process of a self-study at the request of the head of the program. The program had not undergone a review since its inception in the 1950s. Thus, the self-study was intended to measure where we were after many years and numerous changes in the various courses offered in the program. Its objective was not to pass judgment on or find fault with the program, the courses, or its members but to gather information through a collaborative process on the current status of the program's various courses and components to highlight strengths and concerns. It was hoped that the results would be used to further strengthen the program.

Less than a year later, the final reports were submitted and a meeting was scheduled to present the results of the study. How did we accomplish this feat? Is a goal-free, formative, and process-oriented self-study really possible in a tertiary institution with a large ESL program? Is it indeed less threatening and does it provide useful, comprehensive, and honest feedback? What actions and behaviors turn the concept of a self-study into reality and encourage a cooperative and productive undertaking?

In this case study I describe the curriculum self-study experience of OSU's ESL Composition Program. I discuss the review process we followed, including key actions and decisions, data-gathering procedures and instruments, and analysis techniques developed that are compatible with a self-study process. Next, I point out five features that distinguish our case study. Finally, I suggest practical tips for conducting a similar self-study based on the lessons we learned from the experience.

◈ CONTEXT

The ESL Composition Program at OSU is one of three ESL units in the College of Education's School of Teaching and Learning. The program is one of the largest postadmission ESL programs in the United States, with approximately 1,400 students attending its courses every year. The other units are the American Language Program, which provides intensive courses for international students who need English language instruction before entering a U.S. university or college, and the Spoken English Program, which screens and trains international teaching assistants in communication skills for teaching purposes.

A director and an assistant director head the ESL program. During the self-study period, there were six full-time instructional staff and varying numbers of teaching assistants and part-time instructors. Full-time instructors have master's degrees and most have doctorates. In addition to teaching full-time, instructors also coordinate individual courses and mentor graduate teaching assistants who are working on advanced degrees in fields such as foreign and second language education, English, and linguistics.

The program offers an undergraduate sequence of three courses, a graduate sequence of three courses, and special courses for publication and thesis and dissertation writing. It follows the university's quarter system (10 weeks) schedule. Its goal is to help students improve their academic writing to a level at which they can be successful in regular university courses (*ESL Composition Program*, 1998). Our students come mostly from Asia; a growing number are from the Middle East. Most completed their high school diplomas in their home countries and are in the United States as students for the first time; a few attended 1 to 4 years of U.S. high school. Most of those taking the graduate sequence completed their undergraduate and graduate degrees in their home country; a few have advanced degrees from a U.S. college or university.

◈ DESCRIPTION

For our program self-study, selected members of the academic community investigated three aspects: (a) curriculum, (b) instructional staff, and (c) program assessment. Full-time instructors were assigned to form three work groups, one for each area of study. Of these three, the curriculum review, which had three members, was the most extensive and complex and the one I was most closely involved with as convener; hence, its work is the main focus of this case study.

When the program director announced that we were to conduct a self-study, there were no related internal documents or program reports to guide us because no review of the program and curriculum had been done since its inception in the 1950s. The only potentially useful documents were student evaluations and instructor self-assessments done at the end of each academic quarter. Due to confidentiality issues, the self-assessments could not be used. Figure 1 identifies the general steps and timetable we followed.

Our curriculum group's initial meetings were focused on clarifying the task objectives. Were we going to evaluate the curriculum and determine its strengths and weaknesses? Were we merely describing the state of the curriculum without judging it? We needed to address these important concerns early in the task. Without this stage, I doubt that our work would have gone smoothly. We discussed the meaning of terms used to describe the program review we were about to undertake, such as *focused, not comprehensive, goal free,* and *self-study.* We received assurance that our study was to examine merely the program's instructional aspects and that it was not to be evaluative or judgmental. Our study was to gather information about specific aspects of the current curriculum, including participants' needs and concerns, rather than focus on comparing stated goals and outcomes. In this sense it was goal free (Wintergerst & Kreidler, 1995). Finally, the results of our case study were for internal use only.

The second stage, planning the study, involved conceptualizing the general design and direction of the curriculum review. For this we turned to the basic elements that form a curriculum. According to the *Longman Dictionary of Applied Linguistics* (Richards, Platt, & Weber, 1985), a curriculum involves

(a) the educational purpose of the programme (the ends)

(b) the content, teaching procedures and learning experiences which will be necessary to achieve this purpose (the means)

(c) some means for assessing whether or not the educational ends have been achieved. (p. 70)

To cover these three aspects, our inquiry included seven areas of inquiry: (a) program goals and objectives, (b) course objectives and syllabus, (c) classroom approaches and methodology, (d) textbooks and materials, (e) teacher participation, (f) student needs and progress, and (g) assessment. Lacking previous records of the program's history, we conducted interviews with the current director and various

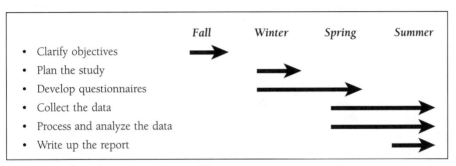

FIGURE 1. Self-Study Stages and Timetable

course coordinators about the historical development of the program and the individual courses. These formed the basis for the questionnaires as well as the framework for data analysis and presentation.

Our plan involved gathering information by interviewing the director and course coordinators, conducting a survey of former students, analyzing existing student evaluations, and conducting a teacher survey. The development of questionnaires along with data collection and analysis were the most challenging and time-consuming stages, covering 6 of the 10 months of the self-study.

In the third stage, we designed interview and survey instruments to be sensitive to our particular needs and to accurately reflect our priorities. Using the seven areas of inquiry specified above as guides, we began by drafting a list of general questions, guided in part by those suggested in the TESOL self-study questions for the review of a curriculum (TESOL, 1992). We then reviewed and modified this list and used it to construct the director and coordinator interview questionnaires (see Appendix A).

After we completed the interviews, we developed the teacher survey questionnaires, guided by the interview results as well as the seven areas of inquiry. Each group member, working with two assigned courses, drew up a list of course goals and objectives; descriptions of class activities and strategies; and comments about materials, textbooks, teacher involvement, and the assessment process. These lists were shared and reviewed by the group and turned into six questionnaires (see Appendix B), corresponding to the six main courses offered by the program. In the process we established similar phrasing and similar categories for easier analysis later. We also devised a well-designed and reader-friendly questionnaire.

Once the questionnaires were ready, they were distributed to the teachers. Anonymity was protected. The original list of general questions was modified slightly to include or disregard certain areas to suit the nature of the subject's position. For example, questions related to program development and maintenance, as well as program links to other academic departments and programs within the university, were included in the interview with the program director, whereas questions related to teacher involvement were included in the teacher survey. As a result, no two questionnaires were alike. It also meant the teacher survey was developed and conducted only after all interviews had been transcribed and analyzed.

The questions were meant to elicit mainly descriptive information (e.g., what are the main goals of the course?). However, some questions were formulated to elicit evaluative and reflective comments (e.g., do assessment approaches influence teaching?). See Table 1 for the areas covered in the various questionnaires.

No instrument was developed to gather data from current students; the program's end-of-course evaluation survey results were used instead. The first section of the student evaluations requires students to express agreement or disagreement on a Likert-type rating scale[1] with statements describing their experiences with the composition course, whereas, in the second section, students provide discursive answers to open-ended questions.

However, we still had to develop the survey questionnaire for post-ESL students. Five graduate students enrolled in a syllabus design course piloted the student

---

[1] A Likert-type rating scale contains an item to which a subject "responds with varying degrees of intensity on a scale ranging between extremes such as agree-disagree" (Isaac & Michael, 1981, p. 142).

TABLE 1. GENERAL TOPICS COVERED BY QUESTIONNAIRES

Areas Covered	Director Questionnaire	Coordinator Questionnaire	Teacher Questionnaire
Program history/course history	yes	yes	
Goals and objectives	yes	yes	yes
Underlying theories and approaches	yes	yes	
Program development and maintenance	yes		
Student assessment	yes	yes	yes
Syllabus		yes	
Materials/textbooks		yes	yes
Classroom methodology		yes	yes
Teacher involvement and participation			yes

questionnaire. Our group then used feedback from this pilot to modify the questionnaire, including formatting changes to accommodate sending and returning the survey responses via e-mail.

The final version of the questionnaire had two parts. Part 1 asked respondents to provide their graduate status, their major, the number and type of ESL courses taken, and the amount of writing they do or have done in courses other than ESL composition. Part 2 asked questions similar to those found in the composition program's end-of-course evaluation form. We added two questions: one on use of source texts and the other on ability to complete a variety of writing tasks. Responses in this section were designed on a 5-point Likert-type/summated rating scale.

The fourth stage, data collection, was divided up within our group, based on familiarity with specific courses. Interviewees were provided a copy of the interview questionnaire before the interviews to acquaint them with the areas of inquiry. Interview sessions lasted about 45 minutes on average and were audiotaped, transcribed, and summarized by the individual in charge.

At the same time that the interviews were taking place, we began the survey of post-ESL students. We sent the student questionnaire electronically to more than 500 post-ESL students. Students e-mailed completed questionnaires to one of the volunteer graduate students who then collected and analyzed the results.

The teaching staff sample was drawn from 24 teachers who had taught ESL composition courses at least twice in the last 2 years. The 2-year limit was for practical purposes. We wanted feedback that would be relevant to the courses as they are currently being taught, and we wanted the memories of their teaching experiences to be as vivid as possible. We gave subjects 2 weeks to return the questionnaire but accepted and incorporated late forms in the analysis.

For current students, we used end-of-term course evaluations from 2 years before the study because they best reflected the contents and approaches presently used in the program's six courses. Because of time constraints and other practical reasons, we used only 60% of the student evaluations from two courses with high enrollment. In the other four courses, all student evaluations were included in our analysis. We analyzed a total of 2,050 student evaluations.

In the fifth stage, analysis of the data, we used different strategies depending on the type of data being processed. Interview data were transcribed and summarized using the same general areas of inquiry outlined early in the project. We also agreed to highlight strengths of the program and concerns expressed by the interviewees. Support staff, who were given release time from their regular office responsibilities, retrieved, tallied, and collated the data from student evaluations. Their involvement solved the problem of confidentiality, which would have been compromised to a certain extent had one of us or any of the teachers or teaching assistants handled the data. In the meantime, one team member, using statistical software for means and standard deviations, analyzed the data from the teacher survey.

By summer 1998, the 7th month of the self-study, we began the final stage of the project: writing the report. Our group considered ways to streamline the analysis and write-up of the report but decided that the most efficient and satisfying procedure was to divide up the courses among the group members. I drafted a sample report, and our team agreed on a detailed framework for presenting each course review.

Simultaneously with our group's data collection on curriculum, the two other groups were occupied with their own assignments. The instructional staff group collected information from both full and part-time teachers on their professional qualifications and experience, their responsibilities and involvement as part of the ESL program, the university community, and the wider field of ESL and composition. The third group interviewed faculty and administrative staff from 20 different units within the university that were chosen because of their contact with international students.

Despite the amount of data to be presented and written up in as clear and organized a form as possible, all three groups completed their tasks as planned.

◈ DISTINGUISHING FEATURES

Internal Motivation

One of the key features of our program self-study was that it was internally motivated. The impetus for studying the program was not brought about by external accountability or accreditation pressures; no such situation was present at that time or even in the foreseeable future. Instead, because the ESL program had not undergone any form of review or assessment since its inception, the program head felt that it would benefit from one. This impetus may be less ideal than the situation where participants themselves, in our case, the instructional staff, initiate the self-study process or unanimously vote to undergo the process (compare, for example, the case of the American Language Program at Columbia University by Numrich, Boyd, & Jerome, 1995).

However, considering the realities and constraints a review can place on an academic program, a staff- and faculty-initiated review is not altogether typical. Rather than avoiding one completely until a state or university mandate or crisis forces a unit or program to conduct a study, a more positive alternative probably is for someone inside the program to suggest it. As our case demonstrates, with the right leadership and motivation, support from the members of the program can be won and the self-study can be accomplished successfully.

Staff and Student Participation

A second distinguishing feature of our study was that all those involved were members of the program. All full-time instructors were active members of work groups: forming the objectives; planning the methodology; developing the instruments; collecting, gathering, and analyzing data; and designing and writing the report. In some stages of the process, administrative staff within the program even provided support.

Getting members of a program involved in all facets of the self-study encourages ownership of the self-study process, which in turn leads to a strong interest in getting things done well and seeing the process through until the end. It was especially important to have the instructional staff completely involved in planning and designing the study because of their familiarity with the program. Our combined insider knowledge allowed the instruments we used to be designed to fit the features of each course reviewed. Insider knowledge led to interview and survey questions and answers that were directly relevant and valuable to the members of the program. In addition, as the goal of the self-study was to get members of a program to look within and reflect on areas of strength and weakness, not having an outsider involved encouraged more openness and honesty.

Internally Developed Review Design and Instruments

A third distinguishing feature of this self-study was that we followed no specific existing model for the review process or data gathering. Although the *TESOL Standards and Self-Study Questions for Postsecondary Programs* (TESOL, 1992) provided the group with some initial guidance on the areas to cover, we found no suitable review or program evaluation models for ESL composition. This project, therefore, was as much a development of a formative model for reviewing a university-based, postadmission ESL composition program as it was a curriculum review report.

The process we followed reflected the organizational features of our specific program. We developed unique assessment instruments that grew out of the priorities, features, and areas of concern within the program. For example, we had a program director who had more institutional memory than most of us and who saw the program as a whole; we had course coordinators whose knowledge of the program came from their intimate acquaintance with the courses for which they were responsible; and we had teachers, both full- and part-time, who had contact with the students and the classroom situation and who interpreted and implemented the course coordinators' plans. Therefore, in planning what areas to investigate and in what order, we considered these layers of authority and responsibility in our design.

Moreover, it was important to us that our investigation focused on the curriculum areas most important to us as members of the ESL program. Thus, we initially drew up a list of questions we wanted answered in relation to program objectives, course objectives and syllabus, materials and textbooks, classroom methodology, and assessment. This became our basis for interview and survey questions.

Finally, having no models for the process and data-gathering instruments, the study developed these organically (i.e., each instrument was informed by instruments designed and results gathered from earlier stages). For example, we awaited the results of the director and course coordinator interviews before designing the teacher questionnaires. This allowed us to identify areas of concern expressed by the director and coordinators and then to match these with teachers' perceived critical areas and issues, such as awareness of program and course goals and objectives, perceptions on the accomplishment of objectives set out by coordinators, and perceptions on the amount of teacher input in the development of a course.

Smart and Creative Data Collection

We also were aware that information about the program already existed in the form of student evaluations. These were readily available and kept for at least 3 years. It made no sense to reinvent the wheel. We used the section on program evaluation but not instructor evaluation. Because confidentiality issues kept us from perusing the actual evaluation forms ourselves, this situation became another boon to our group as administrative staff collected and collated the mass of data we desired.

We also found assistance from graduate students who were working on a related course project. This was a case of well-timed opportunity. An instructor on leave from our program and teaching a graduate course in needs assessment and syllabus design offered students to help us. In turn, these students would use the data they collected to fulfill part of the course requirement. Most of them were international students who had contact with some of the students we wanted to study. In addition, the students were on a tight course schedule, were acquainted with computers, and were well motivated. They also contributed information to the study that would have otherwise not been collected, including in-depth data from face-to-face interviews with former students in their native language. Although the number of participants was small, their opinions about the program confirmed the positive trends of the general student survey.

Because time was important to us, we took advantage of the Internet to disseminate our student survey. Our graduate students piloted and later sent the survey questionnaire as e-mail attachments to 500 former students. These surveys were completed and returned the same way. Although the return rate was merely 20%, we considered this successful considering the 1-week turnaround requirement.

Time Management

The whole self-study process was accomplished in less than a year, from the time the initial discussion was held to the submission of the final reports. The most comprehensive and most complex of the reviews, the curriculum review, took 9 months. How was this possible? The curriculum study efficiently gathered information from members of the program who were willing to share information because they themselves were involved in the process.

Collective Reflection

In the early stages of the self-study, we wondered what useful results an information-gathering approach would yield. Did we not already know what we were supposed to know about the courses we taught? The answer became obvious from our first set of interviews that provided the history of the program and the evolution of the various courses. For new instructors and even those who had been teaching with the program for some years, it was most interesting to know how the various courses evolved; what theories influenced the course coordinators and courses; and what the motives were behind the choice of textbooks and materials, assignments, and tasks. Information and insights from this study led to positive steps for program improvement such as discussions to clarify the goal and mission of the ESL program and the development of a program overview packet.

My colleagues pointed out the usefulness of taking time out to reflect on the whole program, rather than on the individual courses under different coordinators. The self-study emphasized the importance of consensus among teachers of the same course on issues such as the use of technology, the balance between rhetoric and grammar, and rubrics for student assessments. Consequently, there has been an increase in communication among the course coordinators, which has strengthened the rhetorical, discourse, and grammar connections between and among the writing courses.

◈ PRACTICAL IDEAS

Consider a More Focused Study

If the idea of a program review is too intimidating, perhaps look at only one or two specific aspects of a program (e.g., history and goals, syllabus, materials) instead of a comprehensive review. Having feedback about some aspect of the program is better than not having any at all. A smaller study can certainly be more manageable and might encourage follow-up studies on other aspects of the program.

Create Ongoing, Formative Evaluations

Aside from supplying current and relevant feedback of instruction and materials, end-of-term assessments by students and teachers provide useful data for later program reviews and reduce the amount of data gathering.

Investigate What Information Is Already Available

Do not reinvent the wheel. Course syllabi and materials, program brochures, and previous program evaluation reports, if they exist, contain valuable information and, by their existence or lack thereof, indicate the health of a program. In addition, good communication between groups involved in different aspects of the investigation can also yield fruitful sharing of information.

Develop Your Own Data-Gathering Instruments

Begin with basic questions about the area you intend to study. Use, reuse, and modify the same questions for various interview or survey purposes. Gather information first from those who have the broadest perspective of and longest experience in the program.

Seek Release Time and Support From Administration

Some of my colleagues noted that having one less course to teach or some form of release time would greatly help those involved to focus on the project. This in turn would have an impact on the quality of the work produced. Giving release time also increases the profile of the project, especially within the program, as the review project is viewed as having enough importance to justify diverting funds from existing resources.

Use Technology Creatively

The use of technology in data analysis is widely acknowledged. We have found e-mail extremely useful in communicating with group members and in circulating drafts of the various instruments and the final report for review. Word-processing programs helped prepare well-designed questionnaires, which were delivered to students via email.

Double-Check Your Figures and Statistics

Despite computers and computer-savvy users, the old axiom of "garbage in, garbage out" still applies. It is good practice to look closely and perform spot checks of statistical and numerical data. Although doing so may be tedious and boring, catching anomalies early will save both time and embarrassment.

Establish a Mechanism to Encourage Communication

All the major participants in this study noted the importance of communication in a self-study. Setting aside time for informal discussions in groups at the onset to discuss reactions to the self-study plan and to clarify objectives and parameters helps to clear up misconceptions or misinterpretations and allay fears. Similarly, communicating the results of the study, encouraging discussion of the results and the process, and following up on the suggestions and recommendations of the final report are necessary to justify the self-study process.

❖ CONCLUSION

One of the attractions of a self-study as opposed to an externally driven formal program evaluation is that the former is theoretically less stressful and intimidating. Our experience is that stress or pressure is unavoidable even in a self-study and that it is unrealistic to expect otherwise. There will be pressure from having a timetable and deadline and from having to take on work that is over and above one's regular responsibilities. Ideally, giving teachers some release time can compensate for the new task. However, scheduling and budget constraints cannot always accommodate this, as was true in our case. Adjustment in teaching assignments, however, can be made to lighten the load. It is also natural within an institutional context to expect people to feel intimidated when asked to reveal information about their professional practices and beliefs, despite attempts to reassure them that their privacy will be protected and that information will not be used against them.

However, pressure was reduced in our case because the self-study was initiated within the program and conducted by a majority of the participants themselves. The situation would have been more intimidating had an outsider done the interviews and surveys. Also, because the surveys and interviews dealt specifically about program courses, they were, to a certain extent, particularly interesting and enjoyable to most of those who took part. Although there was a deadline set to complete our study, the groups were in almost complete control of their schedules. Aside from the final report, no initial or progress reports were required for submission.

A self-study, despite being different from a program evaluation in a number of ways, is still by its nature an investigation of the self. As such, it is not only an intellectual exercise, but, at some stages of the study, an emotional and psychological activity, with people's personalities, needs, and concerns coming into play. To a great extent, the success of a self-study, its completion and impact, depends on how well participants work together and how open, trustful, and cooperative they are. To engender such a situation, some of my colleagues stressed the importance of anticipating and acknowledging different personalities and points of view. They also felt the need for an established mechanism by which questions, doubts, and dissent can be accommodated and addressed.

We set out to conduct a review of our ESL program guided by the idea of a goal-free, internally motivated self-study. It was successfully completed less than a year later with the use of smart and creative data collection and analysis techniques and efficient time-management strategies. Its members were committed to the task and achieved a harmonious working relationship. In the end, the study provided information and insights that helped highlight the program's strengths, raise awareness of its shortcomings, and guide the main participants in making important decisions to improve curriculum and teaching.

◈ ACKNOWLEDGMENTS

The author wishes to thank Joel Bloch and Natalie Herdman, who formed part of the curriculum review group. Special thanks also go to other colleagues at the ESL Composition Program at OSU, Diane Belcher, Alan Hirvela, Jack Rouzer, and Patricia Weiland, for sharing their valuable insights on the self-study project.

◈ CONTRIBUTOR

Edwina S. Carreon is the assistant director of the ESL Composition Program at Ohio State University in Columbus, Ohio. She has also taught writing and language education courses at the University of the West Indies in Jamaica and at De La Salle University in Manila, Philippines.

◈ APPENDIX A: SAMPLE GUIDE QUESTIONS FOR COURSE COORDINATOR INTERVIEWS

Program Objectives and the Syllabus

1. What is the main goal of the course? What are the objectives and dimensions to reach the goal?

2 How did these objectives come about? Who makes decisions about them?

3. What problems have emerged as the objectives are carried out?

4. How has the course changed over time to reflect changes in students (i.e., language/writing needs and the needs or expectations of their academic departments/disciplines)?

5. What theories of language and learning underlie the objectives of the courses in the program? How does the program ensure that its curriculum and methodology reflect the best, current knowledge in the field of ESL writing?

6. How does the course allow for different background, language proficiency, abilities, ages, and levels of achievement, learning styles, goals, and communicative needs of the students?

The Syllabus

1. What kind of information does the syllabus contain?

2. What language skills does it address?

3. How are the skills and objectives in the course differentiated from those of other courses? What motivates the differentiation?

4. Who designs the course? Who else participates in designing it?

Materials/Textbooks

1. What textbooks have been used so far in the course?

2. What are the procedures for selecting, updating, and modifying textbooks in this course?

3. What purposes do commercially published textbooks serve in the course?

4. What purposes do homegrown or in-house materials serve?

5. What kind of feedback from students is given about them?

Classroom/Teaching Methodology

1. How does the course approach the teaching of genre writing, discourse organization and development, the composing process, and grammar and syntax?

2. What are the dominant activities and techniques suggested or envisioned for the course?

3. What common procedures do teachers generally adapt and use in class?

4. Is there one approach to writing underlying these activities and strategies?

5. What provision is made to link this course to other relevant university courses?

Assessment

1. What measurement instruments are used in this course?

2. Why were they chosen? What theories of language and learning underlie these instruments?

3. How are validity and reliability achieved?

4. Do the assessment approaches influence teaching?

5. What problems have been encountered in using the assessment instruments in the course? What has been done to address the problems?

◈ APPENDIX B: EXCERPT FROM TEACHER QUESTIONNAIRE CURRICULUM REVIEW

Part A: ESL Program

1. Rank the following statements from 1 to 5, according to how well they reflect the main goal/s of the ESL Composition Program.

	1 = Best reflects the goal 5 = Least reflects the goal
Bring students' expository writing skills to a level at which they can perform successfully as writers in university courses.	1 2 3 4 5
Help our students produce comprehensible text (i.e., text that can be understood by readers across the curriculum).	1 2 3 4 5
Help students develop vocabulary and grammatical control/accuracy.	1 2 3 4 5
Enable students to express themselves as learners and writers.	1 2 3 4 5
Other:	1 2 3 4 5

Part B: EDU T&L 107

2. Do you think the goals listed in Part A are reflected in 107?

Yes   No   Not Sure

3. Do the 107 course descriptions (and if provided, the course syllabus) provide enough information to help you teach the course effectively?

Yes   No   Not Sure

4. Please use the space below to write down any information you would like to see added to the syllabus to help you better teach 107.

_____

_____

5. Which of the following do you think are the most important goals of the course? Please circle the most appropriate response.

	1 = Very important 2 = Somewhat important 3 = Neutral *4 = Less important 5 = Not important*
a. Teach students that writing is a process	1 2 3 4 5
b. Accommodate cultural differences among students	1 2 3 4 5
c. Help students see writing and reading as related activities	1 2 3 4 5
d. Teach students how to write a response paper	1 2 3 4 5

e.	Help students be better readers and writers for academic purposes	1 2 3 4 5
f.	Teach students how to write a thesis-driven paper	1 2 3 4 5
g.	Teach students how to write a comparison/contrast paper	1 2 3 4 5
h.	Teach grammar/editing	1 2 3 4 5
i.	Teach students how to synthesize information	1 2 3 4 5
j.	Teach literary texts	1 2 3 4 5
k.	Teach students how to work and write collaboratively	1 2 3 4 5
l.	Teach students how to cite from a source	1 2 3 4 5
m.	Teach students the responsibility of being a writer	1 2 3 4 5
n.	Teach personal writing	1 2 3 4 5
o.	Teach students about plagiarism	1 2 3 4 5
p.	Other:	1 2 3 4 5

6. In the space below, please write the letter corresponding to those goals from the list above that you believe you are <u>actually able to accomplish</u> in 107.

7. In the space below, please write the letter corresponding to those goals from the list above that you think are the <u>three primary goals of 107.</u> (These will not necessarily correspond with your own top goals.)

8. To what extent does each of the following statements reflect what is taking place in your 107 classes? Please circle the most appropriate response.

	1 = Very true 2 = True 3 = Not sure/neutral 4 = Somewhat false 5 = False	
a.	When students have to write, they write in response to reading.	1 2 3 4 5
b.	Grammar is always taught in the context of producing a text and making meaning.	1 2 3 4 5
c.	There is not enough grammar taught.	1 2 3 4 5
d.	Individual language needs and differences are dealt with (*adequately*) in the tutorials.	1 2 3 4 5
e.	The course emphasizes both process and product.	1 2 3 4 5
f.	Teachers take into account that the midterm and final essays exams are first drafts.	1 2 3 4 5
g.	Students are *generally* placed at the appropriate level through the prequarter testing.	1 2 3 4 5

CHAPTER 12

Evaluation of Training in an ELT Project in Egypt

Barbara Thornton, Robert Burch, and Dina El-Araby

Not everything that can be counted counts, and not everything that counts can be counted.

—Albert Einstein

◈ INTRODUCTION

In today's world, managers, directors, and other decision makers need to show bona fide results to justify their training programs. As a result, more organizations in both the public and private sectors are carrying out evaluations to determine the effectiveness of their training programs, to document that program objectives have been met, to provide feedback to their staff and clients, and to make changes that improve program effectiveness.

The Kirkpatrick model is one model used to evaluate training programs. It was first developed in the 1950s by Donald Kirkpatrick and is still the most widely used model for evaluating training, particularly in the area of business (Kirkpatrick, 1998). However, it has not received much attention in the field of language training. In this case study, we describe how the Kirkpatrick evaluation system was used in the monitoring and evaluation of training conducted under the auspices of a United States Agency for International Development (USAID)-funded project in Egypt. We look at how the method has been used to assess a range of training courses across the country and offer insights into the strengths and weaknesses of the Kirkpatrick model.

◈ CONTEXT

The Egyptian Ministry of Education places a great deal of importance on the development of skills in its teachers, teacher trainers, and supervisors, which is achieved through training. However, the expectations of such training are changing. No longer is it enough to train the individual; the Ministry of Education, like other educational systems throughout the world, wishes to achieve broader, systemwide objectives. Such a change in shift requires a change in the way courses are planned, conducted, and evaluated. Although most educators would agree that evaluation is necessary for effective training, principled evaluation of training usually has been lacking. This has meant that there is little useful information for leaders and decision makers within the Ministry to determine the value of the training activities offered, to make improvements, or to justify the continued existence of these activities.

Similarly, other sectors of education in Egypt, including universities and private educational providers, have become increasingly aware of the importance of training. Such training, however, is also most frequently evaluated using customer satisfaction questionnaires, the results of which rarely feed into future planning.

A number of aid-funded projects are also involved in education in Egypt and many such projects involve training interventions such as face-to-face training, one-on-one training, or mentoring. With increased emphasis on issues connected with accountability, evaluation of such interventions has assumed increasing importance.

The Integrated English Language Project II (IELP-II) is a USAID project administered by the Academy for Educational Development and Amideast. The main goal of IELP-II is to promote the use of the English language in Egypt by improving the quality of English language teaching and learning. This is achieved by organizing workshops, seminars, conferences, and courses for those involved in the teaching of English in Egypt. Audiences include teachers, supervisors, managers, and leaders.

IELP-II works closely with the Ministry of Education, faculties of education, and English for specific purposes (ESP) units in universities throughout the country. In addition, it collaborates with partners from the private sector such as language institutes and career development centers. Leaders from these organizations are involved in all aspects of course and program development including overall approach and design, content of events, and logistics.

IELP-II has been providing face-to-face training to large numbers of Egyptian teachers in big cities such as Alexandria and Cairo as well as to teachers outside these metropolitan areas. In an effort to reach rural audiences, IELP uses a training of trainers (TOT) model. Supervisors from various areas in Egypt are selected to attend a regional 3-day TOT workshop. They observe demonstrations of materials and techniques presented by trainers from both IELP-II and the Ministry. They receive sets of trainer's notes and copies of the material to be distributed to other supervisors, senior teachers, and teachers in the schools in their areas. This step-down model has enabled IELP-II to reach far more professionals in Egypt than would have been possible through direct training. However, it makes the evaluation of any impact more difficult because direct intervention is one or more steps removed from the central IELP-II office in Cairo.

It is apparent that the variety of programs offered through IELP-II is complex and wide ranging and the numbers of interested parties significant. It was also recognized from the project's inception that monitoring and evaluation should not be an optional add-on but should be an integral part of all activities. As a result, IELP-II was structured with three main divisions: (a) the program development and implementation division (PDI), (b) the monitoring and evaluation division (M&E), and (c) the finance and operations division.

PDI is responsible for designing training courses and developing appropriate materials. M&E is responsible for planning, managing, and implementing the monitoring and evaluation process to systematically provide feedback to our partners, stakeholders, and funding agency on the results of the IELP-II training activities. M&E also investigates the impact and utility of its training activities.

Each training activity within IELP-II is assigned an activity manager from PDI and an activity monitor from M&E. Evaluations are planned together, although M&E carries out the evaluation that feeds directly into future decision making within PDI.

IELP-II adopts an Egyptian-centered approach to staffing. Unlike in the past, where expatriate personnel would tend to staff entire projects, IELP-II contains a mix of American and Egyptian staff, all with higher degrees in their areas of specialization. In addition, both expatriate and Egyptian consultants are used where needed.

The Egyptian-centered approach carries over into all aspects of planning and implementation. However, the involvement of all parties in the monitoring and evaluation has been a gradual process that is only now bearing fruit.

◈ DESCRIPTION

Evaluating training, which is so broad in its range and complexity, is not an easy task. For comparisons to be made across programs, it was necessary to employ a system that was powerful enough to be applicable to programs at a range of levels yet simple enough in its applicability to be used by expatriate and Egyptian staff and consultants who might not be familiar with the model. Central to the system are the concepts of strategic training and the Kirkpatrick model.

Strategic Training

IELP-II employs a strategic approach to its training interventions. As Denakpo, Hart, Flederman, Gilboy, and Sanders-Smith (1997) describe, strategic training is training that directly impacts the trainees, their job performance, and the results of this performance on their institutions. It emphasizes performance change; in other words, it strives to change the professional behavior of those being trained.

Strategic training involves assessment and evaluation even before a course has begun. This is done by investigating performance gaps. For example, IELP-II asked questions such as:

- What is it that the Egyptian English teachers are not doing now that we believe they should be doing to provide quality English education to their students?

- What are the supervisors not doing that would enable them to do a better job in providing guidance and direction to their teachers?

These questions, when compared with actual performance, lead to what are known as performance gaps, as shown in Figure 1.

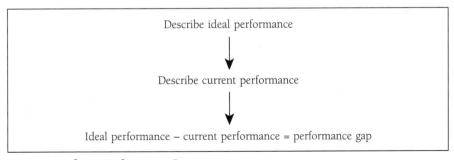

FIGURE 1. Defining Performance Gaps

Once performance gaps are identified and prioritized, it is necessary to reflect on whether such gaps can be closed by training. For example, in the early stages of the program, a training needs assessment was carried out to find out what particular performance gaps existed for teacher educators preparing primary English teachers in Egypt. Analysis showed that understanding and utilizing communicative language teaching techniques for young learners and supervising teachers of young learners were among the most frequently identified performance gaps. Clearly, training was the appropriate means to close performance gaps in these areas.

Training is not always the best way to target performance improvements. For example, individual mentoring schemes, small working parties, or alternative means might on occasion be more appropriate. A specific instance involves school-based training organized for teachers in remote areas in which supervisors attend a central training course. After that, a mentoring (rather than a training) model is utilized as it is felt to be the most appropriate means of intervention. Each supervisor teaches a senior teacher from each school in the district. The senior teacher then also becomes a mentor, responsible for transferring the training to colleagues in school.

On other occasions, changes in educational policy or procedures may be needed to ensure that performance improves. When we asked senior staff members within the Ministry of Education to explore performance gaps in the population of supervisors, they raised a number of systemic issues that were inextricably linked to social and economic factors. For example, we were told that supervisors were underpaid and spent much of their time traveling great distances to reach the vast number of schools under their supervision. Clearly we could do little about this through training alone.

There is a tendency for trainers to conduct a needs assessment and then immediately design a training course to fulfill that need regardless of constraints. Strategic training ensures that the training not only addresses a real need but also involves assessment of whether that need can be met more effectively and efficiently in ways other than direct face-to-face training.

Kirkpatrick Model

The Kirkpatrick model is based on four levels as shown in Figure 2. Level 1, reaction, measures trainee satisfaction. This can include satisfaction with any aspect of the course including content, methods, trainer, logistics, venue, and materials. However, measuring satisfaction tells us nothing about whether trainees have actually learned anything. Even if we ask trainees if they feel they have learned anything, this tells us only about their own perception. Allwright (1984) talks of a conspiracy in the classroom: If the teacher does his or her job and the students enjoy the lessons, then learning is deemed to take place. The same is even truer of the training context.

Level 2, learning, measures what participants have actually learned in terms of new knowledge, skills, and attitudes (KSA). It is commonly administered at the end of the training event and is most usually in the form of a criterion-referenced test. However, because strategic training aims at changing individual job performance, it is still not enough to look only at learning. We need to see whether the learning can be used on the job.

Level 3, behavior, looks at whether or not the trainees have been able to apply what they have learned in their schools and institutions. In other words, we look at

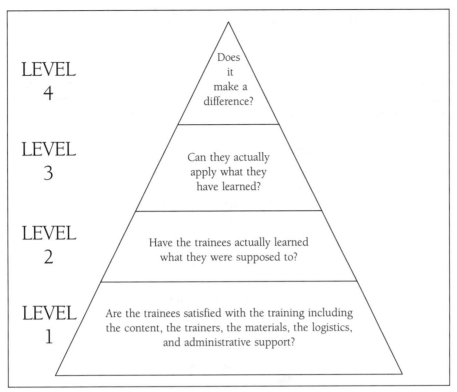

FIGURE 2. Kirkpatrick's Four Levels

whether the trainee has been able to transfer the learning from the training room to the workplace, in this case the classroom or school.

In common with other aid-funded initiatives, many large-scale English language training (ELT) projects wish to look not just at the effects training has had on the individual but also at the broader impact of training. Level 4, results, looks at any wider change—institutional or systemwide—that has come about as a result of strategic training (Kirkpatrick, 1998). It is closely allied to a so-called *impact evaluation* that looks at the longer lasting and intended or unintended effect of training in a broader community. In practice, this level can be extremely difficult to apply because it is costly, the outcomes can be difficult to observe, and it can be time consuming. In addition, because institutional change takes place over time and involves a greater number of people, it is often difficult to attribute the institutional changes to a particular training activity or to a series of training activities.

Evaluation Within IELP

The M&E division ensures that realistic monitoring and data management systems are in place and that evaluation data are collected for all activities. The unit is crucial to the IELP-II performance-based approach to strategic training.

M&E's primary objective is providing timely feedback concerning the status of its many activities. It is important to note that M&E does not work in a vacuum. The unit coordinates closely with the PDI division to (a) design, test, and implement appropriate instruments to collect data and information; (b) provide reports and feedback to program staff, management, and USAID; and (c) identify best practices in teaching English as a foreign language so that activities can be improved. At IELP-II, planning, implementation, and evaluation go hand in hand. The process IELP-II follows is a cycle of activity design, implementation, monitoring, feedback, and decision making that occurs repeatedly over time (see Figure 3).

Application of the System

According to Denakpo et al. (1997), "training planned in isolation from stakeholders could be strategic in theory but condemned to failure or mediocrity in practice" (p. 16). IELP-II adheres to a participatory approach with stakeholder involvement by regularly meeting with its primary stakeholders to develop and provide the most effective training programs possible. Only with this close collaboration will the stakeholders have a vested interest in individual and institutional performance improvements.

During the planning stages of any IELP-II training activity, those responsible for the activity's implementation meet with those responsible for the monitoring and

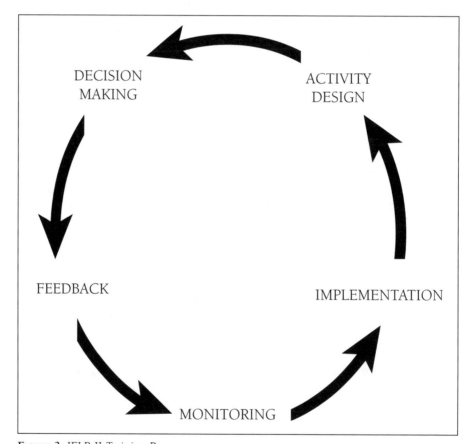

FIGURE 3. IELP-II Training Process

describe in precise terms the objectives on which the success or lack of success of the activity will be measured. They begin by developing a Level 1 instrument to measure satisfaction. During the final hours of the training activity, a member of the M&E staff distributes the instrument to the participants. M&E has a set of established conventions that it adheres to when a training evaluation or Level 1 instrument is administered, although a range of traditional and less traditional methods can be used to gather such information. Finally, M&E analyze and interpret the data.

M&E also manages the development and administration of the Level 2 instrument to check if learning has taken place. This may be accomplished in several ways. Most often, when a training provider carries out the activities, IELP-II writes the Level 2 monitoring activities into the trainer's contract. The M&E staff member assigned to the particular activity must carefully examine the instrument to be sure that it does indeed measure learning. In addition to pencil-and-paper tests, we often use other means of testing such as exit interviews, demonstrations, or projects to try to tap into the skills that our participants have acquired.

So far, IELP-II has been directly responsible for all Level 3 evaluations carried out. To help ensure that workplace transfer takes place, IELP-II training activities often involve action plans. Before completing the training activity action plan, the participants are asked to reflect on the new KSA acquired during training and to produce a plan that demonstrates exactly how they will incorporate the new KSA into their particular workplace (e.g., classrooms, training rooms). By creating these plans, the participants create contracts between themselves and IELP-II, thus increasing the likelihood that transfer will occur.

At some point after the training, preferably between 3 and 6 months later, IELP-II staff members go into the field to determine whether training has transferred into the workplace. The Level 3 evaluation may include classroom observation, focus groups, individual interviews, and participant narratives. No matter which method is employed, it also helps to measure the responses of a control group who did not receive training. Although this is not always feasible, it does increase reliability when carried out.

◈ DISTINGUISHING FEATURES

IELP-II Training Is Not Planned and Carried Out in Isolation

Through the application of strategic training, IELP-II has developed enhanced partnerships with the Ministry of Education, university faculties of education, and components of the private sector in Egypt. Our partners have worked carefully with us in determining the performance gaps and addressing these gaps, developing the training programs' objectives, selecting the trainees, administering the training, and monitoring of training activities.

Training Activities Are Evaluated at a Variety of Levels

This is to ensure quality-training programs to our clients. Not only are trainees asked to provide feedback on their satisfaction with the course or training activity, they are also required to demonstrate the acquisition of KSA and to show how the training has resulted in workplace performance changes.

Evaluation System's Positive Effect

We have found that the evaluation system had a positive effect on the nature of the training itself. Instead of concerning themselves merely with satisfying the participants, trainers have had to focus on achievement of tangible objectives and bear in mind broader aspects of organizational change. Trainers are accountable not just for satisfying the trainees but for making sure that the time spent on training results in learning.

Model Is Widely Applicable and User Friendly

Kirkpatrick provides us with a uniform system that has a wide applicability over a range of contexts. It works well for technical skills as well as soft-skills training.

Evaluation System Provides a Feedback Loop

The evaluation system employed by IELP-II provides detailed information on how people are performing as a result of training as well as how they are reacting. The system allows for a feedback loop where results of the evaluation feed directly into decision making for the future.

System Was Easily Transferable Into Our Context

Perhaps the most valuable feature that makes this evaluation program different from others is that it has easily transferred to our clients with very little effort on our part. The system is clear and easily understood. Indeed, Levels 1, 2, and 3 have entered the vocabulary of many of the participants who have been trained through the project. In addition to the vocabulary, many of our participants have taken the very model we have used to assess the training that they carry out in the classrooms and training rooms across Egypt, routinely administering Levels 1 and 2 instruments at the end of each training activity. The evaluation culture that exists within IELP-II has spread to its partners.

◈ PRACTICAL IDEAS

Develop a Checklist of Responsibilities

The following checklist, a 12-step process, summarizes possible steps in planning and carrying out an evaluation. The individual or group responsible can carry out the different steps depending on available expertise and interest. Decisions can be based on focus groups, interviews, questionnaires, and consultations with partners:

1. Identify performance gaps.
2. Determine if performance gaps can be closed through training.
3. Prioritize performance gaps if necessary.
4. Plan training event in conjunction with evaluation.
5. Establish course objectives and related indicators for the evaluation.
6. Write SMART objectives (explained below).
7. Select and write instruments.

8. Conduct training.

9. Analyze.

10. Interpret and report on results.

11. Conduct Level 3 instrument after the training event to see if training has transferred.

12. Analyze and interpret results of Level 3 instrument to feedback into the design of training programs.

It is useful to put the above checklist into a planning grid to fix timings and assign tasks to individuals.

Prioritize Training Needs at the Planning Stage

We have used a range of techniques to prioritize training needs. Table 1 illustrates one example in which educators from Egyptian faculties of education were encouraged to look at their own strengths and weaknesses relating to training possibilities available and prioritize areas for their own development. Although this example requires individuals to set their own priorities from a menu of options, these surveys are useful tools we have used on a number of occasions to set wider priorities.

Set SMART Course Objectives

The setting of clear and measurable course objectives is important if the evaluation is to be useful. All trainers are instructed to provide SMART objectives for the courses they are running. These objectives should be:

- *specific* (S): in terms of what trainees should know or should be able to do rather than what the trainer intends to do in the session

- *measurable* (M): phrased in terms of measurable actions

- *agreed* (A): objectives requiring the involvement of others in the educational hierarchy need to be agreed on beforehand

- *realistic* (R): given the training population and the constraints we operate within

- *time bound* (T): change needs to be linked to a time period

Plan Appropriate Instruments

Level 1 instruments we have used ranged from questionnaires to more creative assessments of satisfaction. Unlike Level 1 questionnaires, the Level 2 instrument must be unique for each activity. The items in this instrument should be a summative measure of the material covered during the training activity to determine if the objectives of training are met.

Sample Level 2 instruments include paper-and-pencil tests; presentations; demonstrations; simulations; case studies; problem-solving scenarios; and products such as lesson plans, tests, teaching materials, posters, curriculum outlines, and journals. In deciding what type of evaluation activity is appropriate at Level 2, it is necessary to ask the following questions (see p. 175):

TABLE 1. PROFILE QUESTIONNAIRE

Consider how confident you feel about your practice in the following areas: 1 = not very confident; 5 = very confident					

Pedagogy

• Familiarity with the first language acquisition process	1	2	3	4	5
• Knowledge of children's learning styles and strategies	1	2	3	4	5
• Presenting a language lesson to children	1	2	3	4	5
• Games, songs, and chants for children in English	1	2	3	4	5
• Arts and crafts activities for children	1	2	3	4	5
• Providing context for target language	1	2	3	4	5
• Teaching vocabulary to children	1	2	3	4	5
• Teaching listening skills to children	1	2	3	4	5
• Enabling children to acquire the grammar of English	1	2	3	4	5
• Providing a variety of motivating and interesting learning experiences for children	1	2	3	4	5
• Providing clear directions in English	1	2	3	4	5
• Asking questions in English	1	2	3	4	5
• Managing large classes for children efficiently	1	2	3	4	5
• Assessing children's language progress accurately	1	2	3	4	5
• Motivating children to enjoy language learning	1	2	3	4	5
• Other:					

Observation

• Familiarity with observation instruments	1	2	3	4	5
• Evaluating usefulness of observation instruments	1	2	3	4	5
• Focusing on the important within a lesson	1	2	3	4	5
• Providing feedback after a lesson	1	2	3	4	5
• Other:					

Evaluation

• Evaluating teachers against agreed criteria	1	2	3	4	5
• Other:					

Administrative

• Ability to liaise with senior teachers	1	2	3	4	5
• Ability to liaise with the Ministry and Faculty of Education	1	2	3	4	5
• Managing time	1	2	3	4	5
• Completing routine administrative tasks	1	2	3	4	5
• Other:					

- What are the learning objectives to be assessed in the activity?
- What are the time constraints to be considered?
- Are there other constraints that need to be considered (e.g., space)?
- What is the most suitable assessment tool for measuring the success of the activity?
- Are there multiple indicators of performance for each learning objective? What are they?
- Should pre- and postassessments be used?

Use an Administration Protocol

Given that the Level 1, 2, and 3 instruments are administered by so many different individuals in different settings in different parts of the country, it is important to follow a protocol to ensure that the administration of these instruments is reliable.

The word *protocol* when used in this context refers to the steps or guidelines that must be followed when a trainer is administering an evaluation to trainees. In other words, a monitoring and evaluation protocol is the set of conventions that should always be followed carefully when a training evaluation is administered (see Table 2).

Organize the Transition to the Workplace

It is important not to assume that workplace transfer will take place automatically. It is essential to provide support and encouragement during the transition stage. Support starts in the training room with the development of action plans outlining the participant's projected implementation goals. Part of the action plan may include support required on the part of IELP-II to make job place performance changes. After participants return to their schools or training rooms, follow-up visits or correspondence are often necessary. This contact helps to identify if participants are actually

TABLE 2. LEVEL 1 EVALUATION PROTOCOL

Trainee Satisfaction Questionnaire
1. Explain the purpose of this questionnaire (i.e., to get feedback on trainees' level of satisfaction and the degree to which they feel that they mastered the learning objectives of the training). Trainees are actually expressing their personal assessment of the value of the training.
2. Tell the trainees that they should **not** write their names on this questionnaire.
3. Mention that there is no right or wrong answer. The trainees should feel free to express their opinions regarding the training. Explain how this will assist in improving or changing the training.
4. Explain the rating scale to the trainees if there is one.
5. Ask the trainees to complete this questionnaire individually. They may not discuss specific items with other trainees.
6. Make sure that the trainers are not in the room when trainees complete this evaluation, and ask someone to collect all of the forms and put them in an envelope.

applying their new KSA in the field. It also gives us the opportunity to discover barriers that participants may face and allows for corrective action.

⬦ CONCLUSION

Kirkpatrick (1998) claims that his model is the most widely used approach to training evaluation in the corporate, government, and academic worlds. Despite this claim, his four-level model seems to have been largely ignored by the world of language teaching.

In this case study we wished to show how this model could be applied in an ELT training context. We also wished to show the importance of involving partners, tutors, and course managers at all stages of the evaluation process so that evaluation is an integrated participatory experience.

We believe that in adopting the Kirkpatrick framework, we are more confident about the effectiveness of our training. We are more confident in providing our sponsors with concrete evidence of the training's value. We believe that our efforts to provide quality effective training continue to improve. Although Einstein's quote at the beginning of this chapter will always have some truth, by adopting and adapting the Kirkpatrick framework, we are confident that we are counting what counts.

⬦ CONTRIBUTORS

Barbara Thornton is a consultant based in London, United Kingdom. She was previously the coordinator of the MA TESOL program at Leicester University, United Kingdom, and has published widely in teacher education.

Dina El-Araby has been involved in teacher training for 22 years and manages the Educational Resources Unit at IELP-II.

Robert Burch works on a USAID-funded training program in Egypt. He has extensive experience as a teacher, teacher trainer, and evaluator of TEFL programs in the United States and abroad.

CHAPTER 13

Consensus, Control, and Continuity in a University ESOL Program

James Campbell, Julie Howard, Judith A. Kent, Ana King, Kristin Lems, and Gale Stam

◈ INTRODUCTION

This chapter discusses assessment in a five-level, semi-intensive, grammar-based, integrated skills English for speakers of other languages (ESOL) program at National-Louis University (NLU), a private institution in Chicago. A major goal of the ESOL program is to provide students with academic English necessary to succeed in undergraduate studies at the university. Both qualitative and quantitative assessment practices are used to determine if this goal is being met. This case study covers the regular assessment of three areas: program, faculty, and students. It describes the program's unique system of coordination that allows for participation of all faculty in the examination and revision of curriculum in the classroom, language lab, and computer lab components. This program has grown from a 40-student weekday program in 1979 to its current status, with over 300 students from more than 20 countries who attend morning, evening, or weekend classes. Its strength has depended on the systematic assessment of the three aforementioned areas.

◈ CONTEXT

The Department of Applied Language (DAL) and the Language Institute (LI) represent the university's special commitment to those students for whom English is an additional language. The DAL is the academic unit to which faculty, courses, and programs belong. The LI provides administrative support to the department by maintaining records, coordinating schedules, and compiling program data. The five-level ESOL program constitutes the major thrust of the DAL, which is an integral, recognized unit within the College of Arts and Sciences, one of three colleges within the university.

The ESOL program's primary purpose is to provide quality instruction to individuals who need English skills to achieve personal, professional, and academic goals. Located in a major metropolitan area, the program strives to make students aware of the multicultural society that surrounds them and to help them participate in it. The purpose and goals of the program are consistent with the university's history of service to urban, immigrant, and minority populations.

The target population of the ESOL program is full-time freshmen who are admitted to the university and who are found to have limited English proficiency. The vast majority of ESOL students are recent immigrants. All students who enroll in the program must have the equivalent of U.S. high school diplomas. Students come from a variety of academic backgrounds. Some have engaged in postsecondary study, whereas others are more traditional college freshmen. A majority of students are between 20 and 24 years old, but ages may range from 18 to over 60. Regardless of age, nearly all of the students are employed in full or part-time jobs. A 2000 departmental survey found that students are highly motivated, reasonably comfortable with their life situations, and appreciative of the opportunity to study in a multicultural environment.

The five-level program is grammar based and academic, with emphasis on the skills that will allow students to succeed in baccalaureate programs. ESOL Level 1–5 courses range from zero to low-advanced proficiency and are semi-intensive, meeting 14 hours each week. Eleven of these hours are spent with a single classroom instructor, and the remaining hours are spent in computer and language labs. Students may choose a weekday (morning or evening) or weekend schedule.

The courses are credit bearing, and students may apply up to 39 quarter hours (i.e., 39 hours of class during an academic quarter) of ESOL credit as free electives toward a baccalaureate degree. Levels 1 and 2 issue grades on a pass/fail basis; Levels 3–5 issue grades of A, B, C, and U (unsatisfactory), following the university's grading scale. The department chooses not to issue the grade of D. Students who complete ESOL Level 5 are immediately eligible to enroll in degree program coursework at the university; no special testing is imposed by the colleges.

Bridging activities designed to increase retention of students beyond ESOL Level 5 are implemented at Levels 3, 4, and 5. The activities consist of informing students about the U.S. university system, careers, and degree options at the university. In addition, students at Level 5 are surveyed regarding their future study plans and are invited to meet individually with full-time DAL faculty mentors to discuss their educational needs and goals. Data gathered from these surveys and mentoring appointments are forwarded to advisors in the respective degree programs at NLU. Writing Skills Development, a post-Level 5 writing course, is offered by the department to support continuing students.

In addition, the DAL faculty and LI staff collaborate on specific-purpose, noncredit programs to serve the needs of students who cannot be accommodated by the five-level ESOL program. These efforts include English for working professionals and for learners who need preparation before entering Level 1 of the ESOL program.

The DAL also has designed and consulted on a series of courses in English as a foreign language (EFL) and business EFL at Wyzsza Szkola Biznesu–NLU in southeastern Poland. NLU has had an articulation agreement with this postsecondary business school since 1992.

◈ DESCRIPTION

Program

The ESOL program is assessed and approved at several levels of the university, including the department, the college, the university-wide curriculum and program review committees, and the office of the provost.

NLU recently engaged in an assessment review as part of a reaccreditation process. This provided the department with the opportunity to look at the ESOL program's many and varied assessment instruments, describe them, evaluate their effectiveness, and propose improvements. In 1993, the DAL initiated and conducted a self-study using TESOL postsecondary guidelines. Observations by outside evaluators from the profession and from other disciplines have helped the department identify its strengths and weaknesses.

The curriculum is tightly controlled for quality. Most of the ongoing evaluation of the ESOL curriculum takes place by means of the program's special coordination system (see Figure 1). Each course and lab component of the program has a coordinator who is responsible for its curriculum and who serves as a mentor and facilitator to faculty at the level. The group of coordinators meets each term to discuss articulation among the levels. At these meetings, proposals that come from the levels are discussed and initiatives are presented and considered. The coordinators may also undertake long- and short-term multilevel projects such as curriculum review; writing across the curriculum; comparison of final exam scoring systems; and a reexamination of the reading, writing, and oral components.

In addition, coordinators hold quarterly meetings with the instructors at their respective levels. Agenda items such as consistency in grading and modifications to final exams may be discussed. Moreover, it is at these meetings that needs are assessed and proposals take shape. More significant items, such as changes in course competencies or textbooks, are agreed upon and referred to the coordinators for action.

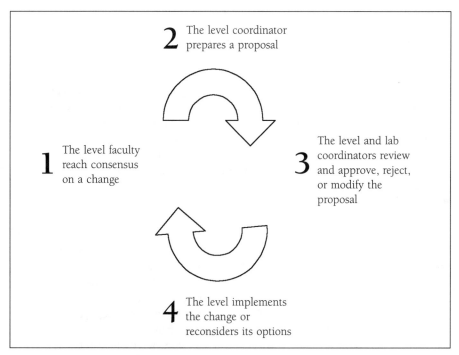

2 The level coordinator prepares a proposal

1 The level faculty reach consensus on a change

3 The level and lab coordinators review and approve, reject, or modify the proposal

4 The level implements the change or reconsiders its options

FIGURE 1. The ESOL Coordination System at Work

The university registrar keeps a complete set of master course outlines, updated every 5 years. The department also has a complete list of course competencies and a syllabus for each course. In addition, the department maintains a current list of required texts, including a core grammar text for each course, a reader, idioms books, and other supplementary materials, which include faculty-generated resource books and a list of language and computer laboratory materials used at each level. Each level has a substantial resource file from which instructors may obtain individual handouts or quizzes. The resource file is regularly enriched by faculty who contribute to it.

Assessment of program success is aided through extensive record keeping by the LI. Each quarter, student retention rates within the program are charted. Retention rates and grade point averages (GPAs) of former ESOL students who continue at the university are tracked as well. The department examines these data regularly for trends both within and beyond the program.

Finally, the program is assessed through an annual setting of goals by the department faculty. Faculty members brainstorm these goals in the spring, prioritize them in the fall, and refer to them throughout the year. At the end of the year, the faculty assess which goals have been fully accomplished, which are ongoing items, and which should be abandoned or revised in light of recent developments. The ongoing goals are carried over to the next year, and new ones are added as needs arise.

Faculty

The ESOL program benefits from a highly qualified faculty, who have graduate degrees in teaching English as a second language (TESL) or related fields and at least 2 years of postsecondary teaching experience. Six of the seven full-time faculty members are tenured. All full-time positions are tenure-track and ranked. Although adjunct faculty are hired on a per-quarter basis, many have more than 5 years of continuous service with the department. The stability within the faculty promotes the commitment, consistency, and academic quality of the program. All new faculty are oriented by the department chair, who provides a copy of the department handbook, which contains information pertinent to performing instructional responsibilities and understanding the organizational context.

In addition to teaching, full-time faculty are responsible for the coordination of a level or lab component of the program. Most adjunct faculty have only the contractual obligations associated with teaching the section or sections assigned and attend a limited number of meetings, but some participate in other program initiatives. Adjunct faculty coordinators receive stipends for their duties.

All faculty are assessed through student course evaluations completed at the end of each quarter. A staff member administers the evaluation, which consists of separate forms for the classroom instructor, the language lab instructor, and the computer lab assistant. The instructor does not see the evaluations until after grades have been turned in, and students must complete the evaluations before the final exam takes place, resulting in a double-blind assessment. Both the level coordinator and the department chair view the course evaluations, and any issues raised in them are addressed in a timely fashion. Instructors also receive a copy of the summary of the evaluations for their records.

Classroom observation of untenured full-time and all adjunct faculty occurs annually. The department chair observes all new adjunct faculty during the first term of employment. Tenured faculty may request that the department chair or another departmental colleague observe them. The peer observation process includes four phases: (a) the determination of an observer, (b) a preobservation meeting, (c) an observation of an hour or more, and (d) a postobservation meeting that takes place within a week following the observation. The two parties discuss the observer's written comments on a form and both sign and retain a copy. The form consists of 16 items pertaining to knowledge of the subject matter, clarity and organization of presentation, methodology, and engagement of students in the learning process.

Level and lab coordinators fill out a self-assessment form that summarizes the duties they have performed during the year, including new faculty trained, level projects undertaken, textbook selection, materials writing, and other activities. This formative assessment gives coordinators an opportunity to take stock of their work annually.

Furthermore, full-time faculty are required by the institution to engage in an annual performance review. It is based on a developmental plan and a setting of goals for each academic year. A self-review is written by the full-time faculty member and submitted to the department chair, who issues a summative rating and then submits it to the college dean. The performance review document is divided into four areas, which are also used for the university tenure and promotion system: (a) quality of instruction, (b) service to the institution, (c) service to the profession, and (d) professional growth and development.

Students

The first assessment of students takes place before program enrollment. A full-time faculty member interviews each student during one of many regularly scheduled assessment sessions, and, at that time, gives the student both an oral screening and a written test. The oral screening is a version of the Oral Language Proficiency Interview (OLPI) used by the Foreign Service Institute, U.S. Department of State, and other U.S. government agencies to evaluate prospective expatriate personnel and has a rubric that assigns six levels of competence in five areas: (a) grammar, (b) vocabulary, (c) accent, (d) fluency, and (e) comprehension. The OLPI is abbreviated because faculty familiar with the program need less than the recommended time period to form an opinion as to placement. The test is scored holistically during or immediately after the 5- to 10-minute audiotaped interview. The interviewer follows up the oral interview by administering a 30-minute writing sample for those at the low-intermediate level or beyond, or a three-part grammar and vocabulary test designed for beginners. The in-house test has 10 multiple-choice items, 10 fill-ins, and a short writing task.

The interviewer evaluates the writing sample or test alongside the ratings on the oral interview and decides into which of the five levels of the program the student should be placed. There is also the option of placing the student beyond the program if his or her proficiency level is sufficiently advanced. The placement process is thoughtful and often involves gathering the opinions of several faculty members.

The placement is reconfirmed with a written pretest given at each level on the first day of class. If a student receives a particularly high score on the pretest, he or she will be given the option of taking the final exam of the level and will be allowed to move to the next level if a score of 80% or above is obtained. Likewise, students who perform poorly on the pretest may be moved down a level. This method of double-checking ensures that placements are highly accurate.

Within the levels, numerous assessment instruments are used, many of them created by the individual instructors. These include a midterm exam, quizzes, and a number of compositions. In addition, a level-standardized final exam is administered in each course, and a score of 70% or above is required to move on to the next level. Each course also has level-specific requirements that are factored into the final grade. These may include attendance, participation, the language lab final exam score, oral presentations, quizzes, or compositions.

Students in Levels 3 and 5 have an end-of-term oral interview, using the modified OLPI. A day is taken out of the schedule for Levels 3 and 5 faculty, trained by their coordinators, to interview each other's students. The OLPI is scored and the result is furnished to the classroom instructor but is not formally factored into the final grade.

Each level also administers a final impromptu writing sample. The samples are placed in students' individual files, along with placement exams, interview results, and grade records. At Level 5, the writing samples are used to help faculty make post-ESOL English coursework recommendations.

Quantitative and qualitative measures of assessment are used in the reporting of students' final course grades and progress during a course. In addition to the standard university grade sheet, ESOL instructors complete summary sheets that are maintained in the program's files. On a grid form, instructors provide information about each student, including the oral interview score (for Levels 3 and 5), final exam and language lab exam scores, and the course grade. An important feature of this evaluation form is the comment section. Instructors document students' strengths and weaknesses in all skill areas. In addition, information regarding attendance, participation, overall performance, and pertinent personal situations (e.g., employment, physical limitations) may be noted. This ultimately serves to facilitate students' learning in that subsequent instructors have access to the information and are thus able to respond to individual learning and, perhaps, personal needs.

Finally, the department holds an annual award ceremony, honoring both current and former students of the ESOL program. Both quantitative and qualitative measures are used to evaluate students' achievement within the program, in undergraduate studies at the university, and through professional accomplishments beyond the baccalaureate degree.

An honor roll recognizes current ESOL students who have received high scores on final exams. Students who have scored 93% or above on one final exam during the previous four terms receive achievement awards; those who have done so twice or more receive high achievement awards. A writing award, established in memory of a former DAL faculty member, recognizes excellence in writing among students in Levels 4 and 5. The selection of honorees for writing awards involves qualitative criteria and a nominating process. Faculty at Levels 4 and 5 identify outstanding writers in their classes. They submit a nomination form along with examples of a student's writing, at least one of which has been done in class. An award committee, composed of ESOL faculty not teaching Levels 4 or 5 and an outside reader, discusses each writer's portfolio and determines award recipients.

Students who have completed the program and gone on to achieve academic and professional success within or beyond the university receive distinguished alumni awards. These distinguished alumni are recognized in two categories: (a) current undergraduates at the university and (b) graduates with either baccalaureate or master's degrees. The department invites nominations from the university community. The quantitative and qualitative criteria for nominations are GPA, academic honors, professional success, contributions to the community, and attribution of success to the ESOL program. Full-time department faculty evaluate the nominations and select the recipients of these awards.

This combination of student assessment practices reveals a system of careful, constant, and ongoing tracking of student achievement and progress that extends beyond the confines of Levels 1 through 5. This tracking relies on the input of a very large group of faculty and on the efficiency of record keeping by staff in yet another example of a multifaceted, synchronized system.

◈ DISTINGUISHING FEATURES

Coordination

The program-wide system of coordination is at the core of a finely tuned system of checks and balances at various levels that strengthens the assessment of the program, the faculty, and the students. Its organization and immediate channels of communication provide for a regular and direct connection among adjunct faculty, individual full-time and adjunct faculty coordinators, and the group of coordinators. It provides a voice to all faculty and thus maintains and enhances their investment in the program.

Although proposed changes may originate at either the departmental or coordination level, the quality and extent of changes are controlled. This system of checks and balances allows for seamless change within the context of the program but controls the quality and the extent of change. It is important because the levels are intricately interwoven, and any change can affect another level whether it is contiguous or not.

Because coordinators report on a regular basis on their respective levels and labs, it is possible to have a program-at-a-glance perspective that allows for ongoing, natural assessment. This system of coordination allows for strong integration among classroom, language lab, and computer lab components. It takes advantage of the multiple perspectives of faculty through creation and compilation of level- or lab-specific workbooks. These tailor-made texts reduce teacher preparation time, provide uniformity of supplementary materials, and focus directly on course competencies and objectives.

Bridging

Bridging is done at Levels 3 through 5 and is designed to increase ESOL student retention at the university. There are two significant aspects of the program's bridging activities. The first is the three-phase approach, which moves along a continuum, increasing in linguistic complexity and becoming more individualized as students near completion of the ESOL program. At Level 3, both classroom and language lab activities involve students in reading, listening, and note-taking tasks as they learn about the U.S. university system and become familiar with key terms such as *major* and *GPA*. At Level 4, classroom teachers use graphic organizers and print materials to present students with information about NLU's degree options and the types of courses they will take as they make the transition from ESOL to degree-related coursework. At Level 5, students meet individually with full-time ESOL program faculty, who serve as mentors by helping them identify future fields of study and by explaining how they will work with undergraduate advisors to select courses within their degree areas.

The second aspect of bridging is the recommended course listing created by DAL faculty in consultation with degree program and content faculty. To optimize successful integration into the mainstream, undergraduate advisors are provided with a rubric that delineates courses and sequencing of courses appropriate for former ESOL students at various points in their studies. These guidelines have helped to ensure that, for example, students are enrolled in math and computer courses before philosophy and art history courses in which the language load is heavier. The listing of recommended courses is periodically reviewed and updated in cooperation with the departments that offer them, and faculty provide feedback regarding the preparation and performance of former ESOL students in their programs.

Data Collection and Analysis

The data gathered by DAL/LI assist in the recruitment of new students and the retention of enrolled students. They also indicate the degree of success obtained by students who complete the ESOL program. Basic enrollment information reveals total numbers of students per term or academic year, their countries of origin, new or returning status, and length of time in the United States. In addition, information as to how students become aware of the program is gathered at the time of placement, during the oral interview. The results demonstrate that word of mouth is the program's most effective recruiter and supports confidence in the quality of the program.

Tracking of students' progress throughout the program, previously mentioned in the discussion of internal quarterly grade and summary sheets, extends to interest surveys of Level 5 students pertaining to their future plans. Tracking of students also continues beyond the program and into students' NLU degree coursework. Records of the retention of former Level 5 students are kept, and the GPAs of those students are compared with those of other on-campus undergraduates.

Although labor intensive, the gathering of data allows the program to know the students it serves, and the examination of enrollment trends may indicate marketing or curricular issues to be addressed. Most important, the data can demonstrate the value of the program to the larger institution and community.

Handbook

Early in its history, the program identified and addressed the need for a faculty handbook. Disparate teaching schedules—mornings, evenings, and weekends—and a large number of adjunct faculty, many of whom also taught at other institutions, led to the production of this orientation tool and resource. The *DAL Faculty Handbook* contains several kinds of information. Background information on the program and its organization offers context. The *Handbook* describes the campus, its facilities, and various offices and provides a quick reference guide with telephone extensions. It also includes copies of NLU policies on academic honesty, disruptive classroom behavior, and other instructional issues and exhibits sample grade sheets and lab assignment forms. All of these features serve to help new faculty acclimatize.

However, for assessment of instructional staff, the most significant portions of the *Handbook* deal with faculty responsibilities and evaluation. During one-on-one orientation sessions, the department chair indicates relevant role descriptions (e.g., adjunct, full-time, coordinating faculty) and discusses the student course evaluation and peer observation forms. By informing faculty of expectations related to their performance, the *Handbook* helps to ensure that meeting those expectations, and even exceeding them, is a common occurrence.

Peer Observation

DAL has strengthened faculty voice through the revision of its classroom observation process. The observation process allows faculty to participate actively in a formative evaluation as opposed to a summative one. A committee composed of adjunct and full-time faculty revised the observation form to eliminate quantitative criteria and to encourage more specific narrative feedback. It also developed the four-phase process mentioned in the previous section. First, faculty members may approach a colleague of their choice at the beginning of the academic year to arrange the observation. Should a faculty member not wish to choose, the observer is determined on a volunteer basis from among the coordinators. Second, in the preobservation conference, faculty have the opportunity to discuss expectations of the upcoming observation and personal instructional goals. It is at this time that they may request the observer to focus on specific aspects of the lesson. Third is the scheduled classroom visit of 1 hour or more. The process concludes with a postobservation conference in which both parties reflect on and discuss the session. The observed faculty member may elect to respond in writing to the written comments or points of discussion.

Award Ceremony

A special feature of student assessment in this program culminates in the Annual ESOL Student and Alumni Award Ceremony, a public event held to recognize the academic and professional achievements of current and former students. The planning and organization of the ceremony follow specific guidelines and timelines as established by the department. The department selects and contacts the honorees and guest speakers. Academic administrators, students, faculty, staff, donors, and the media are invited. A program book that features biographical information on the distinguished alumni and writing awards winners is published and distributed at the event.

Inception of the ceremony in 1997 began a tradition that has resulted in increased exposure for the program, a closer connection to the community, and an increased sense of loyalty between the institution and former students. The occasion further provides an opportunity for marketing and advertising. Perhaps the most rewarding by-product of the awards ceremony is the visible evidence of considerable pride on the part of students and their families, faculty, and staff.

◈ PRACTICAL IDEAS

Implement a Comprehensive System of Coordination

A comprehensive system of course or component coordination should be implemented and should involve all faculty employed in the program. When a variety of individuals have program responsibilities, diverse perspectives are brought forth, and having a say in curricular decisions and how they are implemented can boost morale and create a sense of ownership and belonging.

Create a Program-Specific Faculty Handbook

The *Handbook,* which is periodically updated and revised, provides background information about the university, the department, and the program and also serves as a guide to the facility, key personnel, and their functions. The handbook is an essential element in the orientation of new faculty, both full-time and adjunct, and because it contains role descriptions, course evaluation and classroom observation forms, and relevant university policies, ensures that all instructional staff are aware of what is expected of them and how they will be evaluated.

Institute a Peer Observation Process

The classroom observation of one colleague by another results in the professional growth of both parties through demonstration and exchange of strategies and materials. Moreover, by extending the opportunity to observe to all instructors, the faculty as a whole is better informed about various courses and components of the program. In a large program, the system also facilitates interaction among faculty who might otherwise never get to know each other.

Honor Successful Students Through an Award Ceremony

Public recognition delights and even amazes some students, who assume their efforts and accomplishments have gone unnoticed. The ceremony also provides role models and inspiration for other students, who may be struggling with life changes and studies. Be sure to invite faculty from other disciplines and administrators, who will be impressed with the quality of your students and program. Do not forget to include former awardees to maintain contact with them and to strengthen the sense of community.

◈ CONCLUSION

The purpose of assessment is to validate and measure specific outcomes for the program, faculty, and students. The department must consider whether the program is fulfilling its mission and purpose, how well it is doing so, and how assessment practices are used to revise and improve the program within the framework of the college and university.

The assessment practices of this ESOL program take place within the context of a strong, central system that is composed of multiple layers and a significant number of equal partners. The complexity of the network does not encumber the smooth functioning of the various aspects of the program, nor does it impose undue restrictions on the participants. On the contrary, each element is so firmly in place that it serves to sustain others.

DAL faculty constantly seek ways to build upon success and find new ways to enhance the ESOL program. Future directions focus on assessment in two areas: program and students. In addition, the wealth of data collected on all students in the ESOL program has the potential to provide a rich source of information for various types of research, and many faculty members have expressed interest in this area.

The department has demonstrated that it has an abundance of outcomes and expectations for all aspects of the ESOL program. It has shown how these are assessed; it uses measures that are qualitative and quantitative, formative and summative. All results are filtered through a unique system of coordination, which then focuses on addressing all aspects of the program. The system functions with checks and balances, consensus, and focused purpose. The DAL faculty and LI staff have implemented an efficient, thorough, comprehensive, and ongoing program of assessment.

◈ CONTRIBUTORS

James Campbell has been with the Department of Applied Language (DAL) at National-Louis University (NLU) since 1988. He has been active in learning and teaching languages for 25 years. Before coming to NLU, he had taught in Zurich, Switzerland, and elsewhere in the United States. Further interests include materials development for English as a second language (ESL) and native speaker learners, particularly in grammar and writing.

Julie Howard has been employed in NLU's ESOL program since 1980 and has taught nearly all of the courses offered by the DAL. She is the author of an ESL textbook and maintains a special interest in materials and curriculum development.

Judith A. Kent joined the DAL in 1989. Her experience includes teaching in France, Italy, and the United States. A coresearcher with James Campbell in individual characteristics and learning styles, she is also interested in ESL writing and accent modification.

Ana King has been working in NLU's ESOL program since its inception and has taught at many levels and in the language laboratory component. She has also developed curriculum for and taught in the EFL program at NLU's campus in Poland. Her areas of interest include the teaching and development of oral proficiency.

Kristin Lems spent 2 years as a Fulbright scholar in Algeria doing postsecondary in-service EFL teacher training before coming to NLU. She is pursuing a doctorate in reading and language and is interested in issues related to music, rhythm, and reading. She is also a performing folksinger with several recordings.

Gale Stam has taught and coordinated several ESOL levels and writing skills development courses at NLU since 1985. In addition to her work with nonnative speakers, she teaches grammar to native speakers. Her research focuses on gesture and second language acquisition as well as gesture and lexical retrieval and failure in second language development.

References

Abdal-Haaq, I. (1998). *Professional development schools: Weighing the evidence*. Thousand Oaks, CA: Corwin.

Academic English Program. (1998). Retrieved February 14, 2003, from Texas Tech University Web site: http://www.ttu.edu/esl

Alexander, P. A., & Parsons, J. L. (1991). Confronting the misconceptions of testing and assessment. *Contemporary Education, 62,* 243–249.

Allan, J. (1996). Learning outcomes in higher education. *Studies in Higher Education, 21*(1), 93–109.

Allwright, R. L. (1984). Why don't learners learn what teachers teach? The interaction hypothesis. In D. M. Singleton & D. G. Little (Eds.), *Language learning in formal and informal contexts* (pp. 3–18). Dublin, Ireland: Irish Association of Applied Linguistics.

American Educational Research Association. (1999). *Standards for educational and psychological testing*. Washington, DC: Author.

Bachman, L. F., & Palmer, A. S. (1996). *Language testing in practice: Designing and developing useful language tests*. Oxford: Oxford University Press.

Bahr, M. W., & Bahr, C. M. (1997). Educational assessment in the next millennium: Contributions of technology. *Preventing School Failure, 41,* 90–94.

Basturkmen, H. (1999). Discourse in MBA seminars: Towards a description for pedagogical purposes. *English for Specific Purposes Journal, 18*(1), 63–80.

Basturkmen, H. (2000). The organization of discussion in university settings. *Text, 20*(3), 249–269.

Belanoff, P., & Dickson, M. (1991). *Portfolios: Process and product*. Portsmouth, NH: Boyton/Cook.

Bereiter, C., & Scardamalia, M. (1996). Cognition and curriculum. In P. W. Jackson (Ed.), *Handbook of research on curriculum* (pp. 517–542). New York: Macmillan.

Berry, V., & Lewkowicz, J. (2000). Exit-tests. Is there an alternative? *Hong Kong Journal of Applied Linguistics, 5*(1), 19–49.

Bolton, S. (2000, November). *Response to student writing in large-scale assessment*. Paper presented at the annual conference of the Japan Association of Language Teachers, Shizuoka City, Japan.

Bonham, S. W., Beichner, R. J., & Titus, A. (2000). Education research using Web-based assessment systems. *Journal of Research on Computing in Education, 33*(1), 28–45.

Boulima, J. (1999). *Negotiated interaction in target language classroom discourse*. Amsterdam, Holland: John Benjamins.

Bowers, D. A., & Bowers, V. M. (1996). Assessing and coping with computer anxiety in the social science classroom. *Social Science Computer Review, 14,* 439–443.

Brady, L. (1997). Assessing curriculum outcomes in Australian schools. *Education Review, 49*(1), 57–66.

Brindley, G. (1998). Outcomes-based assessment and reporting in language learning programmes: A review of the issues. *Language Testing, 15*(1), 45–85.

Brindley, G. (2001). *Teaching, learning, and assessment in the language curriculum: Towards an embedded model*. Plenary presented at the Fifth Current Trends in English Language Testing Conference, Dubai, United Arab Emirates.

Brown, J. D. (1989). Improving ESL placement tests using two perspectives. *TESOL Quarterly, 23*(1), 65–83.

Brown, J. D. (1990). Where do tests fit into language programs? *JALT Journal, 12*(1), 121–140.

Brown, J. D. (1993). A comprehensive criterion-referenced language testing project. In D. Douglas & C. Chapelle (Eds.), *A new decade of language testing research* (pp. 163–184). Alexandria, VA: TESOL.

Brown, J. D. (1995). *The elements of language curriculum: A systematic approach to program development*. New York: Heinle & Heinle.

Brown, J. D. (1996a, February 5). Japanese entrance exams: A measurement problem? *Daily Yomiuri*, p. 15.

Brown, J. D. (1996b). *Testing in language programs*. Upper Saddle River, NJ: Prentice Hall Regents.

Brown, J. D. (1997). Computers in language testing: Present research and some future directions [Electronic version]. *Language Learning and Technology, 1*(1), 44–59. Retrieved February 14, 2001, from http://llt.msu.edu/vol1num1/BROWN/default.html

Brown, J. D., & Hudson, T. (1998). The alternatives in language assessment. *TESOL Quarterly, 32*, 653–675.

Brown, J. D., & Yamashita, S. O. (Eds.). (1995). In D. T. Griffee (Series Ed.), *JALT applied materials: Vol. 1. Language testing in Japan*. Tokyo: Japan Association of Language Teachers.

Buell, J. (1996). Testing English—What for? *On CUE, 4*(2), 24.

Bugbee, A. C. (1996). The equivalence of paper-and-pencil and computer-based testing. *Journal of Research on Computing in Education, 28*, 282–299.

Calfee, R. C. (1994). Cognitive assessment of classroom learning. *Education and Urban Society, 26*, 340–351.

Calfee, R. C., & Hiebert, E. H. (1988). The teacher's role in using assessment to improve literacy. In C. U. Bunderson (Ed.), *Assessment in the service of learning* (pp. 45–61). Princeton, NJ: Educational Testing Service.

Calfee, R. C., & Hiebert, E. H. (1991). Classroom assessment in reading. In R. Barr, M. Kamil, P. Rosenthal, & P. D. Pearson (Eds.), *Handbook of research on reading* (2nd ed., pp. 281–309). New York: Longman.

Carle, E. (1998). *Hello, red fox*. New York: Simon & Schuster.

Chou, C. (2000). Constructing a computer-assisted testing and evaluation system on the WWW: The CATES experience. *IEEE Transactions on Education, 43*(3), 266–271.

Clay, M. M. (1979). *The early detection of reading difficulties: A diagnostic survey with recovery procedures* (2nd ed.). Portsmouth, NH: Heinemann.

Cohen, E. G. (1994). *Designing groupwork: Strategies for the heterogeneous classroom.* (2nd ed.). New York: Teachers College Press.

Colleges to add hearing skills to tests. (2000, March 22). *Asahi Evening News*, p.1.

Courtney, A. M., & Abodeeb, T. L. (1999). Diagnostic-reflective portfolios. *The Reading Teacher, 52*, 708–714.

Cumming, A. (1990). Expertise in evaluating second language compositions. *Language Testing, 7*(1), 31–51.

Darling-Hammond, L. (2000). How teacher education matters. *Journal of Teacher Education, 51,* 166–173.

Darling-Hammond, L., & Sykes, G. (1999). *Teaching as the learning profession.* San Francisco: Jossey Bass.

Denakpo L., Hart, D., Flederman, P., Gilboy, A., & Sanders-Smith, M. (1997). *The HRDA best practices series: A collection of eight practical manuals for human resource development professionals.* Washington, DC: AMEX International.

Devereux, J. R., Cooper, A., & Ng, L. G. (1992). *Technical institute graduates, English, and the workplace: Executive summary and recommendations.* Hong Kong: Hong Kong Bank Language Development Fund/Institute of Language in Education.

Dewey, J. (1997). *Experience and education.* New York: Simon & Schuster. (Original work published 1938, Kappa Delta Pi.)

Dewsbury, A. (1994). *Reading: Resource book.* Portsmouth, NH: Heinemann.

Dickenson, L. (1987). *Self instruction in language learning.* Cambridge: Cambridge University Press.

Douglas, D. (2000). *Assessing languages for specific purposes.* Cambridge: Cambridge University Press.

Doyon, P. (2001). A review of higher education reform in modern Japan. *Higher Education, 41,* 433–470.

Educational Testing Service. (1997). *TOEFL test and score manual.* Princeton, NJ: Author.

Ehrman, M., & Dornyei, Z. (1998). *Interpersonal dynamics in second language education.* London: Sage.

Eigo listening juushi [Attaching greater importance to English listening test]. (1999, August 20). *Chunichi Shinbun,* p. 34.

Elbow, P. (1993). Ranking, evaluating, and liking: Sorting out three forms of judgment. *College English, 55*(2), 187–206.

Elbow, P., & Belanoff, P. (1991a). State university of New York at Stony Brook portfolio-based evaluation program. In P. Belanoff & M. Dickson (Eds.), *Portfolios: Process and product.* Portsmouth, NH: Boyton/Cook.

Elbow, P., & Belanoff, P. (1991b). Using portfolios to increase collaboration and community in a writing program. In P. Belanoff & M. Dickson (Eds.), *Portfolios: Process and product.* Portsmouth, NH: Boyton/Cook.

English Language Institute. (1962). *Michigan Test of English Language Proficiency manual.* Ann Arbor, MI: Author.

English Language Institute. (1986). *English Language Institute Listening Comprehension Test manual.* Ann Arbor, MI: Author.

ESL Composition Program self-study final report. (1998). Columbus, Ohio: Ohio State University.

Fair assessment of advanced research needed. (2000, November 11). *Daily Yomiuri,* pp. 1, 3.

Falvey, P., & Coniam, D. (1997). Introducing English language benchmarks for Hong Kong teachers: A preliminary overview. *Curriculum Forum, 6*(2), 16–35.

Fitzpatrick, K. A. (1995). Leadership challenges of outcome-based reform. *Education Digest, 60*(5), 13–17.

Flood, J., & Lapp, D. (2000). Teaching writing in urban schools: Cognitive processes, curriculum resources, and the missing links—management and grouping. In R. Indrisano & J. Squire (Eds.), *Perspectives on writing: Research, theory, and practice* (pp. 233–250). Newark, DE: International Reading Association.

Flood, J., Lapp, D., Flood, S., & Nagel, G. (1992). Am I allowed to group? Using flexible patterns for effective instruction. *The Reading Teacher, 45,* 608–616.

Forey, G. (1996, March). *Communication in the professional workplace project—Interim report.* Hong Kong: University of Hong.

Fountas, I. C., & Pinnell, G. S. (1996). *Guided reading: Good first teaching for all children.* Portsmouth, NH: Heinemann.

Frey, N., & Hiebert, E. H. (2002). Teacher-based assessment of literacy learning. In J. Flood, J. M. Jensen, D. Lapp, & J. R. Squire (Eds.), *Handbook of research on teaching the English language arts* (2nd ed.). Mahwah, NJ: Lawrence Erlbaum Associates.

Fulcher, G. (1999). Computerizing an English language placement test. *ELT Journal, 53*(4), 289–299.

Fulcher, G. (2003). *Resources in language testing page* [On-line]. Retrieved April 23, 2003, from http://www.dundee.ac.uk/languagestudies/ltest/ltr.html

Fullan, M. (1999). Leading change in professional learning communities. *Education Update (ASCD), 41*(8), 1.

Furneaux, C., Locke, C., Robinson, P., & Tonkyn, A. (1991). Talking heads and shifting bottoms: The ethnography of academic seminars. In P. Adams, B. Heaton, & P. Howarth (Eds.), *Socio-cultural issues in English for specific purposes* (pp. 75–88). London: Macmillan.

Gaies, S., Bolton, S., & Lyons, C. (2002, April). *Proficiency testing of secondary school EFL.* Paper presented at the annual conference of TESOL, Salt Lake City, UT.

Gaies, S., Johnson, D., Lyons, C., & Bolton, S. (2001, March). *Interrelationships among skill areas in standardized testing.* Paper presented at the annual conference of TESOL, Salt Lake City, UT.

Genesee, F., & Upshur, J. A. (1996). *Classroom-based evaluation in second language education.* Cambridge: Cambridge University Press.

Goldberg, M. A. (1997). WebCT (Version 1.3) [Computer software]. Vancouver, Canada: University of British Columbia.

The good and bad of AO exams. (2001, February 5). *Daily Yomiuri,* p. 7.

Gorsuch, G. J. (1999). Monbusho approved textbooks in Japanese high school EFL classes: An aid or a hindrance to educational policy innovations? *The Language Teacher, 23*(10), 5–15.

Gorsuch, G. (2000). EFL educational policies and educational cultures: Influences on teachers' approval of communicative activities. *TESOL Quarterly, 34,* 675–710.

Gorsuch, G. (2001). Japanese EFL teachers' perceptions of communicative, audiolingual and yakudoku activities: The plan versus the reality [Electronic version]. *Educational Policy Analysis Archives 9*(10). Retrieved February 14, 2003, from http://epaa.asu.edu /epaa/v9n10.html

Gravatt, B., Richards, J., & Lewis, M. (1998). *Language needs in tertiary studies: ESL students at the University of Auckland* (Occasional Paper No. 10). Auckland, New Zealand: Auckland University Press, Department of Applied Language Studies and Linguistics.

Groulx, J., & Thomas, C. (2000). Discomfort zones: Learning about teaching with care and discipline in urban schools. *International Journal of Educational Reform, 9,* 59–69.

GSLPA: English scales for reporting student performance. (n.d.). Retrieved March 29, 2003, from Hong Kong Polytechnic University Web site: http://www.engl.polyu.edu.hk /ACLAR.default.htm

Guest, M. (2000). "But I *have* to teach grammar!": An analysis of the role "grammar" plays in Japanese university English entrance examinations. *The Language Teacher, 24*(11), 23–28.

Hamp-Lyons, L. (1991a). *Assessing second language writing in academic contexts.* Norwood, NJ: Ablex.

Hamp-Lyons, L. (1991b). Scoring procedures for ESL contexts. In L. Hamp-Lyons (Ed.), *Assessing second language writing in academic contexts* (pp. 241–276). Norwood, NJ: Ablex.

Hamp-Lyons, L. (1997). Washback, impact, and validity: Ethical concerns. *Language Testing, 14*(3), 295–303.

Hamp-Lyons, L., & Lumley, T. (1998). *Expectations of exit language proficiency of university graduates in Hong Kong.* Paper presented at the 20th Language Testing Research Colloquium, Monterey, CA.

Hamp-Lyons, L., & Lumley, T. (2000). *Ethical dilemmas in language testing: What can we actually do?* Paper presented at the 22nd Language Testing Research Colloquium, Vancouver, Canada.

Hatch, E. 1992. *Discourse analysis and language education.* Cambridge: Cambridge University Press.

Heinssen, R. K., Glass, C. R., & Knight, L. A. (1987). Assessing computer anxiety: Development and validation of the Computer Anxiety Rating Scale. *Computers in Human Behavior, 3,* 49–59.

Hoberman, M. A. (1999). *And to think we thought we'd never be friends.* New York: Crown.

Hoey, M. 1991. Some properties of spoken discourse. In R. Bowers & C. Brumfit (Eds.), *Applied linguistics and English language teaching* (pp. 65–84). London: Macmillan.

Hong Kong Polytechnic University. (1996). *GSLPA (Graduating Students' Language Proficiency Assessment)-English strand. UGC project code HKP 17.* Hong Kong: Author.

Hong Kong Polytechnic University. (1997). *Report on the GSLPA project extension. Further development and trialling, 1996–97. Report submitted to the UGC.* Hong Kong: Author.

Hong Kong Polytechnic University. (2000). *GSLPA-English: Learning package.* Hong Kong: Author.

Hughes, A. (1989). *Testing for language teachers.* Cambridge: Cambridge University Press.

Institutional Research and Information Management. (2000). *Applied and admitted: Fall 2000.* Retrieved February 20, 2003, from Texas Tech University Web site: http://www .irs.ttu.edu/FACTBOOK/Applied/2000/index.htm

International Reading Association (2000). *Making a difference means making it different: Honoring children's rights to excellence in reading education* [Position statement]. Newark, DE: International Reading Association.

Isaac, S., & Michael, W. (1981). *Handbook in research and evaluation.* San Diego: EdITS.

Ito, K. (2001, January 13). Entrance exam questions test nation's patience. *Daily Yomiuri,* p. 8.

Jacobs, E. L. (1998). KIDTALK: A computerized language screening test. *Journal of Computing in Childhood Education, 9,* 1043–1055.

Johnson, D. W., & Johnson, R. T. (1994). Cooperative learning in second language classes. *The Language Teacher, 18*(10), 4–7.

Johnson, D. W., & Johnson, R. T. (1999). Cooperative learning and assessment. In D. T. Griffee (Series Ed.) & D. Kulge, S. McGuire, D. Johnson, & R. Johnson (Vol. Eds.), *JALT applied materials: Vol. 23. Cooperative learning.* Tokyo: Japan Association of Language Teachers.

Jordan, R. R. (1997). *English for academic purposes.* Cambridge: Cambridge University Press.

Kirkpatrick, D. L. (1998). *Evaluating training programs: The four levels.* San Francisco: Berrett-Koehler.

Kitao, S. K., & Kitao, K. (1996). Testing communicative competence. *The Internet TESL Journal, 2*(5). Retrieved February 13, 2003, from http://iteslj.org/Articles/Kitao-Testing.html

Kluge, D. E. (1994). An interview with Roger and David Johnson. *The Language Teacher, 18*(10), 30–31, 37.

Knight, S. L., Wiseman, D. L., & Cooner, D. (2000). Using collaborative teacher research to determine the impact of professional development school activities on elementary students' math and writing outcomes. *Journal of Teacher Education, 51,* 26–38.

Kokkouritsu daigaku nyuushi [National and public universities' entrance exams]. (2001, August 23). *Asahi Shimbum,* p. 12.

Kolb, D. A. (1984). *Experiential learning: Experience as the source of learning and development*. Englewood Cliffs, NJ: Prentice Hall.

Krashen, S. D. (1992). *Fundamentals of language education*. Beverly Hills, CA: Laredo.

Leamnson, R. (1999). *Thinking about teaching and learning*. Sterling: Stylus Publications.

Levine, M. (1992). *Professional practice schools: Linking teacher education and school reform*. New York: Teachers College Press.

Linacre, J. M., & Wright, B. (1992–1996). *FACETS*. Chicago: MESA Press.

Lipson, M. Y., & Wixson, K. K. (1997). *Assessment and instruction of reading and writing disability*. New York: Longman.

LoCastro, V. (1996). English language education in Japan. In H. Coleman (Ed.), *Society and the Language Classroom* (pp. 40–58). Cambridge: Cambridge University Press.

Long, M. (1984). Process and product in ESL program evaluation. *TESOL Quarterly, 18*, 409–425.

Lumley, T. (1999). *Exit assessment for Hong Kong university students? The implementation of the GSLPA-English*. Paper presented at International Language in Education Conference (ILEC), Chinese University of Hong Kong, Hong Kong.

Lumley, T., & McNamara, T. F. (1995). Rater characteristics and rater bias: Implications for training. *Language Testing, 12* (1), 54–71.

Lynch, B. (1996). *Language program evaluation: Theory and practice*. Cambridge: Cambridge University Press.

Lynch, T., & Anderson, K. (1991). Do you mind if I come in here? A comparison of EAP seminar/discussion materials and the characteristics of real academic interaction. In P. Adams, B. Heaton, & B. Howarth (Eds.), *Socio-cultural issues in English for academic purposes* (pp. 99–99). London: Macmillan.

Mabry, L. (1999). Writing to the rubric: Lingering effects of traditional standardized testing on direct writing assessment. *Phi Delta Kappan, 80*, 673–679.

Mariotti, A. S., & Homan, S. P. (2001). *Linking reading assessment to instruction: An application worktext for elementary classroom teachers* (3rd ed.). Mahwah, NJ: Lawrence Erlbaum.

McCarrier, A., Pinnell, G. S., & Fountas, I. C. (2000). *Interactive writing: How language and literacy come together, K–2*. Portsmouth, NH: Heinemann.

Micheau, C., & Billmyer, K. (1987). Discourse strategies for foreign business students: Preliminary research findings. *English for Specific Purposes, 16*(2), 87–97.

Ministry against prep schools setting college entrance exam. (2000, May 14). *Daily Yomiuri*, p. 1.

Ministry of Education. (1989). *Course of study for junior high schools: Foreign languages–English*. Tokyo: Shoseki.

Ministry of Education. (1990). *Course of study for senior high schools: Foreign languages–English*. Tokyo: Shoseki.

Mulvey, B. (1999). A myth of influence: Japanese university entrance exams and their effects in junior and senior high school reading pedagogy. *JALT Journal, 21*(1), 125–142.

Murphy, S. (1995). Revisioning reading assessment: Remembering to learn from the legacy of reading tests. *Clearing House, 68*, 235–239.

Murphey, T. (1993, January). Why don't teachers learn what learners learn? Taking the guesswork out with action logging. *English Teaching Forum*, 6–10.

Murphey, T. (1997). The perversion of perfectionism: Foreign language anxiety. *Nanzan's Language Teacher Briefs, 7*, 24–25.

Murphey, T. (1998). *Language Learning Histories I and II*. Nagoya, Japan: South Mountain Press.

Murphey, T. (1999). For human dignity and aligning values with activity. *The Language Teacher, 23*(10), 39, 45.

Murphey, T. (2001a). Asking may be a moment's shame; not asking is a lifelong regret. What can YOU do to change the entrance exam system? Dare to ask some embarrassing questions. *Avenues—The Magazine for Central Japan, 95,* 13.

Murphey, T. (2001b). Face validity. In E. F. Churchill & J. W. McLaughlin (Eds.), *Qualitative research in Japan: Japanese learners and contexts* (pp. 188–206) (Temple University Japan Working Papers in Applied Linguistics). Tokyo: Temple University Press.

Murphey, T. (2001c). Nonmeritorious features of the entrance exam system in Japan. *The Language Teacher, 25*(10), 37–39.

National Association of Secondary School Principals. (2000). *NASSP board of directors position statement on standards and assessment.* Retrieved March 26, 2003, from http://www.principals.org/news/05-02-03.html

National Evaluation Systems. (1993). *The official TASP test study guide.* Amherst: Author.

Niederhauser, D. S., Reynolds, R. E., Salmen, D. J., & Skolmoski, P. (2000). The influence of cognitive load on learning from hypertext. *Journal of Educational Computing Research, 23*(3), 237–255.

Niwa, T. (2000). *Entrance exams filled with bad questions.* Tokyo: Shueisha.

Numrich, C., Boyd, F., & Jerome, M. (1995). Academic program review: A focused self-study. In A. Wintertgerst (Ed.), *Focus on self-study* (pp. 79–94). Alexandria, VA: TESOL.

Nunan, D. (1992). *Research methods in language learning.* Cambridge: Cambridge University Press.

Nunan, D. (2002, April). *English as a global language: Counting the cost.* Paper presented at the annual conference of TESOL, Salt Lake City, UT.

Ogle, D. M. (1986). K-W-L: A teaching model that develops active reading of expository text. *The Reading Teacher, 39,* 564–570.

Olaniran, B. A., Stalcup, K. A., & Jensen, K. J. (2000). Incorporating computer-mediated technology to strategically serve pedagogy. *Communication Teacher, 15*(1), 1–4.

O'Loughlin, K. (1995). Lexical density in candidate output on direct and semi-direct versions of an oral proficiency test. *Language Testing, 12*(2), 217–237.

O'Loughlin, K. (1997). *The equivalence of two versions of an oral proficiency test.* Unpublished doctoral dissertation, University of Melbourne, Australia.

Overton, R. C., Harms, H. J., & Taylor, L. R. (1997). Adapting to adaptive testing. *Personnel Psychology, 50,* 171–185.

Oxford, R., & Green, J. (1996). Language learning histories: Learners and teachers helping each other understand learning styles and strategies. *TESOL Journal, 5*(1), 20–23.

Ozok, A. A., & Salvendy, G. (2000). Measuring consistency of Web page design and its effects on performance and satisfaction. *Ergonomics, 43*(4), 443–460.

Peck, R. (1998). *A long way from Chicago.* New York: Puffin.

Perkins, R. F. (1995–1996). Using hypermedia programs to administer tests: Effects on anxiety and performance. *Journal of Research on Computing in Education, 28,* 209–220.

Poon, W. (1992). *An analysis of the language needs of accountants and company administrators in Hong Kong* (Research Report No. 21). Hong Kong: City Polytechnic of Hong Kong, Department of English.

Powell (Eller), R. G. (1998). Johnny can't talk, either: The perpetuation of the deficit theory in classrooms. In M. F. Optiz (Ed.), *Literacy instruction for culturally and linguistically diverse students: A collection of articles and commentaries* (pp. 21–26). Newark, DE: International Reading Association.

Reischauer, E. O. (1988). *The Japanese today.* Tokyo: Charles E. Tuttle. (Original work published 1977, Boston: Harvard University Press.)

Richards, J. (1990). *The language teaching matrix.* Cambridge: Cambridge University Press.

Richards, J., Platt, J., & Weber, H. (Eds.). (1985). *Longman dictionary of applied linguistics.* Essex, England: Longman.

Roemer, M., Schultz, L. M., & Durst, R. K. (1991, December). Portfolios and the process of change. *College Composition and Communication, 42,* 455–469.

Sato, K. (2002). Practical understandings of communicative language teaching and teacher development. In S. J. Savignon (Ed.), *Interpreting communicative language teaching: Contexts and concerns in teacher education* (pp. 41–81). New Haven, CT: Yale University Press.

Sato, K., & Kleinsasser, R. C. (1999). Communicative language teaching (CLT): Practical understandings. *The Modern Language Journal, 83,* 494–517.

Sebesta, S. L., Monson, D. L., & Senn, H. D. (1995). A hierarchy to assess reader response. *Journal of Reading, 38,* 444–450.

Seligman, M. (1990). *Learned optimism.* New York: Pocket Books.

Shohamy, E. (1997a). *Critical language testing and beyond.* Plenary presented at the American Association of Applied Linguistics, Orlando, FL.

Shohamy, E. (1997b). Testing methods, testing consequences: Are they ethical? Are they fair? *Language Testing, 14,* 340–349.

Smith, R., & Stalcup, K. A. (2001). Technology consulting: Keeping pedagogy in the forefront. In K. Lewis & J. P. Lunde (Eds.), *Face-to-face* (pp. 227–246). Stillwater, OK: New Forums Press.

Stake, R. E. (1995). *The art of case study research.* Thousand Oaks, CA: Sage.

Stalcup, K. A. (1999). *Technology predispositions and attitudes.* Unpublished manuscript. (Available from Katherine Austin at kathy.stalcup@ttu.edu.)

Stringer, E. T. (1999). *Action research* (2nd ed.). Thousand Oaks, CA: Sage.

Student Affairs Office. (1996). *Graduate employment survey 1995.* Hong Kong: Hong Kong Polytechnic University.

Sweedler-Brown, C. O. (1993). ESL essay evaluation: The influence of sentence level and rhetorical features. *Journal of Second Language Writing, 2*(1), 3–17.

Tapper, J. (1996). Exchange patterns in the oral discourse of international students in college classrooms. *Discourse Processes, 22,* 25–55.

Taylor, C., Kirsch, I. S., & Eignor, D. (1999). Examining the relationship between computer familiarity and performance on computer-based language tasks. *Language Learning, 49*(2), 219–274.

TESOL. (1992). *TESOL standards and self-study questions for post-secondary programs.* Alexandria, VA: Author.

TESOL. (2002). *TESOL member resolution of English entrance exams at schools and universities.* Retrieved February 20, 2003, from http://www.tesol.org/assoc/abm-resolutions/2000-entrance.html

Tsui, A. B. M. (1994). *English conversation.* Oxford: Oxford University Press.

Tsui, A. B. M. (1995). *Classroom interaction.* London: Penguin.

Tsuido, K. (2000). Kyoin yosei no jittai [Research on preservice training]. *Eigo Kyoiku, 49*(10), 17–19.

Universities strive to survive age of fewer students. (1999, November 30). *Mainichi Daily,* p. 10.

U.S. Department of Education. (1998). *The educational system in Japan: Case study findings* [Electronic version]. Retrieved February 20, 2003, from http://www.ed.gov/pubs/JapanCaseStudy

van Lier, L. (1996). *Interaction in the language classroom: Awareness, autonomy, and authenticity.* New York: Longman.

Viorst, J. (1991). *Alexander, que era rico el domingo pasado* [Alexander, who use to be rich last Sunday]. New York: Atheneum.

Weigle, S. C. (1994). Effects of training on raters of ESL compositions. *Language Testing, 11*(2), 197–223.

Weir, C. (1990). *Communicative language testing.* London: Prentice Hall.

Weir, C. (2000). *Alternatives or existing necessities: New directions or old? Language testing in the 21st century.* Plenary presented at the Fourth Current Trends in English Language Testing Conference, Dubai, United Arab Emirates.

Weissberg, B. (1993). The graduate seminar: Another research process genre. *English for Specific Purposes, 12,* 23–35.

Wesche, M. (1992). Performance testing for work-related second language assessment. In E. Shohamy & R. Walton (Eds.), *Language assessment for feedback: Testing and other strategies.* Washington, DC: National Foreign Language Center.

White, E. M. (1995, February). An apologia for the timed impromptu essay test. *College Composition and Communication, 46,* 30–45.

Wintergerst, A., & Kreidler, C. (1995). The TESOL self-study program. In A. Wintergerst (Ed.), *Focus on self-study* (pp. 7–20). Alexandria, VA: TESOL.

Wolcott, W., & Legg, S. M. (1998). *An overview of writing and assessment.* Urbana, IL: National Council of Teachers of English.

Wright, P. C., Fields, R. E., & Harris, M. D. (2000). Analyzing human-computer interaction as distributed cognition: The resources model. *Human-Computer Interaction, 15,* 1–41.

Yamashita, S. O. (1996). *Six measures of ESL pragmatics* (Report). Honolulu: University of Hawaii.

Yin, R. K. (1994). *Case study research: Design and methods* (2nd ed.). Thousand Oaks, CA: Sage.

Yoneyama, S. (1999). *The Japanese high school: Silence and resistance.* London: Routledge.

Zammit, K. (2000). Computer icons: A picture says a thousand words. Or does it? *Journal of Educational Computing Research, 23*(2), 217–231.

Zandvliet, D., & Farragher, P. (1997). A comparison of computer-administered and written tests. *Journal of Research on Computing in Education, 29,* 423–438.

Zayed University. (2001). *The Zayed University academic model.* Dubai, United Arab Emirates: Author.

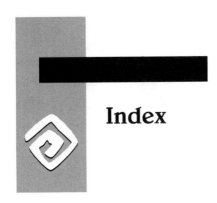

Index

Page numbers followed by *n*, *t*, and *f* refer to notes, tables, and figures respectively.

A

Abdal-Haaq, I., 69
Abodeeb, T. L., 73
Academic discussion, 127
Academic English Program (AEP), 78–79, 84
Academic integrity contract, 81, 84
Academic interaction, 54–56
Academic Listening Test (ALT), 15
Academic speaking course, 91–102
Academic Writing Test (AWT), 15
Accuracy
    of scoring, 75
    of self-assessment, 94
Achievement awards, 182
Achievement stage of assessment at UHM, 16
Achievement tests, 10, 18, 19
ACT, Inc., 27
Action plans, 171
Action research, 64
Additional assessment, 124, 130
Adjunct faculty, 180–181, 185
Administration, of Web-based tests, 82, 84
Administration protocol, 175
Administrators, 18, 19, 20
Admissions office (AO) type of entrance exams, 42
AEP. *See* Academic English Program
Agreed objectives, 173
Alexander, P. A., 64

Alexander, Que Era Rico el Domingo Pasado (Viorst), 66
Allwright, R. L., 168
ALT. *See* Academic Listening Test
Alternative assessment, 124
Alumni awards, 183
American Language Program, 152, 156
American usage, edited, in essay, 107, 108*t*, 117
Anchor essays, 109–110
Anderson, K., 96
And to Think We Thought We'd Never Be Friends (Hoberman), 71
Apathetic users, Web users as, 77
Aptitude tests, 9, 10
Argument, as rhetorical purpose, 109
Assessing Second Language Writing in Academic Contexts (Hamp-Lyons), 105
Assessment, language. *See also* Self-assessment
    additional, 124, 130
    alternative, 124
    communicative, 27–39
    competency-based, 4
    comprehensive, 1, 7–23
    computer-based. *See* Computer-based assessment
    in context, 3–5
    cooperative, 49–59
    cultural norms and values and, 4, 35–36, 38
    cyclical nature of, 5
    data gathering for, 70–71, 155, 158, 159
    data interpretation for, 71–72
    data processing for, 156

of discussion skills. *See* Discussion skills, assessment of
for employment, 2, 135–147
end-of-program, 2, 119–147
ensuring quality of, 144
high-stakes, 3, 4, 5, 43, 49, 50
holistic, 47, 106–107, 181
informal, 64, 70
in-program, 1–2, 61–117
of international students, 13–16, 181–183
in Japan, 1, 3, 5, 27–59
linking with instruction, 63–74, 99
linking with teacher development, 97–98
of listening skills. *See* Listening skills, assessment of low-stakes, 31, 49, 51–52, 94
matching to instructional practices, 72
multidimensional, 107
multiple-measures, 3, 22, 47, 127–128
outcomes-based, 124, 129
performance-based, 4, 143
for placement. *See* Placement tests
planning instruction after, 73
portfolio. *See* Portfolio assessment
program evaluation as, 2, 149–188
purposes of, 30
of reading skills. *See* Reading skills, assessment of recursive, 73
student's point of view of, 16–18, 19
task-based, 94–95, 142–143
teacher-based, 18, 19, 20–21, 63–74, 99
themes in, 1–6
transparent process of, 130
visa system of, 2, 121–134
workplace-oriented, 142–143
of writing skills. *See* Writing skills, assessment of
Assessment checklist, 96, 99, 101
Assessment pilot, 105–106, 111, 112
Assessment protocols
  reliability of, 129–130
  validity of, 128–129
Assessment training, 110
Assistant director, 20
Assistant language teachers, 44
Auckland University, 91–102
Audience, of essay, 115
Audiotape, 31, 82, 98, 140, 143, 181
Aural computer testing tutorials, 80
Austin, K. A., 1, 4, 75–89
Australian Board of Senior School Secondary Studies, 28

Award ceremony, 182–183, 185–186, 186
AWT. *See* Academic Writing Test

 B

Bachman, L. F., 139
Bahr, C. M., 75
Bahr, M. W., 75
Band system of grading, 97
Basturkmen, H., 1–2, 3, 91–102, 96
BEC. *See* Business English Certificate
Behavior of trainees, 168–169, 171
Beichner, R. J., 77
Belanoff, P., 105, 110
Beneficial washback, 125
Benesse Corporation, 27
Bereiter, C., 69
Berry, V., 137
Billmyer, K., 96
Bolton, S., 1, 4, 5, 27–39, 38
Bonham, S. W., 77
Bottom-up processing, 54
Boulima, J., 96
Bowers, D. A., 77
Bowers, V. M., 77
Boyd, F., 156
Brady, L., 122
Brain drain, 47
Bridging, 183–184
Brindley, G., 129, 137
Brown, J. D., 1, 3, 9–23, 43, 50, 76, 77, 94, 111
Buell, J., 44
Bugbee, A. C., 77
Bullying, 43
Burch, R., 2, 4–5, 165–176
Business English Certificate (BEC), 142–143
Business letter writing, 139

 C

Calfee, R. C., 68, 69, 73
Calibration sessions, 110, 129
Campbell, J., 177–188
Carle, E., 67
Carreon, E. S., 2, 5, 151–164
Cause/effect, as rhetorical purpose, 109
Center Activity Rotation System (CARS), 66
Center Test, 41, 43
Cheating, 80–81, 84
Checklist, assessment, 96, 99, 101
Checklist of responsibilities, 172–173

City Heights K-16 Educational Pilot, 69

Classroom learning, 53

Classroom observation, 181, 185, 186

Clay, M. M., 70

CLO. *See* Course learning outcome

Cloze Procedure (test), 15

Coding symbols for interlocutor skills, 97, 97*t*

Cohen, E. G., 52

College of Education's School of Teaching and Learning, 152

Color-coding, 54–56, 57

Color reversal, 67

Columbia University, 156

Communicative curriculum, 27–28

Communicative language teaching, 27–28, 45, 46, 50

Communicative language testing, 27–39

Communicative quality, 96, 101

Communicative test, 36

Company-administered examinations, 49

Comparison/contrast, as rhetorical purpose, 109

Competency-based assessment, 4

Comprehensive assessment, 1, 7–23

Computer anxiety, 77, 80

Computer-based assessment, 1, 4, 75–89
  advantages of, 77
  context of, 76–79
  description of, 79–82
  disadvantages of, 77, 84–85
  distinguishing features of, 83–84
  practical ideas of, 84–85
  reliability of, 76
  validity of, 77, 83

Computer-based scoring, 75

Computer experience and attitude questionnaire, 83–84

Computer screen display design, 78

Coniam, D., 137

Consistency, 37

Content, on assessment checklist, 96, 101

Content areas, literacy across, 64, 66–68

Content validity, of assessment protocols, 128

Context, language assessment in, 3–5

Continuous quality improvement (CQI), 103

Coombe, C. A., 1–6

Cooner, D., 69

Cooper, A., 138

Cooperative assessment, 49–59

Cooperative learning, 3, 52

Cooperative written tests, 3, 52, 53–56

Coordination system, 179, 179*f*, 183, 186

Counterbalancing, 15, 16

Course concepts, recycling, 53

Course coordinator interviews, 154, 161–163

Course learning outcome (CLO), 123, 124, 126, 130

Courtney, A. M., 73

Cox, T., 81

CQI. *See* Continuous quality improvement

CQI Exit Criteria Task Team, 105

Cram schools, 43, 46, 49

Creativity, 58

Criterion-referenced scoring, 58

Criterion-referenced tests, 10, 15–16, 18, 19, 168

Cultural norms and values, assessment and, 4, 35–36, 38

Cumming, A., 107

Curriculum
  assessment of, 152–156, 179–180
  communicative, 27–28
  components of, 11, 153
  problems with, 21–22
  systematic design of, 11–13, 12*f*

Curriculum committee, 12, 13, 21

Curriculum washback, 1, 25–59, 136

Cyclical nature of language assessment, 5

◈ D

Daily teaching events, 64–66, 72

DAL. *See* Department of Applied Language

Dalton, D., 2, 3, 121–134

Darling-Hammond, L., 48, 69

Data
  reliability of, 71–72
  validity of, 72

Data analysis, 184

Data gathering, 70–71, 155, 158, 159, 184

Data-gathering instruments, 158, 159

Data interpretation, 71–72

Data processing, 156

Davidson, P., 2, 3, 121–134

Defense Language Aptitude Test, 10

Deficit theory of schooling, 64

Definition, short talk of, 95

Delivery, on assessment checklist, 96, 101

Denakpo, L., 167, 170
Department of Applied Language (DAL), 177, 178, 179, 184
Department of Education (U.S.), 42
Description, as rhetorical purpose, 109
Descriptors, proficiency, 141, 144
Descriptors for portfolio assessment, 107, 108t, 115–117
Development, of essay, 107, 108t, 116
Developmental writing program, 104
Devereux, J. R., 138
Dewey, J., 53
Dewsbury, A., 71
Diagnostic tests, 10, 18, 19
Dialogic forms of speaking, 93
Dialogues, 31, 36
Dickenson, L., 94
Dickson, M., 105
Dictation (test), 15
Director, 20
Direct speaking test, 143
Direct writing assessment, 28
Discussion skills
  assessment of, 2, 91–102, 127
    context of, 91–92
    description of, 92–94
    distinguishing features of, 94–98
    practical ideas of, 99–100
  development of, 91
  research on, 95–97, 99
Distinguished alumni awards, 183
Dogger, B., 2, 3, 103–117
Domain-referenced scoring, 58
Dornyei, Z., 46
Double-blind scoring, 108
Douglas, D., 95
Doyon, P., 42, 43
Durst, R. K., 105

◈ E

Economics, of entrance exams in Japan, 43, 46, 50
Edited American usage, in essay, 107, 108t, 117
Educational Testing Service (ETS), 127–128
EFL. *See* English as a foreign language
Egypt, 165–176
Ehrman, M., 46
Eignor, D., 77
Einstein, A., 165
El-Araby, D., 2, 4–5, 165–176

Elbow, P., 105, 107, 110
ELG. *See* English Language Center
ELI. *See* English Language Institute
ELILCT. *See* English Language Institute Listening Comprehension Test
ELIPT. *See* English Language Institute Placement Test
ELT. *See* English language training
Employment, assessment for, 2, 135–147
End-of-course evaluation survey, 154–156
End-of-program assessment, 2, 119–147
English as a foreign language (EFL), 127
English as a Foreign Language (EFL) Readiness Program. *See* Readiness Program
English as second language/English as foreign language (ESL/EFL) assessment, 29, 75
English as second language (ESL) Composition Program, self-study of, 2, 151–164
English for publishing course, 123
English for speakers of other languages (ESOL), 2, 103, 177–188
English for specific purposes (ESP), 1, 123
English for specific purposes (ESP) assessment, 49–59
English Language Center (ELG), 123, 138
English Language Institute (ELI), 10–22, 79
English Language Institute (ELI) courses, 11f
  context of, 11–13
  description of, 13–18
  distinguishing features of, 18–19
  practical ideas of, 19–22
English Language Institute Listening Comprehension Test (ELILCT), 79, 80–84
English Language Institute Placement Test (ELIPT), 10, 13, 14–15, 14f, 18
English language proficiency test. *See* Michigan Test of English Language Proficiency
English Language Program, 91–102
English language training (ELT), 165–176
Entrance exams. *See also* Japanese University entrance exams
  admissions office (AO) type of, 42
  economics of, 43, 46, 50
  norm-referenced, 50
  reliability of, 46
  validity of, 46

Error correction task, 139
ESL/EFL assessment, 29
ESOL. *See* English for speakers of other
  languages
ESP. *See* English for specific purposes
Essays
  anchor, 109–110
  assessment of, 33. *See also* Portfolio
    assessment
  impromptu, 79, 109
  in-class, 108, 109
  out-of-class, 108, 109
  rhetorical purposes of, 109
  rhetorical structure of, 126
ETS. *See* Educational Testing Service
Evaluation. *See also* Assessment, language
  impact, 169
  as rhetorical purpose, 109
Evaluative portfolio, 108
Examination-oriented English, 45
Exit requirements. *See* Visa system of
  assessment
Exit test, 2, 4, 135–147, 144
Explanation of innovation, 94, 95

◈ F

FACETS (software program), 142
Face validity, of assessment protocols, 128
Faculty. *See* Teachers
Falvey, P., 137
Farragher, P., 76
Feature explorers, Web users as, 77
Feedback
  double-blind scoring and, 108
  formal, 57
  informal, 57
  in Japan, 35, 50, 56–57, 58
  from students, about program, 154–156,
    157
  from teachers
      about program, 154, 155, 157
      about writing, 35, 124
  from trainees, 169–170, 171, 172
  verbal, 57
  written, 57
Fields, R. E., 78
Field testing, 34
Finance and operations division of IELP-II,
  166
Fisher, D., 1, 5, 63–74
Fitzpatrick, K. A., 122, 129

Flederman, P., 167, 170
Flexibility, 37
Flood, J., 66, 70
Flood, S., 70
Focus, of essay, 107, 108*t*, 116
Focused holistic assessment, 106–107
Focused study, 159
Forey, G., 138
Formal accuracy, 34
Formal feedback, 57
Formative evaluation, regularly conducted,
  11, 12*f*
Fountas, I. C., 64, 66, 72
Frey, N., 1, 5, 63–74, 69, 71
Fulcher, G., 2
Fullan, M., 42
Functional fluency, 34
Furneaux, C., 96

◈ G

Gaies, S., 1, 4, 5, 27–39, 38
General education learning outcomes, 122–
  123
Genesee, F., 53
Gilboy, A., 167, 170
Glass, C. R., 77
Goals specification, 11, 12, 12*f*
Goldberg, M. A., 78
Goodman, M., 1, 3, 49–59
Gorsuch, G. J., 1, 4, 43, 50, 75–89
Grades
  group, 52, 56, 57
  individual, 56, 57
Grading. *See also* Scoring
  band system of, 97
  standardized, 97–98, 99
Graduate assistants, 21
Graduate students, helping with self-study,
  154, 158
Graduating Students' Language Proficiency
  Assessment (GSLPA), 135–147
Graduating Students' Language Proficiency
  Assessment (GSLPA) Reporting Scale, 141
Grammar-based language program, 178
Grammar questions, 44
Grammar rules, memorization of, 50
Grammar-translation practice, 50
Gravatt, B., 91
Green, J., 44
Groulx, J., 69
Group grades, 52, 56, 57

Grouping
  heterogeneous, 70
  homogeneous, 70
Groupwork, 52–57
GSLPA. *See* Graduating Students' Language
  Proficiency Assessment
Guest, M., 41
Guided reading, 64, 66, 67*f*

◈ H

Hamp-Lyons, L., 105, 107, 135, 136
Handbook, 184–185, 186
Handwritten comments, 35
Hardware, 51
Harms, H. J., 77
Harris, M. D., 78
Hart, D., 167, 170
Hatch, E., 93
Heinssen, R. K., 77
Hello, Red Fox (Carle), 67
Heterogeneous grouping, 70
Hiebert, E. H., 68, 69, 71
High achievement awards, 182
High-stakes assessment, 3, 4, 5, 43, 49, 50
Hoberman, M. A., 71
Hoey, M., 96
Holistic assessment, 47, 106–107, 181
Holistic rubric construction, 34–35
Homan, S. P., 72
Homogeneous grouping, 70
Hong Kong, 2, 135–147
Hong Kong Polytechnic University (PolyU),
  135–147
Hong Kong University, 137
Honor roll, 182
Howard, J., 177–188
Hubley, N. J., 1–6
Hudson, T., 94, 111
Hughes, A., 112, 125

◈ I

Idea development, 34
IELP-II. *See* Integrated English Language
  Project II
IELTS. *See* International English Language
  Testing System
I-ITF. *See* Inter-Institutional Task Force
Ijime, 43
Illusions, 67, 68
Illustrations, 31

Impact evaluation, 169
Impromptu essays, 79, 109
Impromptu writing sample, 182
In-class essay, 108, 109
Individual grades, 56, 57
Informal assessments, 64, 70
Informal feedback, 57
Information literacy, 127
Informative report card, 144–145
In-house exit test, 144
Initial screening stage of assessment at
  UHM, 13–14
Innovation, explanation of, 94, 95
In-program assessment, 1–2, 61–117
Institutional Research and Information
  Management, 78
Instruction, linking with assessment, 63–
  74, 99
Instructional practices, matching assessment
  to, 72
Instructional tools, assessment of, 72
Instructors. *See* Teachers
Instruments, 157, 159, 173–175, 182
Integrated English Language Project II
  (IELP-II), 165–176, 170*f*
Interaction, 58
Interactive writing, 64–66, 66*f*
Inter-Institutional Task Force (I-ITF), 137
Interlocutors, 93, 95
Interlocutor skills, 94, 96, 97, 97*t*, 98, 99
Internal motivation, 156
International English Language Testing
  System (IELTS), 4, 92, 125, 142
International Reading Association, 73
International students, language assessment
  of, 13–16, 181–183
International visitors, speaking with, 140
Interrater reliability, 106, 109, 110, 129,
  141
Interview
  as assessment, 13–14, 140, 181
  course coordinator, 154, 161–163
  with failing students, 16
  for self-study, 154
  summarizing information from, 140
Item banks, 47
Ito, K., 42

◈ J

Jacobs, E. L., 77
Japan

characteristics of exam system in, 46
language assessment in, 1, 3, 5, 27–59
problems in education system in, 42–43
revenue from entrance exams in, 43, 46, 50
Japan Association of Language Teachers (JALT), 38
Japanese students, 47, 50–51, 53, 54
Japanese University entrance exams, 41–48, 50–51
Jensen, K. J., 77
Jerome, M., 156
Johnson, D., 38
Johnson, D. W., 52
Johnson, R. T., 52
Jordan, R. R., 96
Juku. See Cram schools

❧ K

Kawai Juku, 42
Kent, J. A., 2, 5, 177–188
Kindergarten, writing in, 64–66
King, A., 177–188
Kirkpatrick, D., 165, 169, 176
Kirkpatrick model, 165, 168–169, 169f
Kirsch, I. S., 77
Kitao, K., 28
Kitao, S. K., 28
Kleinsasser, R. C., 28
Kluge, D. E., 52
Knight, L. A., 77
Knight, S. L., 69
Knowledge, skills, and attitudes (KSA), 168, 171
Knowledge seekers, Web users as, 77
Krashen, S. D., 54
Kreidler, C., 151, 153
KWL chart, 67–68, 68f

❧ L

Language aptitude tests, 9, 10
Language Institute (LI), 177, 178, 180, 184
Language placement tests. *See* Placement tests
Language proficiency tests, 9, 10, 27–39. *See also* Michigan Test of English Language Proficiency
Lapp, D., 66, 70
Lead teacher, 18, 20
Leamnson, R., 51, 54, 56

Learner profile, 130, 133–134
Learning
  classroom, 53
  cooperative, 3, 52
  interaction and, 58
  measuring, in trainees, 168, 171
  motivation and, 56
Learning Enhancement Center (at Zayed University), 124
Learning outcomes, 122–123, 124–125, 126, 130
Lecture, listening to, 126
Legg, S. M., 34, 35
Lems, K., 177–188
Letter writing, 139
Levine, M., 69
Lewis, M., 91
Lewkowicz, J., 137
LI. *See* Language Institute
Likert-type rating scale, 154, 155
Linacre, J. M., 142
Lingnan University, 137
Lipson, M. Y., 63–74
Listening
  to lecture, 126
  questions about, for test development, 29
Listening comprehension test, 79, 82
Listening exams, 41
Listening skills, assessment of, 14f, 28, 31, 32t, 44, 126, 139
Listening subtest, 31, 32t, 36–37
Literacy
  across content areas, 64, 66–68
  information, 127
  teachers' beliefs about, 70
Literacy block, 66
LoCastro, V., 27, 28
Locke, C., 96
Long, M., 151
Longman Dictionary of Applied Linguistics (Richards, Platt, Weber), 153
A Long Way From Chicago (Peck), 71
Low-stakes assessment, 31, 49, 51–52, 94
Lumley, T., 2, 4, 110, 135–147, 136
Lynch, B., 151
Lynch, T., 96
Lyons, C., 1, 4, 5, 27–39, 38

❧ M

Mabry, L., 72
Macro-level learning outcomes, 122

"Magic eye" painting, 66–67
Mariotti, A. S., 72
Master teachers, 69
Materials adoption, adaptation, or
    development, 11, 12*f*, 13
McCarrier, A., 64
McNamara, T. F., 110
Measurable objectives, 173
Memorization of grammar rules, 50
Memo writing, 139, 146
Metacognition, 104
Michaeu, C., 96
Michigan Test Academic Integrity Contract,
    81
Michigan Test of English Language
    Proficiency (MTELP), 75, 77, 78–79, 80–
    84, 86–89
Ministry of Education, Culture, Sports,
    Science, and Technology (Japan), 27, 41,
    42, 45, 46, 49, 50
Ministry of Education (Egypt), 165–166,
    168, 171
Mode, of essay, 107, 108*t*
Monbukagakusho. *See* Ministry of
    Education, Culture, Sports, Science, and
    Technology (Japan)
Monitoring and evaluation (M&E) division
    of IELP-II, 166–167, 169–170, 171
Monologic forms of speaking, 93
Monologues, 36
Monson, D. L., 71
Motivation
    internal, 156
    and learning, 56
Moy, J., 2, 3, 103–117
MTELP. *See* Michigan Test of English
    Language Proficiency
Multicultural elementary school, linking
    assessment with instruction in, 1, 63–74
Multidimensional assessment, 107
Multiple-choice examinations, 54
Multiple-measures assessment, 3, 22, 47,
    127–128
Multiple rating, 143–144
Multiple-trait scoring, 106–108, 108*t*, 110
Mulvey, B., 28, 41, 50
Murphey, T., 1, 5, 41–48
Murphy, S., 72, 78

❖ N

Nagel, G., 70
National Association of Secondary School
    Principals, 73
National Evaluation Systems, 104
National-Louis University (NLU), 5, 177–
    188
Needs analysis
    at Auckland University, 91
    at Hong Kong Polytechnic University, 138
    at Richland College, 111
    strategic training and, 168
    at University of Hawaii, 11, 12, 12*f*
    at Zayed University, 125
Neiderhauser, D. S., 77
New item types on test, 36–37
Ng, L. G., 138
Niwa, T., 42
Nogami, M., 2, 3, 103–117
Noncommunicative training, 36
Norm-referenced tests, 9–10, 18, 19
Norm-referenced university entrance exams,
    50
Notes, taking, 126
Numrich, C., 156
Nunan, D., 36

❖ O

Objectives, 173
Objectives-referenced scoring, 58
Objectives specification, 11, 12, 12*f*
Observation, classroom, 181, 185, 186
Ogle, D. M., 67, 70
Ohio State University (OSU), 151–164
Olaniran, B. A., 77
Old item types on test, 36–37
O'Loughlin, K., 140
One-on-one conferences, 124
Operational prompts, 34
Optical illusions, 68
Oral Language Proficiency Interview
    (OLPI), 181, 182
Organization
    on assessment checklist, 96, 101
    of essay, 107, 108*t*, 116
Organizational pattern, 34
Outcomes-based assessment, 124, 129

Outcomes-based education, 121, 122–123
Out-of-class essay, 108, 109
Overton, R. C., 77
Oxford, R., 44
Ozok, A. A., 78

❧ P

Palmer, A. S., 139
Paper-and-pencil test, 53–56
  computer adaptation of, 1, 4, 75–89
Parsons, J. L., 64
PDI, 166–167, 170
PDS. *See* Professional development system
Peck, R., 71
Peer correction, 54–56
Peer observation, 181, 185, 186
Performance-based assessment, 4, 143
Performance gaps, 167–168, 167*f*
Performance indicators (PIs), 123
Performance reports, 16
Performance review, 181
Performance test, 138–139
  of speaking, 135, 140–141, 146–147
  of writing, 135, 139, 146
Perkins, R. F., 77
Pilot, assessment, 105–106, 111, 112
Pinnell, G. S., 64, 66, 72
PIs. *See* Performance indicators
Placement stage of assessment at UHM, 14–15
Placement tests
  at National-Louis University, 181–182
  purpose of, 9
  at University of Hawaii, 10, 13, 14–15, 14*f*, 18, 19
Planned forms of speaking, 93
Platt, J., 153
Poggendorf, J., 67
"Poggendorf's Illusion," 67
PolyU. *See* Hong Kong Polytechnic University
Poon, W., 138
Portfolio
  evaluative, 108
  streamlined, 105, 106
  working, 108, 109
Portfolio assessment, 3, 103–117
  context of, 103–104
  criteria for, 107, 108*t*, 115–117
  description of, 104–106
  distinguishing features of, 106–111

practical ideas of, 111–112
  at Zayed University, 124–125
Portfolio committee, 109, 111
Portfolio content selection, 108–110
Portfolio exit procedure, 112
Portfolio handbook, 110
Portfolios: Process and Product (Belanoff and Dickson), 105
Postobservation conference, 185
Powell (Eller), R. G., 64
Preobservation conference, 185
Presentation of findings from written source, 140, 146–147
Presentation of findings of survey study, 95
Presentation skills, 91, 94
Preservice teacher education, 69
Pretest, 181–182
Price Charities, 69
Problem solving, 139
Process writing, 104
Professional development system (PDS), 69
Professional letter writing, 139
Proficiency descriptors, 141, 144
Proficiency Test of English Communication (PTEC), 27–39, 32*t*
  and communicative language testing, 28
  context of, 27–28
  description of, 29–35
  distinguishing features of, 35–38
  practical ideas of, 38
  purposes of, 30
Profile, learner, 130, 133–134
Profile questionnaire, 173, 174*t*
Program development and implementation (PDI) division of IELP-II, 166–167, 170
Program evaluation, 2, 149–188
Progress tests, 10
Prompt construction, 32*t*, 33–34
Prompts, writing, 109
Prompt topic, 33–34
Proofreading
  Web-based tests, 81, 84
  of writing, 139
PTEC. *See* Proficiency Test of English Communication
Purpose, of essay, 107, 108*t*, 109, 115

❧ Q

Qian, D., 2, 4, 135–147
Qualitative measures of assessment, 182
Quantitative measures of assessment, 182

Questionnaire
computer experience and attitude, 83–84
profile, 173, 174t
for self-study, 154–155, 163–164
trainee satisfaction, 175t

◈ R

Radio interview, summarizing information from, 140
Rasch analysis, 142, 143–144
Rater reliability, 106, 109, 110, 129, 141
Raters, 129, 142
Rater training, 35
Rating, 142
institutions, 47
multiple, 143–144
Rating sheets, 109, 114–115
RCT. *See* Reading Comprehension Test
Reaccreditation, 179
Readiness Program, 2, 121–134, 123
Reading
guided, 64, 66, 67f
questions about, for test development, 29
Reading comprehension test, 79
Reading Comprehension Test (RCT), 15
Reading response log, 71
Reading skills, assessment of, 14f, 28, 32t, 33, 44, 70–71, 126–127
Reading subtest, 32t, 33, 36
Realistic objectives, 173
Recordings, 31, 82, 98, 140, 143, 181
Recycling course concepts, 53
Reflection notes, 98
Reflection tasks, 98, 100, 101–102
Regularly conducted formative evaluation, 11, 12f
Rehearsing, Web-based tests, 81, 84
Reischauer, E. O., 50
Release time, 159–160
Reliability
of assessment protocols, 129–130
of computer-based assessment, 76
of data, 71–72
of entrance exams, 46
interrater, 106, 109, 110, 129, 141
of questions, 37
of WebCT, 79–80
Remediation courses, 104
Repeat students, 51
Report card, informative, 144–145
Report of assessment, 156

Research, on discussion skills, 95–97, 99
Research paper, 127
Research proposal, 127
Response format of test, 54–56, 55f
Responsibilities, checklist of, 172–173
Reteaching, 71
Revenue, from entrance exams in Japan, 43, 46, 50
Review design, 157
Reynolds, R. E., 77
Rhetorical purposes, 109
Rhetorical structure of essays, 126
Richards, J., 91, 96, 98, 153
Richland College, 3, 103–117
Robinson, P., 96
Roemer, M., 105
Rubric, 34–35
Running records, 66, 67f, 70–71

◈ S

Salmen, D. J., 77
Salvendy, G., 78
Sanders-Smith, M., 167, 170
San Diego Education Association, 69
San Diego State University, 69
San Diego Unified School District, 69
Sandlot Science Web site, 67
Sato, K., 1, 5, 28, 41–48
Scanning, 33, 36
Scardamalia, M., 69
Schooling, deficit theory of, 64
School refusal syndrome, 43
Schultz, L. M., 105
Scoring, 35, 56. *See also* Grades; Grading
accuracy of, 75
categories for, 141
computer-based, 75
criterion-referenced, 58
domain-referenced, 58
double-blind, 108
multiple-trait, 106–108, 108t, 110
objectives-referenced, 58
Sebesta, S. L., 71
Second-week assessment stage at UHM, 15–16
Self-assessment (by students), 93–94
accuracy of, 94
incorporating, 3, 98, 100
portfolio assessment and, 105
sample of, 101–102
Self-assessment (by teachers), 181

Self-awareness, 104–105
Self-monitoring, 112
Self-study, 2, 151–164
Seligman, M., 47
Semidirect speaking test, 143
Seminar discussion, 127
Seminar participant, 96–97, 101
Senn, H. D., 71
Sentence structure
  in essay, 107, 108t, 116–117
  in rubric, 34
Server, 78, 82, 83
Shohamy, E., 47, 48, 64
Short talk of definition, 95
Skimming, 33, 36
Skolmoski, P., 77
SMART objectives, 173
Smith, R., 77
Software, 51
Speaking
  forms of, 93
  with international visitors, 140
  performance test of, 135, 140–141, 146–147
Speaking proficiency, descriptors of, 141
Speaking test
  direct, 143
  semidirect, 143
Specific objectives, 173
Spoken English Program, 152
Spontaneous forms of speaking, 93
Staff. See Teachers
Stakeholder involvement in training, 170
Stalcup, K. A., 77, 86
Stam, G., 177–188
Standardized assessment, 63. See also High-stakes assessment
Standardized grading, 97–98, 99
Strategic training, 167–168, 171
Streamlined portfolio, 105, 106
Stringer, E. T., 64
Student Affairs Office, 137
Students
  assessment of. See Assessment, language
  at Auckland University, 92
  feedback from, about program, 154–156, 157
  Japanese, 47, 50–51, 53, 54
  learner profile for, 130, 133–134
  perspective of, 16–18, 19
  repeat, 51
  self-assessment by. See Self-assessment

video and audio recordings of, 98
  as Web users, 77
  working in groups, 52–57
  at Zayed University, 122, 124
Student teachers, 69
Summarizing information from interview, 140
Summary writing, 126
Survey, for self-study, 154
Survey study, presentation of findings of, 95
Sweedler-Brown, C. O., 35
Sykes, G., 48

T

Taking notes, 126
Tape recordings, 31, 82, 98, 140, 143, 181
Tapper, J., 96
Task-based assessment, 94–95, 142–143
Task sheets, 98
Task specifications, 95
TASP. See Texas Academic Skills Program
Taylor, C., 77
Taylor, L. R., 77
Teacher-based assessments, 18, 19, 20–21, 63–74, 99
Teacher education, 69
Teachers. See also Raters
  assessment of, 152–156, 165–176, 180–181, 185
  assistant language, 44
  beliefs about literacy, 70
  completing learning profile, 130
  on entrance exams in Japan, 43–45
  feedback from, about program, 154, 155, 157
  lead, 18, 20
  master, 69
  professional development for, 69
    linking assessment with, 97–98
  self-assessment by, 181
  student, 69
  at Zayed University, 122, 124
Teacher support, 11, 12f, 13
Teacher survey questionnaire, 154, 155, 163–164
Teacher training, evaluation of, 165–176
Teaching, Learning, and Technology Center (TLTC), 78, 80–81, 84
Teaching English as a second language (TESL), 180
Technical English vocabulary, 51–52

Technology instructors, 80
Telephone message, 140
Tenured faculty, 181
TESOL, 45, 154, 157
TESOL Convention (2000), 45
TESOL Resolution on English Entrance
  Exams at Schools and Universities, 45
TESOL Standards and Self-Study Questions for
  Postsecondary Programs, 157
Test certificate, 141
Test content, 53
Test design, 138–141
Test development and improvement
  as ELI curriculum component, 11, 12*f*
  as valid professional field, 47
Test in English for Educational Purposes,
  93
Test items, 53
Test method, response format as, 54–56,
  55*f*
Test of English as a Foreign Language
  (TOEFL), 3, 4, 10, 13–15, 28, 49, 125–
  126, 127–128, 142
Test of English for International
  Communication (TOEIC), 28
Test specifications, 54
Test stimuli review, 36
Texas Academic Skills Program (TASP), 104
Texas Tech University, 78–79
Textbook publishers, 50
Thomas, C., 69
Thornton, B., 2, 4–5, 165–176
Time bound objectives, 173
Time management, 158
Titus, A., 77
TLTC. *See* Teaching, Learning, and
  Technology Center
TOEFL. *See* Test of English as a Foreign
  Language
TOEIC. *See* Test of English for International
  Communication
Tokokyohi, 43
Tonkyn, A., 96
Top-down processing, 54
Trainee satisfaction, 168, 171, 175*t*
Training
  planning, 170–171, 173, 174*t*
  strategic, 167–168, 171
Training activity action plans, 171
Training needs, prioritizing, 173, 174*t*
Training of trainers (TOT), 165–176
Transparency of assessment process, 130

Tsui, A. B. M., 96
Two-decision rubric, 34

◈ U

United Arab Emirates (UAE), 121–134
United States Agency for International
  Development (USAID), 165, 166, 170
University entrance exams. *See* Entrance
  exams
University Grants Committee (UGC), 136
University of Auckland, 3
University of Cambridge Local
  Examinations Syndicate, 142
University of Hawaii at Manoa (UHM), 10–
  22
University of Tokyo, 28
Unplanned forms of speaking, 93
Upshur, J. A., 53
U.S. Department of Education, 42

◈ V

Validity
  of assessment protocols, 128–129
  of computer-based assessment, 77, 83
  of data, 72
  of entrance exams, 46
Van Lier, L., 52
Verbal feedback, 57
Video recordings, 98
Viorst, J., 66
Visa system of assessment, 2, 121–134
Visual computer testing tutorials, 80
Vocabulary, technical, 51–52
Vocabulary list, 31, 33
Vocabulary questions, 44

◈ W

Washback, 105. *See also* Curriculum
  washback
  beneficial, 125
Web-based assessment, 75–89
WebCT, 79–83
Weber, H., 153
Web server, 78, 82, 83
Web users, 77
Weigle, S. C., 110
Weir, C., 93, 124
Weissberg, B., 96
Wesche, M., 139

White, E. M., 111
Wintergerst, A., 151, 153
Wiseman, D. L., 69
Wixson, K. K., 63–74
Wolcott, W., 34, 35
Word choice, 34
Working portfolio, 108
Working portfolio rating sheets, 109, 114–115
Workplace, organizing transition to, 175
Workplace-oriented assessment, 142–143
Wright, B., 142
Wright, P. C., 78
Writer's Corner, 64
Writing
  interactive, 64–66, 66f
  in kindergarten, 64–66
  performance test of, 135, 139, 146
  process of, 104
  questions about, for test development, 29–30
  rating, 35
  summary, 126
Writing award, 182
Writing Center (at Zayed University), 124
Writing portfolios, 2
Writing proficiency, descriptors of, 141
Writing prompts, 109

Writing sample, 181, 182
Writing Sample (test), 15
Writing skills, assessment of. *See also* Portfolio assessment
  direct, 28
  at Hong Kong Polytechnic University, 139
  in Japan, 28, 32t, 33–35
  in kindergarten, 64–66
  at University of Hawaii, 14f, 15
  at Zayed University, 126–127
Writing subtest, 32t, 33–35
Writing task, 146
Written feedback, 57
Written tests, cooperative, 3, 52, 53–56

Y

Yagi, Y., 41
Yamashita, S. O., 50, 94
Yobiko. See Cram schools
Yoneyama, S., 47

Z

Zammit, K., 77
Zandvliet, D., 76
Zayed University (ZU), 121–134

Also Available From TESOL

Academic Writing Programs
Ilona Leki, Editor

Action Research
Julian Edge, Editor

Bilingual Education
Donna Christian and Fred Genesee, Editors

Community Partnerships
Elsa Auerbach, Editor

Content-Based Instruction in Higher Education Settings
JoAnn Crandell and Dorit Kaufman, Editors

Distance-Learning Programs
Lynn E. Henrichsen, Editor

English for Specific Purposes
Thomas Orr, Editor

Grammar Teaching in Teacher Education
Dilin Liu and Peter Master, Editors

Implementing the ESL Standards for Pre-K-12 Students Through Teacher Education
Marguerite Ann Snow, Editor

Integrating the ESL Standards Into Classroom Practice: Grades Pre-K–2
Betty Ansin Smallwood, Editor

Integrating the ESL Standards Into Classroom Practice: Grades 3–5
Katharine Davies Samway, Editor

Integrating the ESL Standards Into Classroom Practice: Grades 6–8
Suzanne Irujo, Editor

Integrating the ESL Standards Into Classroom Practice: Grades 9–12
Barbara Agor, Editor

Intensive English Programs in Postsecondary Settings
Nicholas Dimmit and Maria Dantas-Whitney, Editors

Interaction and Language Learning
Jill Burton and Charles Clennell, Editors

Internet for English Teaching
Mark Warschauer, Heidi Shetzer, and Christine Meloni

Journal Writing
Jill Burton and Michael Carroll, Editors

Mainstreaming
Effie Cochran, Editor

Teacher Education
Karen E. Johnson, Editor

Technology-Enhanced Learning Environments
Elizabeth Hanson-Smith, Editor

For more information, contact
Teachers of English to Speakers of Other Languages, Inc.
700 South Washington Street, Suite 200
Alexandria, Virginia 22314 USA
Tel 703-836-0774 • Fax 703-836-6447 • publications@tesol.org •
http://www.tesol.org/